THE WINNING EDGE 3

Traders' & Investors' Coaching to Excellence

by Adrienne Laris Toghraie, MNLP, MCH

On Target Press
100 Lavewood Lane
Cary, North Carolina 27518
919-851-8288

A Division of Trading on Target

First Published in the United States in 2000
Third Printing, 2006
Fourth Printing, 2008

ISBN 978-0-9661837-4-0

PHOTO BY BILL SPURGEON

About the Author

ADRIENNE LARIS TOGHRAIE, MNLP, MCH, is a trader's coach, an internationally recognized authority in the field of human development and a master practitioner of Neuro-Linguistic Programming (NLP) for the financial and business communities. She is the founder and president of *Trading on Target* and *Enriching Life Seminars,* two companies dedicated to helping traders, sales people, and other high achievers to dramatically increase profits and success in all areas of life. Using her 20 years of study in the science of Modeling Excellence/(NLP) and numerous other forms of psychological development, Ms. Toghraie has helped her clients to push through their self-imposed limitations to extraordinary and documented new levels of success.

Adrienne's articles and interviews have been featured in most of the major financial trade magazines and newspapers throughout the world. She has authored Get A life: *Treasure Diary for Creating Wealth and Happiness, The Winning Edge 2: Traders' and Investors' Psychological Coach in a Book, Dear Coach: Potty Training for Traders, Brokers & Investors,* and co-authored *Traders' Secrets* with Murray Ruggiero and *The Winning Edge, How to Use Your Personal Psychological Power in Trading and Investing* with Jake Bernstein.

Adrienne's public seminars and private counseling, as well as her television appearances and keynote addresses at major industry conferences, have achieved a wide level of recognition and popularity.

Table of Contents

Section Two: Your Mind & Emotions

Section Three: Your Choices

Section Four: Your Habits

Section Five: Creating Balance

Section Six: Life Phases

Dedicated to:

Jim Geuder

Who Makes My Fantasies
Come True

Acknowledgments to:

Rick Morgan

Who gives the TOT Bull his flair and humor.

Wendy Clouse

Who coordinated the assembly and editing
of this book and is my invaluable right hand.

Antonia Weeks

Who taught me how to write and assisted me every
Step of the way by continuously asking,
"So what are you really trying to say?"

Roger Reimer

Who was our invaluable editor.

&

A special thanks to all of the traders who contributed their stories, so that everyone could learn from their lessons.

Preface

The Winning Edge 3, Traders' & Investors' Coaching to Excellence is a collection of my revised articles appearing in financial magazines and newsletters all over the world. Admittedly, sometimes it was a stretch to include a particular article in a section. But, I felt it was more important to be complete and informative than to be consistent. In addition, you will find certain lessons which are repeated throughout this book. Since these lessons are the ones that traders seem to forget and need to be reminded of periodically, I'm sure you will welcome the repetition.

The stories included in the book are about people who are clients, who have been to my seminars and workshops or whom I have met on the phone. I have changed their names and altered their situations slightly. In some cases, when their story was unusual, I asked permission to write about it even though the information surrounding the story was disguised.

Masculine pronouns are used generically, implying his/hers, he/she, him/her in all cases for ease of reading.

Foreword

By Sunny J. Harris

One of Sunny's many bestsellers is

Electronic Day Trading 101

Adrienne Toghraie is an influential force in the lives of traders. Her work in Neuro-Linguistic Programming and in coaching traders, has brought to the forefront the most difficult problem facing traders: discipline. Actually, it is the lack of discipline that is usually the problem.

Whether you call it a recipe, a map, a methodology, a set of rules, a strategy, or a system it is the second half of the two components that are essential to successful trading: a profitable system and the discipline to follow it. You can't have one without the other.

Very few traders get caught in the trap of having too much discipline applied to a bad system. More often, traders find themselves caught in the trap of having a worthwhile system and not having enough discipline to follow it. It is this type of trader that comes to Adrienne for a tune-up. And, it is the tune-up at which she is so masterful.

Adrienne works only with serious traders, who realize the urgency of taking care of the discipline component of successful trading. As such, her counsel is expensive and requires dedication. For those not ready for this depth of commitment, Adrienne has been generous in sharing her first-hand studies of trading psychology. In books such as this one, Adrienne liberally takes examples from her private work, changes the names and circumstances to protect the innocent, and shares these insights with the rest of us. These stories are not fictional; they are real, everyday situations we all face.

You will identify with characters in the book. You will find yourself nodding in recognition as you begin to realize just how similar your problems are to those of other traders. And, as you read, you will gather tools to help you when you encounter the situations again.

Thanks to Adrienne for making her wealth of experiences so readily available to the rest of us.

SECTION 1
Your Past...

Chapter 1

THE PAST DOES EQUAL THE FUTURE, PART I
BURIED ALIVE: UNRESOLVED EMOTIONAL TRAUMAS

"Here's my card," said a trader, extending his unsteady arm at a trade show. It said, "Trader, Financial Advisor, Analyst, Vietnam Veteran." Many veterans bury the wounds of war and enter professions that allow them to do so. However, trading is not a merciful profession when it comes to burying past traumas. A high level of performance requires a great deal of healthy, high energy. When energy is down, the shadows of the past resurface, and then trading becomes a battleground of unresolved emotions.

With a look that brought back shadows of my own past (having been married to a Vietnam veteran), Joe asked, "Can we talk?" It was at a time when speakers were in their sessions. I left my exhibit unmanned, feeling intensity build with each step towards privacy and comfortable seating. And so the story began of how trading was now the Vietcong, the helicopters, the jungle and the terror. Joe is a trader's household name. He built a fortune over the years with his street-smart, savvy, approach to the markets. Then he lost it all and traded his name to keep up a comfortable life-style. He inspired many a new trader by being a guru and mentor. Now in his fifties, with a wife and two sons, he was tired of living the lie. He wanted to be the person everyone thought him to be, the person who made the fortune. Trading became a bottomless pit of disappointment where, in its debts, he found hell. He told me of his nightmares, the ones that haunt him still.

What is Happening?

What happened to Joe and why is his experience important for traders to understand? In the course of nearly everyone's life, the chances are that we will face an experience which will rock us to our core. Since death is a certainty for everyone, we will have to face the death of people we love very deeply. We live in a violent society in which we are faced with the prospect of being a victim of a crime, potentially a violent one. Each and every one of us travels, and as each mile ticks by, the likelihood that we will be in an accident increases. Periodically, we find ourselves in a war like Joe. If we are lucky enough to survive, we are left to face the long-term trauma from wounds and terrifying experiences.

Gulf War veterans, who have their own brand of horrors to bury, are being added to the victims of war. And finally, we live on a planet as guests of mother nature, who periodically throws a fit, just to remind us who is in charge. All of these potentially devastating experiences are predictable, to some extent. There are many others that are not. If and when they occur, how are we going to handle them and how are they going to affect our professional (as well as personal) lives afterwards?

When we experience a living nightmare, it often follows us throughout our lives, undermining our ability to trade because of its powerful and frightening imagery of loss, pain and disaster. The reason that these traumas continue to plague us is because they are often too overwhelming for us to deal with at the time they occur. As a result, we bury them deeply in our subconscious while they are still powerful and full of life, and where they continue to hold the same level of influence over us as long as they are left unresolved . Unfortunately, we never go back to dig them up in order to deal with them because, very simply, they frighten us.

As time passes, we begin to think that we have recovered and go on with our lives. After awhile, we often forget that these traumatic experiences even happened. Then, without warning, we start to have dreams about these past traumas, usually because something happens in our present lives that sparks old associations. Because we are not dealing with the past trauma on a conscious level, our unconscious mind will continue sending us a message that we need to attend to our problems until we finally do so.

The result of this common response to trauma is that even though we have survived the terrible experience, we are essentially buried alive by the trauma of the past that we have attempted to bury alive as well.

The Give-Back Trader

Several years ago, I worked with a trader whose trading was dramatically inconsistent. Val, a brilliant trader in his late twenties, was capable of creating tremendous profits in his trading. Then, after a series of exciting weeks of profit-taking, he would fall apart. He claimed, during these give-back times, that he seemed to lack any energy. In fact, Val was suffering from stress and exhausted adrenals, the small glands above your kidneys which supply the body with the hormones that keep you going during stress. But, the question was, why did this happen to Val? What was so stressful about success that it would deplete him of all of his reserves?

In the course of talking to Val about his family, I asked him about his mother. Val talked animatedly about her for a long time. When I asked where she lived, I was surprised to hear him say that she had died ten years previously. Then, Val changed the subject. But, some instinct prompted me to ask him to return to the death of his mother and tell me what happened. Reluctantly, Val said that she had died of cancer. I continued to probe. Finally, Val began to talk about the final weeks of his mother's life in the hospital, of the frightening things he saw happening to her and of her agony and fear. These images had burned so deeply into Val's mind that he could recall them in tremendous detail, from the smells of the room to the minutes it took her to finally die. When he was finished, Val was sobbing with grief that he had never released.

Val had been a freshman in college when he went to the hospital to visit his mother every day. He had grown up in a sheltered and loving family, never experiencing anything traumatic and painful. Suddenly, he was confronted with the images of suffering and death. Even worse, he was watching it happen to the person who represented all comfort and security in his world. As his father and sisters tried to cope with their own loss, they were unable to help Val cope with his. So, he buried the images and the feelings associated with them deeply in his unconscious mind. But, that was not the end of his suffering.

As time passed, Val began to have dreams about his mother. Sometimes these dreams would follow watching a movie in which someone died or in which a mother who was like his own mother played a prominent role. Sometimes his dreams came after driving by a hospital or after hearing that someone he knew was hospitalized. After awhile, there were more and more things which triggered the associations with his mother.

One of the most interesting associations with his mother's death had to do with Val's trading. Every time Val had an exceptionally good run in his trading, he began to have nightmares about his mother's death. He often awoke feeling stressed and exhausted, knowing that he had tossed and turned all night and not knowing why. Occasionally, he would remember his dreams, and then feel miserable all day.

The association with a successful trading run and the death of Val's mother became obvious after Val talked about the months preceding her hospitalization. Val had been competing in major gymnastic events in the months just prior to his mother's illness. In fact, he had been consistently winning more and more competitions, so that he was standing in line for a place on the U.S. Olympic team. His mother had traveled to each of his competitions. When he won, he would always search the audience for her cheering face.

Burying the Pain

Like Joe, Val had buried alive an experience that was too traumatic to bear. Instead of dealing with their fear and pain, both of these traders learned to protect themselves by pretending that they had healed. The result of this strategy, however, was that they were still suffering from the effects of these experiences many years later.

Are Joe and Val a tiny minority of two? Hardly. Every week, I receive calls from traders who are dealing with the effects of traumas in their lives which have wormed their way into the day-to-day workings of the trading day.

For example, I recently worked with a trader named Riener who grew up in Hitler's Germany. Riener lived on a farm with his parents. Because they were Socialists, his family were outcasts in the community. During the war, his father was stationed away from his family for three or four years at a time and they only saw him, at best, once a year. During that time, as a young boy, Riener ran the farm. He remembers, as a child, the Americans coming, and although they were kind to them, Riener and his family still feared them, not knowing how to react.

Then the Russians came. Riener remembers that they were a lot of fun and treated the German children well, too, but he continued to see strange people coming into his world and he felt much uncertainty. Then, finally, the Communists arrived. Riener managed to escape just before they took over his country. Nevertheless, Riener is haunted by the memories and insecurities of his childhood. Today, when all things are secure and Riener's trading is going especially well, there is always an underlying fear - will there be enough? This fear has some obvious and also some very subtle effects on Riener's trading. The sum of which adds up to sabotaged performance.

What to Do?

We can do our best to minimize the possibility of traumatic experiences from occurring. But, even the most carefully planned life by the most conscientious control freak cannot foresee and avoid a drunk driver coming at you in the wrong lane at 70 miles an hour on a foggy afternoon. This shattering experience, once you have survived it physically, presents you with the challenge of not just surviving it emotionally, but of growing through it. How?

1. **Accept the Unacceptable**

   The first step in healing and growing through a traumatic experience is to accept the fact that it actually happened. Many people live in a state of denial: it didn't happen. With that approach, no healing can ever take place.

   How can you accept the unacceptable? One way, is to talk about it. As you talk about it, it becomes real. Of course, you must be careful with whom you talk about your most vulnerable issues and you cannot wear out friendships and family relationships by expecting them to endlessly hear about your traumatic experience. Joining support groups is a healthy way of opening dialogue about your experience. Other resources that are valuable are trained listeners: clergymen, social workers, therapists, etc. These professionals know the questions to ask and when to be quiet. Writing about it helps, as well. Sometimes, the act of putting your experience and your thoughts about it on paper is the best way to make it real and to put it into perspective for you. Read aloud what you have written and listen for the truth of your own words.

2. **Experience Your Emotions**

   Far too many traders I have worked with are afraid to experience their own feelings. Because they are afraid of losing control of their emotions, they believe that they will give their emotions power over them by expressing them. As a result, they keep them buried deep inside, where they fester and seek to find an outlet whenever opportunity permits. The solution is to cry when you feel grief, to experience your fear when you are afraid, and to feel your outrage and anger when it wells up in you. This does not mean that you act out your emotions in destructive ways. But, feeling your feelings will allow you to bypass the self-destruction that takes place when you don't allow room for your basic emotions. For example, punching a punching bag or slapping water while you're in a pool.

3. **Find Meaning in the Aftermath**
   It is true that bad things happen to good people and that there is no meaning in many of the painful and traumatic things that happen. Nevertheless, it is also true that out of nearly every tragedy evolves some of the most unexpected benefits to those who survive. Sometimes, it takes many years to see the doors that opened for us when the doors we loved so well shut down. However, the act of looking for these newly opened doors can help us heal by looking at the experience through a new paradigm.

4. **Seek Help**
   A common mistake made by people who have lived through a terrible experience is to attempt to recover alone. Licking their wounds like a frightened animal, they go off in their own private, internal world, not letting anyone else know what is happening. Unfortunately, the longer this emotional isolation continues, the more difficult it is for the final healing to take place. At this point, it generally takes a trained therapist or psychological coach to guide an individual back into his unconscious mind and exhume the old trauma. Once this occurs, the therapist can work with the individual to help him put the experience to rest.

5. **Help Others**
   One of the best ways to reconcile a traumatic experience is to help others who have recently gone through the same experience. Flood victims often find resolution by helping others who are going through what they themselves experienced. Cancer survivors find the same source of healing in working with people who are going through chemotherapy.

Conclusion

Traders, in the day-to-day practice of their profession, are highly susceptible to the unconscious forces that are at work under the surface. When traders have buried unresolved traumatic experiences, they find their trading results at the mercy of these submerged memories. Since we are all subject to the vagaries of fate and our mortality, we are all likely to experience, at least once, a traumatic experience. If we have buried this experience alive while it still has power over us, we can still come to terms with this experience later on with help from the outside. Otherwise, it will remain a persistent and damaging negative force in our trading lives.

PAST
FUTURE

Chapter 2

THE PAST DOES EQUAL THE FUTURE, PART II
IDENTIFYING TRADING SABOTAGE

What does the past have to do with successful trading? The answer is "nearly everything." The past, whether from our earliest childhood memories or from our most recent drawdown, has more to do with the future than the present ever will. Our experiences and their interpretation guide our actions throughout the day, sometimes on a conscious level, but more often on an unconscious level. And trading, despite the protestations of the most ardent mechanical trader, is unusually responsive to the influence of the unconscious mind.

Automatic Reactions

On a conscious level, we can only process 7 bits of information, plus or minus two, at any moment. In order to perform multiple tasks during the day, we cannot rely on our conscious mind because there is too much information to process. So, once a pattern becomes familiar, it goes to the unconscious mind as an automatic reaction to a particular set of circumstances. As an example, remember how clumsy you were when you first began to use the mouse on the computer. Now, consider the multitude of operations that you have learned that have become automatic actions.

In trading, certain habits are built in order to identify, execute, and exit a trade. When the responses to a specific set of circumstances are based on following tested rules, which you believe are winning rules, the outcome will reflect the profitability of your system. Unfortunately, if your actions go against your rules, you can be guaranteed that those actions will continue to repeat themselves. Why? Regardless of the outcome, the fact that you have taken a specific action imprints a pathway on your neurology. When you face the same set of circumstances, you will likely follow the same pathway you have just established. Each time you take that pathway, it becomes more deeply worn into your neurology until it becomes an automatic reaction.

Sometimes, you will take actions that violate your trading rules only when you are not in top trading condition, like most traders who follow their rules to the letter until emotions are added to the strategy pattern. When you are not in a top performance state and emotions are used to determine your action, internal conflict is the result. Part of you will want to follow your trading rules and part of you will have an agenda based upon insecurities or addictive tendencies. When a trader has not handled psychological issues from the past, does not have a supportive environment, and has not kept his life in balance, he will not be able to follow his rules and losses will be the result.

Identifying Problems from the Past that Interfere with Your Present Trading

Fear of Loss

In looking back over your life and identifying all of the traumas and times that were uncomfortable in any way, you will find that there was some loss involved in that discomfort. This sense of loss has serious implications for your trading. If a trader views trading as a series of "wins and losses" and not as a long-term plan, which when followed, will produce profit, each trade will come from a state of loss that includes all past losses in the decision. All of the accumulated losses are present because the emotional state of loss has been painfully etched into the trader's neurology. The pain from each loss will be determined by how the trader is feeling physically, emotionally, and mentally at the time of each trade. When logic and emotion are in conflict, emotion usually wins the battle.

The Need for Healing

Wounds, whether they are physical or emotional, will fester if they are not allowed to heal. Physical wounds are easy to see and demand our immediate attention. Emotional wounds are less obvious and are often left alone, but this does not mean that they go away. Most human beings block the details of negative events from the past, but keep the anchors of the pain. We usually deny the fact that a past event haunts our present moment, but these anchors repeat themselves when the physical and emotional body is feeling a sense of loss. Instead, we fool ourselves into believing that we should have healed the past by saying, "I forgive," or "I'll put it behind me." The truth is that most of us carry baggage from the past, which reveals itself when opportunity arises.

This baggage can take many forms. It may come in the guise of headaches, back and joint pain, or any other physical discomfort that has no particular physical cause. This physical discomfort is our body's way of sending us the message to heal the hurt in our heads. If we ignore the message and bury the hurt again, the body, a self-healing mechanism, will simply attract another attention getting situation. This process of final resolution to a loss that has been ignored is the reason that patterns of hurt repeat themselves. Trading losses provide a fertile breeding ground for those opportunities.

The first step in the healing process is to identify the events and recognize that problems in your life or in your trading may have their roots in these past traumatic events. I have listed examples of the traumatic events, which have created trading problems for my clients in the past. When the loss was resolved, the trading problems it caused were relieved. These examples can be used to help identify your own life traumas, which may be holding you back from your next level of trading success.

Please evaluate yourself to see how many of these issues are affecting you. Rate these issues on a scale of 0 to 4 with "0" meaning that it doesn't affect you now to "4" meaning that it continuously comes back to haunt you. There may be a number of issues that you have suffered in one category such as the loss of various people in your life. List each loss separately and how it affected you at the time and how you think the loss still affects you now.

For example: The loss of a parent when you were 6 years old was a "4" to you at the time, but is a "1" to you now.

Important to note:
If you just read through the following evaluation rather than actually completing it, you will not get as much out of it. Therefore, proceed to the next chapter if you are not ready to fill in the blanks at this time.

Also, please note that while you might not think that a loss affects you now, if the loss was very traumatic at the time you experienced it, it could continue to play a significant role in your market struggles. Part of your problem may be unintentionally (or intentionally) denying the loss. There are times that it is not easy to identify past losses because the hurt was too great at the time.

For example:
You attended a boarding school and you were assaulted by one of the other boys or a teacher. You do not think that this experience affects you now, so you do not want to dredge up the old, uncomfortable feelings associated with this experience. Unfortunately, your trading results are not what you think they should be because taking losses are difficult for you in the markets. What you do not realize is that this trading problem is a result of this past, traumatic experience.

1. **The loss of someone** **(0-4)** ______

   Example:
   A boy lost his mother when he was six years old. He felt that she abandoned him, no matter what was said to him to the contrary.

   The effect on this boy when he became a trader was that every time he made profits, he was afraid he was going to lose them. So, he would lose his profits before the market could take them away from him.

2. **The loss of something** ______

   Example:

As a young boy, a cousin stole his piggy bank where he had been saving money to buy a pair of skates. His family refused to recover the stolen bank, so that the young boy could get his skates.

The results were that he gave away his profits before they could be taken from him.

3. **The loss of an ideal** ______
Example:
This trader started his trading career working for a large financial institution. He arrived with high ideals and soon discovered that the only way the traders could make money was to steal from the investors' accounts.

He found that he could not enter the market for fear of losing even more money from innocent people's accounts.

4. **The loss of innocence** ______
Example:
A trader discovered that his mentor, who had sold him a supposedly winning system, was not trading his own account and had only made money by selling from his successful reputation of the past to people like himself.

The result was a lack of trust in trading professionals and a loss of faith in himself for picking the wrong person to trust.

5. **The loss of competitive spirit** ______
Example:
This young man raced automobiles but lost the most important race of his life because he could not push himself past his fear.

This loss haunted him when he became a trader. He took risks that he should not have taken in order to make up for this loss in the past.

6. **The loss of face** ______
Example:
The only time this young boy was allowed to come off the bench and play in his Little League game, he dropped the ball.

This episode left him so risk-averse that he was afraid to enter a trade for fear of "dropping the ball."

7. **The loss of the sense of security** ______
Example:
As a child, this futures trader was forced to flee his homeland with only the clothing on his back. The loss of security forced him to find financial security at any price.

This need, in turn, caused him to become so reckless in his trading that he nearly lost everything he was able to amass.

8. **Loss of health** ______
   Example:
   Having asthma as a child led this young man to depend on others to take care of him. As a result, he was unable to depend on himself when making decisions.

   When he became a trader and his energy was low, he could not trust his own judgment or his system. He looked to others to make the decisions.

9. **Loss of ability** ______
   Example:
   A successful, long-term floor trader wanted to make the proactive choice of becoming an electronic trader before the choice was forced on him. He tried to use the same rules from the floor in electronic trading and failed desperately.

   Afterwards, fearful of having lost his ability to make money, he was unable to successfully trade on the floor.

10. **Loss of independence** ______
    Example:
    This young man lost his sense of security when he was treated like an outsider instead of a member of the family.

    Later, he searched for a sense of security and was unable to complete a system for fear that it would not be profitable.

11. **Loss of marriage** ______
    Example:
    A trader who lost his wife and children through a bitter divorce was suddenly forced to live alone.

    Once, he made a tremendous living, but now he had lost the reason to make any money and had no motivation to succeed.

12. **Loss of self-values** ______
    Example:
    The words of an ex-jock father still haunted this trader when he remembered how he was supposed to have the emotional detachment of his father, "The Man." His father's voice was always telling him that he would never measure up and that he was a wimp.

    The result was that the son could never make more than an average trader. There is nothing wrong with being an average trader, in fact, it's commendable. The problem was that he was not happy with himself.

13. **Loss of control** ______
Example:
This trader's father was an irresponsible gambler who lost his family's money.

Now, he follows the lead of his dad whenever his energy is low. Out of control, he gambles in the markets, losing all of his hard-earned profits.

14. **Loss of livelihood** ______
Example:
A trader worked, unlicensed, for an abortion clinic to get through school. When his lack of credentials was discovered, he lost his right to become a doctor.

Entering the field of trading, he continued this pattern by starting out with inadequate capital and repeated his pattern of failure.

15. **Loss of freedom** ______
Example:
A once successful floor trader was falsely accused of a crime committed by another.

After he had served time for this crime, he could not follow his rules because he no longer believed in the legitimacy of rules.

16. **Loss of trust** ______
Example:
A father abandoned his family. The son traded well until he pushed his wife with their children into leaving him.

Now, he does not trust his choices in life and in his trading.

17. **Loss of a sexual life** ______
Example:
A trader who was footloose and fancy free, got married to a woman who went into a depression after giving birth to a colicky child. As a result, he lost his sexual life.

He also lost the motivation to trade well.

18. **Loss of human rights and human dignity** ______
Example:
A trader was an unattractive child who was publicly taunted and humiliated in school about his looks.

As a trader, he never made the kind of money he wanted because he felt, on an unconscious level, that he was unworthy.

19. **Loss of joy** ______
Example:

This trader and his wife lost their two-year-old son who represented the joy in their lives.

The trader sabotaged his success because he no longer believed that he could or should be happy again.

Of course, identifying losses will not resolve the issues. It will give you an idea of some of the issues that can be causing problems in your trading. Once you have identified your losses, decide if it is worth the time and money necessary to address them and overcome their effect on your life. Fortunately, a wide variety of treatments are available to help you overcome these issues from the past. In traditional therapies, major trauma can take many years to overcome. A wonderful thing about Neuro-Linguistics is that for most people, major trauma can be dealt with quickly and with very little, if any, emotional distress.

Fear of Success

The fear of success is just as debilitating as the fear of loss for some traders. Many traders sabotage themselves with both fears. When your success depends upon your performance on a daily basis, psychological well being plays a major role in the outcome of profits. In shorter timeframe decision situations, more psychological strength is necessary. Listed below are some types of fear of success experienced by my clients. Continue to rate the issues you can identify with on a scale of 0 to 4, with "4" being the strongest feeling.

1. **Fear of not living up to expectations** **(0-4)** ______
   Example:
   A young boy who was an average student and athlete was compared to his brother who was a super jock and got straight A's as a student. He was told he would never be as good as his brother. Both of them became traders.

   The younger brother was a better trader than his older brother, but sabotaged his trading every time he made more than his brother did. Part of him believed he would never overtake his brother and this part of him made sure that it didn't happen.

2. **Fear of being better than your father** ______
   Example:
   A young boy worshipped his father who was a hard working man.

   As a trader he found it easy to earn money. Part of him did not think this was okay since his father had to work so hard at it. He made choices that did not allow him to exceed his father's earnings.

3. **Fear of losing the people from your past** ______
   Example:

A young man who grew up in the tenements became a trader while his old, supportive friends became laborers.

His salary far exceeded theirs, but he tried not to show it because it put a strain on the their friendships. He did not live up to his potential for fear he would have to make the choice to leave the comforts of his hometown surroundings.

4. **Fear of added financial responsibilities** ______
   Example:
   A floor trader observed that trading results suffered for traders when they upscale their lifestyles by adding big financial responsibilities that they could not afford.

   He sabotaged his best results to avoid assuming these responsibilities by being unable to afford them.

5. **Fear that money will bring out the evil in you** ______
   Example:
   A young man was raised with the belief that "money is the root of all evil." His father justified his own financial limitations by pointing to the unhappiness of the wealthier people they knew.

   Although the young trader consciously realized that his father's beliefs were not rational, he sabotaged his results when he exceeded his financial comfort zone.

6. **Not feeling worthy** ______
   Example:
   A young man was a high school dropout. His family told him, repeatedly, that he wasn't worthy of achieving the level of financial success beyond a blue-collar worker.

   He became a floor trader with a natural ability to scalp. Whenever he earned more than he felt that he is worthy of earning, he unconsciously made a mistake that kept his earnings within the range of his family's expectations.

Continue to collect experiences from your past, which could affect your trading. You may discover examples that are not listed.

Greed

Our emotions can sabotage the very finest trading system and they nearly always have their roots in our past. After fear, greed is the emotion that has the most profound effect on trading results. Although all of us have the potential to feel greed to some degree, the level of greed, which can deeply undermine trading results, is based upon past experiences. A trader must constantly monitor emotional behavior to overcome the natural tendency toward greed. When greed becomes an issue, I usually recommend longer timeframes, preferably with a system that does not require constant monitoring. Market swings often draw a trader into his compulsion by stimulating his awareness of a potential windfall. For traders who experience greed as a continuous addictive behavior, it is better to enter another profession. Trading, for a greedy compulsive, is like tending bar for an alcoholic. You cannot expect the alcoholic to not take a drink, and you cannot expect a trader, who is subject to greed, to trade by his rules. For other traders who are affected by greed but are not addicted to it, a clearing of past events with some behavior modifications will serve to check the tendency towards greed.

Consider the following signs that indicate that you may have a problem with greed.

1. **You have an obsessive, insatiable need for more** **(0-4)** ______
   Example:
   While growing up in the Great Depression, often there was not enough food for this trader as a child. To this day, nothing is ever enough.

   As a trader, whenever he is low on energy, he reverts back to an emotional state of having an insatiable appetite for more. This is when he takes uncalculated risks and gambles instead of trades.

2. **You believe that you deserve more** ______
   Example:
   A young boy is not as attractive as his older brother, but is far more talented. The affection and attention are bestowed on the older brother.

   As a trader, he overrides his system thinking he can get more out of the markets than his system will allow because he thinks he deserves more.

3. **You have a need to be better than others** ______
   Example:
   A young man is viewed as limited in his neighborhood because of his racial background. Always needing to prove everyone wrong, he far exceeds most young men in the old neighborhood scholastically.

   In trading, however, he sabotages his efforts by taking foolish risks in an effort to prove himself better than everyone else.

Hope

While hope is an emotional instability, I feel it deserves a category of its own for traders. Hope and greed are closely related because traders see themselves wishing for something that they do not deserve. What a trader does not deserve is to gain profits from gambling.

Some Examples:

1. **Hoping the present does not equal the future** **(0-4)** ______
   Example:

A young boy observed his mom sticking with his dad who was an emotionally abusive man that she thought would change with time.

When the boy became a trader, he did not believe in putting stops with his orders. He would see his position go through his mental stop and hope that it would come back.

2. **Relying on others to make things happen** ______
   Example:
   Throughout a young man's life, his parents did not allow him to be a part of the decisions that affected his life.

   As an adult investor, he made choices based on everyone else's advice and hoped that the bad choices would turn around and be good choices.

Emotional Instabilities

Losses from the past result in a wide range of emotional instabilities that create unresourceful behaviors which sabotage trading. Many traders experience a lifelong struggle to overcome a host of effects on their trading from various events in their past. Others have a single culprit that is enough to cripple their efforts. One of the most successful remedies for these emotional instabilities is to transform the perceptions that surround the original experience. These perceptions are the conclusions that we form, the way we relate the experience, and the specific details of the experience that we remember or recreate in our minds.

As an example, a trader places his first real-time trade and loses most of his trading capital. The experience is very frightening to him. The trading process does not work in reality the way it did on paper and he has experienced a serious loss. Now, he begins to interpret what happened and talk to himself about the experience. It is very likely that he will see himself as a powerless victim in the process. He will focus on the pain of the loss and the fear he felt as he watched the market go against him. He will talk about how difficult it is to make money in the market and how his system failed him. The result of this self-talk and perception will be emotional instabilities that prevent him from trading well in the future.

Suppose, however, that this same trader reframes the experience and is able to see it in an entirely different way. In this new perception, he sees that he went into trading without completing the proper amount of preparation or study and testing of his system. He also sees that he did not create a business plan to follow. He also failed to work on his own psychology so that he was not prepared for the whipsawing of his emotions. Instead of feeling scared and victimized, he can now feel a different set of emotions: relief, empowerment, determination, and commitment. This is the process of transformation that allows for more resourceful behavior in the future. When this trader is confronted with his next real-time trade, he will be able to react differently. It is important to note that in addition to transformation, diet and other life behaviors need to be addressed in order to support emotional stability.

Here are some emotional instabilities that I have helped clients transform. Add any of these that are appropriate to your list, and rate them on the 0-4 scale as they affect your life.

1. **Need for excitement** **(0-4)** ______
   Example:
   In the Vietnam conflict, a man was constantly in the extremes of emotional drama. Trading is a perfect outlet for emotions that need to be played out. In order to feel the peaks of wins; however, you must feel the pain of losses.

   When he is emotionally drained, this trader plays emotions to their extremes.

2. **Need to express emotions** ______
   Example:
   A young child was taught that he should behave like a man and not cry. By suppressing the display of negative emotions, he developed the need for an outlet of these emotions.

   When he is depressed as a trader, he loses money in order to allow himself to feel bad. He chastises himself for feeling bad and buries the feeling only to repeat the cycle.

3. **Need to overcome feelings of guilt** ______
   Example:
   As a teenager, a young man nearly destroyed his family by using drugs. His father had a heart attack and never recovered completely.

   When he became a trader, his guilt prevented him from becoming a highly successful trader.

4. **Need to control** ______
   Example:
   A trader grew up with parents who were out of control and needed to try to control everything, including him. This produced a child who was afflicted with the same emotional instability.

   A trader wants to control the markets because he cannot tolerate "the loss part" of trading. He therefore limits his success.

5. **Need to be perfect** ______
   Example:
   Whatever this young man did was never good enough for his parents and, as a result, for himself.

As a trader, he could never get the best out of a trade even if he picked the top or bottom of a market. As a result, he took risks that were too great and his results were erratic.

6. **Need to be a martyr** ______
   Example:
   While they lavished their attention on his older and younger siblings, his parents rejected a young man as a child. The only way he could get their attention was through extreme measures of self-sacrifice.

   As a trader, he could run up incredible profits only to sacrifice himself to the market.

7. **Shirking responsibility** ______
   Example:
   Raised in a family that was always too giving of the wrong things, this young man was not taught to take responsibility for anything. His parents hired people to take care of his every whim.

   As a trader, he was looking to brokers and advisors for the answers. He never trusted his own decisions.

8. **Lack of motivation** ______
   Example:
   A boy grew up in a family that did not believe in rewards or celebration for any of his achievements or to commemorate important moments.

   In attempting to become a trader, it was difficult for him to face the challenges because he did not know how to reward himself for his work.

9. **Negative self-talk** ______
   Example:
   Surrounded in stereo by his mother and father, a boy was raised to listen to continuous negative conversation: from what was wrong with the world, the neighbors, themselves, and their son. The seeds of negative self-talk have deep roots in this trader's life.

   As a trader you can imagine the continuous self-inflicted wounds from words that this trader plants in his head each day. It is a wonder that he manages to survive in trading at all.

10. **Anger and rage** ______
    Example:
    A young girl was taught that it is unattractive to display any form of negative emotion in her boarding school. Her parents supported the school in order for their daughter to behave like a perfect lady at all times. Inside her anger and rage fester, periodically exploding in a volley of invectives at servants, animals, and anyone in her path.

As a floor trader, she has good instincts for trading, but her use of foul language gets her in trouble with the people she works with.

11. Loneliness ______

Example:

This only child's parents worked until all hours, and he was not allowed to participate in extracurricular activities, have friends, or siblings to play with. He became very familiar with every food delivery service in the neighborhood.

As an adult, he had no model for creating a happy life. He succeeded at making money as a trader and failed at life. He did not enjoy the fruits of his labor.

12. Negative attitude ______

Example:

A very impulsive young man with an idyllic life made an impulsive decision to marry a fair young lady within a month of their meeting. She was able to disguise her negative attitude and keep her best foot forward until the honeymoon.

After constantly hearing his wife's ranting about everything, he began to join her in her negative attitude. Soon, he started to play the role of victim, which resulted in him not trusting his trading decisions.

13. Lack of trust ______

Example:

A parent needed to override almost every major decision made by his son led this young man to distrust his own decisions.

Later, when he became a trader, he looked to others for their choices. When he found that this did not work, he looked to himself and found in himself someone who was not trustworthy.

14. The need to get even ______

Example:

A skinny kid whose life was made miserable by bullies discovered that weapons worked well as a defense.

Becoming a successful trader was the primary goal of his adult life. But whenever he had a major drawdown, he wanted to get even with the markets. Weapons did not work this time.

15. Need to criticize yourself and others ______

Example:

This boy's father needed to criticize his children because it repeated the pattern of behavior he experienced as a child. (This is one of the most common problems that a trader has to overcome.)

Critical self-talk has haunted this trader's decision-making process. It has made it difficult for him to follow his system.

16. Inability to forgive ______

Example:

A boy grew up with an alcoholic father. He witnessed his father beating and raping his sister in a drunken rage. His father got treatment when the boy was a teenager and became a good husband and father, but the son cannot forgive his father's behavior as an alcoholic.

Unable to release the negative feelings he has toward his father, as a trader he amplifies the problem when things are not going well by entering periods of despair.

Hopefully, you are beginning to see that these categories of sabotage are interrelated. While you can identify a person as having an issue of loss, it can also be identified as an issue of emotional instability and/or a behavioral issue. Keep this idea in mind while you are listing issues that could be plaguing your trading results.

Negative patterns of behavior will continue to repeat themselves in a cyclic manner unless a traumatic event or a metaphor given at the right moment transforms them in the course of life. They can also be changed as a result of a conscious, disciplined decision over a longer period of time. Unfortunately, most people do not stumble on to these changes or are not disciplined enough to make a conscious decision to make changes on their own. In the short term, counseling can be expensive, but in the long term it can be the best choice for a trader when considering all of the alternatives.

Behavioral

Here are some examples of behavioral problems, which sabotage traders' efforts:

1. **Patterns of failure** **(0-4)** ______

   Example:

   A young man experienced his father's struggles to shift from being a blue-collar worker to an entrepreneur. His father made all of the typical mistakes of someone who does not know how to make this happen. He also saw the struggles of his mother scraping to make ends meet. These influenced his desire to become successful in his business life.

   As a businessman, he failed at multi-level marketing and a series of other small enterprises. He discovers trading as the answer to his search, but makes all of the choices of someone wanting to take the fast track to trading success without knowing the correct way to do it.

2. **Out of balance** ______

   Example:

A young man out of college found his niche as a successful broker. He made too much money too fast for him to deal with on a healthy basis.

His life went out of balance with his choices of wine, women, and party activities. His trading began to suffer because his body, mind, and spirit were not supporting him.

3. **Not having a plan** ______
Example:
A successful lawyer who had always worked for others decided he wanted to become a trader. Having never completed a business plan, he proceeded as if he were working for someone else who had the business plan for the company all figured out. (90% of the traders I have evaluated do not have a written business plan. This is the main cause of failure to succeed at running a trading business.)

This trader becomes a money manager who succeeds in profits as a trader, but fails in the business because of lack of planning. Very often a new money manager sees a million dollars under management as "having arrived." With only 2% in fees and 20% of profits, this management account is not enough to run a business when the inevitable drawdown occurs.

4. **Living beyond your means** ______
Example:
Keeping up with the Jones' was an important part of the neighborhood environment where a young man grew up. The only problem was that his family was on the bottom rung of the competition.

As a trader, he was playing a different game. He had the biggest and best toys in his pit. The only problem was that he could not keep up with his lifestyle and his trading suffered. He was soon going to find himself at the bottom of the totem pole again.

5. **Not being consistent** ______
Example:
The home environment of a young man was one in which punishment was threatened, but rarely carried out.

This trader had several good systems. If he followed any one of them, he would be successful in his results. The problem was that he would sometimes follow one and then the other. (Consistency is key to a trader building a more successful system, because when he is consistent, he can see where to improve his system.)

6. **Disorganization** ______
Example:
A trader was raised by a father who was good in every way except being a role model for cleanliness and organization.

As a trader he kept family tradition and lived in chaos. The chaos led to a lack of focus, which made it difficult to follow his rules.

7. **Inflexibility** ______
   Example:
   A trader was raised in a predictable environment where everything was determined by a rigid set of beliefs and values. As long as you adhered to this limited thinking, you were doing your job as a member of the family.

   He was a very successful trader for a number of years, always sticking to the rules he first developed and tested. The markets changed, but he did not have the flexibility to adjust to the new environment.

Stress

Stress results from your neurological system being out of balance. This means that energy gets blocked from flowing naturally through the body. A natural, balanced diet, exercise, restful sleep, and meditation are key ingredients in overcoming stress. Stress piggybacks on all of the issues of sabotage. As a result, additional habits are formed which increase stress.

Here is a listing of some stress traps that traders fall into:

1. **Not enough time and energy** **(0-4)** ______
   Example:
   A dual career couple has two children with one on the way. The father is a member of the Masonic Lodge, coaches his son's baseball team, and spends every ounce of free time surfing on the Web. He gets the flu and has no time in his schedule for handling an illness.

   He is a consistently good trader, but lack of energy and the additional stress caused by being sick creates a problem in his trading choices. His body is trying to tell him to back off, but he is not getting the message.

2. **Not enough rest and relaxation and/or exercise** ______
   Example:
   A trader was obsessed with trading. His behavior took over all the time when he should have been with family and friends while rejuvenating. Everyone in his life learned to fill his or her time without him. His wife decided to leave with the kids to start a life with someone who had a life beyond his profession.

   He finally wakes up to the fact that he is alone and is a very tired person. Relaxing and recreating are foreign to him when he tries to expand his life. He blames trading as the problem and now finds everything too overwhelming and his trading suffers.

3. **Bad food choices** ______
   Example:
   A trader was raised on junk food. Pepto-Bismol is part of his regular diet and is considered a separate food group.

   His physical health is affecting his mental health, and his mental health is affecting his trading decisions.

4. **Addictive substances** ______
   Example:
   This trader drinks 4 cups of coffee before breakfast. He is up to 10 cups during the day.

   As in the above case, his trading eventually is affected. Since he does not believe coffee is an addictive substance, he blames his trading problems on everything else.

5. **Relationships that do not work** ______
   Example:
   A partnership was formed to create a new money management business. One partner was going to concentrate on trading and the other on sales and marketing. The salesman is a closet trader who starts to dabble with the trading side, neglecting the sales side.

   The trader's frustration in dealing with this issue creates a problem in his own trading results.

6. **Need to create pressure in order to get things accomplished** ______
   Example:
   In college, this trader developed a pattern of leaving studies until the last minute and studying all night for the exam or completing the paper. This strategy worked for him. He adopted the idea that he worked best under pressure.

   When he became a trader and created a pressured environment, he produced negative results. Good trading is predicated on having a healthy performance state of mind. Most people work best under a non-pressure environment. (Many people who seem to be thriving under pressure are those who are actually using passion as their motivational force.)

Beliefs

Once again, a major psychological influence on your trading has its roots in your past. The category of "Beliefs" would have too many possibilities to be listed because everything you say is a belief. The extent to which you believe something to be true determines how it will affect your behavior. Beliefs come from the experiences in your life so that you are rarely consciously aware of them. In order to identify your beliefs; listen to your thoughts and the things you say about yourself, trading, and how you feel about money. This exercise will tell you what level of success is possible for your trading.

Become aware of the significant people in your life and listen to what they say about themselves and about you. These people have influenced your language patterns and thoughts.

Beliefs that limit success possibilities or diminish self-worth are destructive to your greatest potential and need to be reframed if you want to increase growing.

Suggestion to overcome negative beliefs:
When you identify negative dialogue coming from yourself or others, reframe it into positive dialogue until it becomes a natural pattern of speaking.

Examples would be:

Negative: I will never be as good as ______________.
Positive: I will be the best I can be.

Negative: I am stupid.
Positive: I make good choices that include the best possible outcome for all concerned.

Negative: I will never be a successful trader because I don't have the killer instinct.
Positive: I will model traders who have successful lives.

Changing language behaviors must be a conscious choice before you can rely on the unconscious to make it a part of how you express yourself. If you are not successful in making these changes on your own, realize that one or more of the issues previously listed could be sabotaging your efforts. These issues would have to be dealt with first.

Conflicts

When one part of you has a belief that is different from another part of you, you have a conflict. The part of you that needs to be healed, the emotional part, will win the conflict when you go into that negative emotional and physical state that I call "The Cesspool." This is the place where your neurology is off balance, when you are sick, or when your energy is very low. It is also the place where all negative past issues are stored, ready to surface when you are in an unresourceful state of mind. Even if you are only in this place on a part-time basis, you can do great damage to your income.

You can best negotiate conflict when you are in a rational state of mind. This takes creating a living and working environment which has the least amount of stress.

Conclusion

Complete your own analysis of possible issues that have their roots in your past and are holding you back from trading success. Even though these sabotaging issues are deeply buried in your past, they do not need to continue to shape your future. Realize that each new level of success will be determined by transforming some part of your thinking and behavior. Some of you might be satisfied with the status quo and will keep doing what you are doing. Realize that with advanced technology the world around you is changing. If you do not keep up with the times, you could be left behind.

Your continued success is dependent upon the choices that you make. The choices you make are dependent upon your mental stability. Keep rediscovering and healing yourself. This is the key to enjoying the process of life and to attaining each next level of success.

ARE YOU OKAY?
TIME-OUT

Chapter 3

IN SHOCK

Recently, I was in an automobile accident. A cab driver sped through a four way stop sign as I was entering the intersection. For a spell, I felt lost in time. I did not know if I had been in an explosion, or where I was. In that moment of unreality, I even thought that it had all been a dream. Whether it is a sudden shock from an accident or the shock of realizing that you are observing your trading account being taken by the markets and you cannot act appropriately - it is the same feeling.

Events in life can cause a state of shock. In the best of all circumstances, a person can go through life without a major shock. This utopian existence is very unlikely. Since successful trading is predicated on good performance, it is important that a trader have contingency plans in place for any event that might create a shocking circumstance. Being unprepared for such an event could financially be very costly.

Sometimes You Just Gotta Let Go

I was sitting in my car, counting body parts and trying to figure out whether the next world war had started. Had Saddam managed to drop a bomb over Cary, North Carolina, or was it something else, perhaps a huge meteor we did not stop in time? At that moment, a gentle, concerned face appeared at my window and asked how I was. For a split second, I thought of all the times I had been asked in a crisis how I was and I just wanted to say, "Obviously, I'm not okay!" But, all I could say was, "I don't know." The one thing I did know was that it was time for me to let go of the control and let others take care of me for a change.

When you are in a state of shock, it is the best time to make NO choices if at all possible. The first thing to do is seek out the first helpful person that you can feel comfortable with and allow him to make the immediate decisions. When something has happened in your trading and you are in a state of shock, you need to know whom you can trust to make the best choices for you. Then, trust those people at that time without question, and follow their advice. For me, after the accident, it was the paramedics, the police and my assistant, Wendy.

Who are the right people to make the choices for you when you are in shock? There is a different answer for each of us. Some of the people in our lives are very good at giving advice, but are not necessarily the people you want to model when something goes wrong. For example, a best friend leads a model life, when you suddenly need answers to some sticky ethical issues these individuals may not be the right people to help you find your way out of the situation you are in. On the other hand, you may remember a friend or family member who was in a similar situation and feel comfortable relying on them for help.

In a shocking situation, you may also find that you have no one in your life whose advice and guidance will be of help. At that time, you may need to look for the expert advice that you need for specific emergencies. For example, a trader needs a person to talk to who will understand his specific situation during times of drawdown or when he has made a foolish mistake.

Recovery

During the first stage of recovery from a shock, you will need to allow yourself to discuss your problem with whomever will listen. It is particularly helpful, however, to pick someone who is compassionate, but who will not add to your problem by emotionally taking on your feelings and adding to your panic and feelings of hopelessness or helplessness.

Once you have talked about the situation initially, it is time to exhaust the subject completely, so that you are tired of hearing your own voice and tired of hearing that same, old story. Make certain, of course, that you are not bending the same ear over and over again. Long term friendships can be tested beyond the strength of their bonds if care is not taken. You do not want to exhaust your precious resources.

Now that you have told and retold your story until you have grown tired of it, let it go, and let your mind release it and occupy your thoughts completely with other things. Participate in vigorous exercise, go to a movie that will capture your full attention, read a great book, or visit with friends, which will serve to divert your attention. It is important that you release your emotions and choose circumstance that will make you laugh.

One positive way to occupy your thoughts during a shock, if this is appropriate, is to focus on the needs of those around you. In an emergency, this if often the most successful strategy for handling a shock. If you can attend to those less well off than yourself, you get to put your experience into a different context. You will still feel the loss and the shock, but you will find that you are better able to handle it.

Shock and the Body

The physiological effects of shock can have a profound effect on your ability to recover quickly. The enormous production of adrenaline by your body during shock and immediately afterwards can exhaust your adrenals. If that happens, your immune system will be temporarily depressed, which sets you up for many types of infection and inflammatory conditions. You will also feel exhausted, unable to sleep, have difficulty concentrating, and prone to tearful outbursts. The smallest sounds or stresses will be too much for you to bear. This is all the result of adrenal exhaustion from shock.

How can you prevent this from happening? Your first line of defense is to provide your body with the nutrients that your depleted adrenal glands need to produce the adrenaline: vitamins C, B2, B6 and particularly Pantothenic Acid, the principle ingredient of adrenaline. These nutrients are readily available at your local health food store. Always check with your doctor first, of course.

Another way to reduce the damaging effects of adrenaline in your body is to exercise rigorously immediately after the shock to use up the adrenaline. To illustrate this point, a woman jogger who had to escape from early morning attackers was in a state of shock by the time she returned to the safety of her apartment. After telling her best friend that she felt sick and shaky from the adrenaline, she was convinced to go back out in the daylight to "run it off". She protested, but her friend insisted that she needed to exercise. Afterwards, the jogger told me that to her great surprise, despite the terrible shock and panic she had experienced in her narrow escape, she never felt any ill effects. In fact, she felt remarkably well afterwards.

Assessing the Damages

After an automobile accident, the parties involved are often unaware of the true extent of their injuries. For example, a woman I knew who had been in an auto accident sought no medical attention afterward because she believed she was uninjured. Nearly a year later, she discovered that a vertebra in her neck had shifted during the impact, and was a hair's breath from severing her spinal cord. She underwent emergency surgery and subsequently, wore a neck brace for many months.

The same principle applies to the psychological damages a trader suffers after a major loss. Sometimes, even though the impact seems slight, the actual damages cause an anchor of fear for other trades. At other times, a trader knows it is time for a vacation to Bora Bora and come back refreshed and start as if nothing had happened.

Taking Control

Prepare a list of things to do when you are ready to begin to trade again after a time of crisis. Complete one task, followed by the next task on the list. Pretty soon you will be back in full swing. Start with the simplest things, like taking out the trash, clearing your desk or updating your charts before starting to trade. And as you do these things, notice how you feel about it. If you are successfully completing these tasks without putting yourself in a state of tension, then you can move on. If not, you need to take breaks in between each task to get your mind and body back into your routine. There is a tendency to try to do everything at once, because time and control have been lost.

People who are good at handling things while in a state of shock have times when everything feels like it is coming apart and afterward has settled down. If you are one of these people, it is important that you arrange for yourself to be the one who gets attention and support at the time when you need to regroup.

How to Help Others in a State of Shock

If someone is not physically harmed, but is in a state of shock, you can help them to handle the shock by creating a situation where they can feel useful. Just as it is helpful to pull yourself out of a state of shock by focusing on helping others, you can help someone else in a state of shock by providing a way for them to be useful. The best way to do this is to give them a task they can easily handle. For example, if someone has just died, you can ask others to make phone calls, or make coffee, or pick up food. Most people want to feel useful and feel like they can do something about the situation. Another thing is to give them a list of things they can do, in sequence. Since people in shock cannot make complex decisions or use higher reasoning, you can reduce their stress by giving them a list. As they check off items completed on the list, they begin to regain a sense of control.

The worst thing to do is to say, "Just sit down and take it easy." Unless the person is too overcome to walk and talk, this may simply force them to focus inwardly on the looped tape of the experience, which they will relive over and over again.

The best help you can give is to be a listener. The person who is in shock needs someone to talk to and that, alone, may be the best thing you can do for him. Listen patiently, without emotion, to what he needs to say. Do not react with anger, tears or advice to what has happened. Just listen. He may need to repeat the story over again. And then, there are those who need to say nothing. Sometimes your presence and sitting with them quietly is the best you can do.

A Death in the Family

Several times a month, I receive phone calls from traders who have lost loved ones. Most of the time, when they are talking to me, they are in a state of shock. Usually people will say, "I wish I had more time," or " I wish I had said this or that." I usually suggest that they go out for a long walk and, in their mind's eye, talk to the person who has just recently departed until there is nothing left to say at that moment. Realizing that this can be a two-way conversation, I instruct them to listen for answers. Knowing their departed well enough, they know what they would say. It is important to have a conversation with the best part of the deceased and the best past of yourself, keeping the exchange very positive.

Coming out of this grieving state is different for everyone. It does not necessarily have to take a long time, but there is a certain amount of time that is needed for overcoming the shock and the grief. THIS IS NOT A TIME TO TRADE. Grieving does not begin until the shock is over. A television news' magazine featured a segment on people who grieve for the rest of their lives when a loved one is lost. Although we get over the initial grief and loss, it is not unusual for people to hold onto their grief forever, because it is a way for them to maintain the relationship.

Contrary to the popular notion that you pass through the various stages of grief, anger, denial, and negotiation, to final acceptance, you can get caught in a loop and go through the various stages over and over again. You first have to want to get out of the loop before a healing can take place. The best way for people to get out of a loop, who will not do it for themselves, is for them to consider the others whose lives are being adversely affected by their being stuck in a negative loop.

Not Up to Speed and Not Knowing It

When people are in a state of shock, they are not able to think clearly enough to know that they are not thinking clearly. The biochemical changes in the brain during shock prevent us from making higher level decisions and from clearly observing our surroundings and making intelligent assessments based on our observations. We are short of memory and find that we cannot remember what just happened or was just said to us. The problem is that we still believe that we are functioning well enough to take care of ourselves. But, too often we are not.

Therefore, when you have just experienced a shock, make sure to allow other people to let you know that you are not functioning at full capacity. When I was in a state of shock, I thought I was perfectly in control and could handle everything. The feedback I got from other people made me realize later how out of sorts I had really been.

Conclusion

When you go through an experience that puts you in a state of shock, whether it is the result of your trading or not, it will affect your trading if you do not deal with the fallout from the shock. First, recognize that you are not functioning at your peak performance and that you should not be making decisions. Find someone you can trust to make decisions for you. Talk out your shock and then find ways to occupy your mind and body. Find a way to be useful and to help others. Take care to replenish the nutrients your body lost during the shock so that you stay healthy. Recognize that you may be in one or more stages or grief for an extended period. If you need to do so, find qualified people to help you work through your shock and grief. And above all else, do NOT trade when you are in this state.

Chapter 4

PATTERN RECOGNITION:
OLD PATTERNS AFFECT TRADING

Trading disturbs comfortable life patterns for many traders because it requires them to think like an entrepreneur, deal with high levels of risk, manage their life on an insecure income, and accomplish this surrounded by friends and family who do not consider trading to be a real job. These demands challenge the traditions, beliefs, and early environment which form the patterns and behaviors we choose for our lives.

These patterns feel comfortable because they are familiar. If the behaviors are strengthened by strong emotional and environmental support, they are difficult to break loose from when they stand in the way of a trader's need to grow. For some individuals, it is better to hang on to the old patterns, rather than suffering the consequences of failing by trying to change the behaviors. However, if a trader is willing to pay the price of discomfort and possible loss, these changes can make the difference between living in passion or settling for one's lot in life.

Settling for Happy

Adam grew up in a happy and stable Kansas family where everyone knew their range of personal choices and the consequences of deviating from this prescribed path. While Adam loved and respected his family and community, he wanted more from life than his Midwestern lifestyle would allow. He decided to become a commodities trader which was a major break from tradition. In a typical response to his decision, Adam's family was both supportive and practical: If he did not get positive results, he would return to the family business with no questions asked. Even with their support, Adam felt guilty for not fulfilling his family's expectations and feared that he would have to give up his dream if he could not achieve immediate success in trading. He felt the need to create "the Holy Grail System" which would guarantee success, and the pressure to create the perfect system made it impossible for him to complete it. Compounding his dilemma was the fact that this earnest young trader was locked in a very unhappy marriage.

While looking for a way out of his never-ending loop, Adam attended one of my seminars. Not only did he discover and overcome the issues which were holding him back from trading, Adam also found the passion of his life in one of the other participants at the seminar. Soon, Adam was legally separated from his wife and living in his own apartment. His wife pleaded with him to return home and offered to seek counseling which she had adamantly refused before his leaving. But, for the first time in his life, he felt alive and was ready to conquer the world. Blinded by his passion, Adam became a modern day Don Quixote, tilting at market windmills.

During this brief period of freedom from his old patterns of behavior, Adam not only completed his system, but successfully attracted outside capital to manage. However, a series of painful experiences and the shattering appeals to his sense of loyalty and family, eventually pulled Adam back to his old reality. Reluctantly, he decided to do the "right thing," and return home. Over time, the "right thing" proved to be the best choice for Adam. Now, five years later, he enjoys a good life in the familiar arms of his solid and traditional Midwestern life. He lives his passionate life in his fantasies, and in the meantime, he has become a steady, good trader.

Selling Out on Yourself

From the time he was a teenager, Larry knew he wanted to be a trader. He had become a successful floor trader in the corn pit when he met Monica who was beautiful, rich and smart. Although she loved Larry, she hated his profession and made it abundantly clear that if they were to have a life together, he would have to give up trading and come into her family's business. Larry found Monica's terms too hard to resist. At first, he enjoyed the challenge and the financial security his new life provided, but eventually, he realized that he had sold out on himself and on his dreams.

Play Now/Pay Later

Pam and Rhoda were identical twin sisters although their behaviors were completely different. According to her mother, Pam was rebellious from her first prenatal kick. Always the center of attention, Pam was a popular teenager. Rhoda, on the other hand, was compliant, studious, and quiet. While everyone in the family loved and appreciated Rhoda, Pam was the apple of everyone's eye. Rhoda invested her trust fund in her education, established a law practice, and married Vincent who was one of Pam's throw-aways. They lived a quiet, successful life.

Pam, on the other hand, was eager to make her fortune in the excitement of the markets. She did not want to waste her valuable time in school, and her unwillingness to prepare herself plus her compulsive need for excitement soon resulted in a series of unwise decisions. The patterns that Pam had established early in life served her and were supported by her environment. However, they were so counterproductive in a successful trading career that, unless they were changed rapidly, Pam would be met with the same swift and unsympathetic fate that carries so many new traders out of the business. Unable to break her addiction to excitement and immediate gratification, Pam lost all of her inheritance in the markets as well as the adoration of her friends and family. Unfortunately, the markets were not nearly so forgiving as her parents.

Focused on the Gold Ring

George's parents had experienced success and failure as restaurateurs. As a young man, he knew that he would eventually enter an entrepreneurial profession because risk-taking was in his blood. George married Athena whose family lived by a very predictable and secure set of patterns. Athena's family could always rely on their father to be home by six every evening with a steady, reliable paycheck every two weeks because of his position as an accountant with a major firm. George was also an accountant who was self employed. This meant that instead of a predictable bi-weekly salary, his business forced him to live with the yearly strain of tax season. However, following the markets, which happened to be George's avocation, made tax season seem like a vacation.

His market activities put continual strain on his relationship with Athena, and when George announced that he was going to become a commodities trader, Athena reacted with anger and tears. His risk-taking family was also against his becoming "a gambler," and tried to discourage him by threatening to disinherit him. George was undeterred. Although the atmosphere of conflict made it difficult for him to trade his rules consistently, he knew that trading was what he wanted to do. The price George paid for following his passion was the loss of Athena, his children, and his family.

Two years later, George met Kathy, a successful equities trader. She was also divorced and caring for one child. They instantly clicked and were soon married while supporting their good trading results. George has been welcomed back into the good graces of his family, and has become good friends with his ex-wife who has also remarried.

Unlike Pam, George was able to trade successfully because the entrepreneurial and risk-taking patterns he developed were consistent with the requirements of trading. He did not have to break any major behaviors to succeed. In fact, his patterns provided him with the resources he needed for success. The people closest to him were severely challenged by his new career, and they were not willing or happy to change their patterns to accommodate his dream. George had seized the gold ring, but much of its glitter was lost in the process.

Weighing the Cost of Success

In making the choices for our lives, we must consider what is at risk and decide whether we are willing to pay the required price. Trading is not the right fit for over ninety percent of the people who come into the markets. What makes you believe that you can beat those odds? Ask yourself these questions and answer them honestly:

1. Do I have the right education to become a successful trader?
2. Do I have a system which has been tested and which I believe will make me money?
3. Do I have the resources necessary to withstand the inevitable drawdowns?

4. Do I have the psychology which will support me in following my rules?
5. Do I have a trader's business plan which I know will lead me to success?
6. Do I have a supportive environment?
7. Do the significant people in my life support me in becoming a trader?
8. Do my attitudes, beliefs, and values support having a trading career?
9. Is it okay for me to lose, knowing I will eventually win because I believe in my system?
10. Is it okay for me to win, knowing that the money I earn brings me, my family, and my community good fortune?

Your honest answers to these questions will identify the hurdles that you need to overcome in order to succeed. They will also tell you whether or not the price of becoming a trader is too high for you to accept.

Recognizing the Patterns

It is important to recognize the patterns that are an integral part of your response to your environment and the people close to you. In reviewing your early responses to environmental influences did you:

- Accept them unquestioningly?
- Unwillingly submit to them?
- Reject them?
- Adapt to them?

When you recognize your patterns, you will be able to identify the obstacles you face in meeting your goals or the resources you have to support you in reaching them. To discover these patterns, ask yourself how you and your family feel about:

- Family ties
- Religion
- Social interests
- Education
- Career
- Money
- Risk
- Trading

Your responses represent the patterns of the past creating the self-defeating behaviors in your trading. Study your list and notice how you react to each pattern. Examples are:

- Most family members divorce because of conflicts over money
- Only the professional people in the family are thought to have any value
- Your family wants you to be a doctor because your grandfather was a doctor and your father is a doctor

- Anyone in the family who tries to become an entrepreneur is discouraged--success is praised, but failure is rejected
- Your family smokes drinks, and is obsessive about food
- Criticism is an accepted form of communication between family members
- When you enter a trade, a part of you questions your ability
- When a trade goes against you, you stay in your position hoping that the market might reverse and go in your favor

Your patterns will either sabotage your efforts or provide the foundation for your success.

Breaking Patterns

Since your patterns are not only long-standing, but deeply rooted in your emotions and identity, changing them can be very difficult. First, you must identify the source of the pattern. Is it:

1. Physical dependence--Is this pattern based upon a physical dependence such as a health issue, food addiction or drugs?
2. Emotional--Is this pattern based upon feelings? For example, you need to hold too tightly to stories about yourself to maintain self-esteem and/or values.
3. Environmental--Is this pattern based upon cultural expectations, pressures, or norms?

Once you have identified the source of the pattern, you can work on changing it by consciously:

1. Becoming aware when engaging in the pattern which limits your success.
2. Determining how a changein your thinking and behavior will affect you and the people in your life.
3. Deciding if the change is worth the price. If it is. . .
4. Repeatedly behave in a new desired way. Or,
5. Reframe your thoughts until the new pattern is a natural part of your behavior.

Highly disciplined individuals who are emotionally balanced are sometimes able to change patterns on their own. However, many individuals who attempt to change behaviors consciously find that they do not have the discipline or emotional balance to change their patterns with much success. If a behavior is in the way of good trading results, get out of trading or seek professional help.

Conclusion

Our patterns are the well-worn paths that lead us to our future. The cost of changing a pattern that leads to failure can be too high for some, while a pattern change that will lead to happiness and success is worth the price for others. A majority of people find that their patterns do not conform to the requirements of a successful trading lifestyle because the fit is uncomfortable and unnatural. It is important to know if you are going with the flow of your natural tendencies or working against your inclinations. Until you can create supportive patterns that lead to success as a trader, you will be sabotaging your discipline and undermining all of your efforts.

WALL STREET JOURNAL 1980's
WOODSTOCK
THE FAB FOUR
Marilyn
WALL ST. JOURNAL
COFFEE
KEEP FOREVER
TAXES 1989
PAINT BY NUMBERS
Herb Alpert
TAXES
TAXE

Chapter 5

HOLDING ON: LETTING GO OF EMOTIONAL CLUTTER

The life-long pattern of obsessively holding on to things in their lives is one of the major reasons that traders:

- Fail to follow their trading rules
- Hold on to trades too long
- Let go of trades too soon
- Fail to take trades
- Stay with a trading system that is outdated

Fueled by deeply held and often unconscious fears of pain, loss, and the unknown, the inability to let go or hold on can result in the failure to follow trading rules. This negative trading behavior leads to a host of other psychological problems, which supports the inability to let go. Although this pattern of behavior is destructive to trading results, it can be replaced with constructive alternatives if the trader is willing to acknowledge that the pattern exists, has a desire to change it, and works on an appropriate solution.

The Cluttered Trader

Jack was having trouble following his trading system because he refused to exit trades when his rules gave him the exit signal. Instead, Jack grimly watched as his profits disappeared with the runaway trades. When he called me for help, I was scheduled to present a seminar in his city, so I agreed to visit him at his home. When he opened the door, I was shocked at the clutter. Having recently divorced, Jack was living in bachelor hell. Everywhere you looked in his living and working environment there were magazines, books, mail, empty pizza boxes, and dirty clothes.

When I offered to help Jack create order out of his chaos, he emphatically declined my offer. He was determined not to let anyone into his life who would force him to throw anything away. His wife had ruthlessly thrown out everything that she perceived as clutter in their lives, which upset Jack and eventually caused their breakup.

Jack's mother had grown up during the Great Depression and had watched helplessly as her family lost their home. Her response to this loss had been to latch on to everything that came into her life for fear of someday being without. Since she did not assign different values to anything, she was unable to let anything go. The result was that her husband and children were forced to live in a home that had no free space. Jack saw uncluttered surfaces as strange, cold, and threatening—and something that needed to be filled. Once the empty space was filled with clutter, Jack was in his comfort zone. The problem was that the newfound clutter in his bachelor hell was undermining his trading efforts. Even though he had hated the wide-open spaces of his marriage, the enforced order around him had caused him to let go of things, including his bad trades.

When Jack realized the connection between his trading and his clutter, he agreed to find a happy balance in his life. He learned how to create order that was not threatening to his need for security and when he did this, his trading came back into balance as well.

Space: The Financial Frontier

If all of the space in your life had value, what would it be to you? Suppose that you looked at your living space in the same way that a newspaper looks at its printed space. You would assign a dollar value to each square foot of it. Suddenly, the space where you lived and worked would take on a whole new meaning. You would begin to see each square foot as a resource in your life. How would you be using that resource? This question lies at the heart of the clutter problem. If you are paying hard-earned money for the space around you, what value are you getting from that investment? Is the utilization of your space supporting your life or is it holding you back, like Jack? If everything around you is cluttered, it prevents you from being able to focus on opportunity and flexibility. As a trader, these two goals must be at the forefront of your consciousness.

What value do you place on each part of your surroundings?

- Do you use your space for equipment and appliances that make your life easier or help you find opportunities?
- Are there pieces of furniture that you look forward to using each day because they give you great comfort?
- Do items in your space remind you of pleasant experiences that make you feel good when you contemplate them?
- Does it make you comfortable when you look at your surroundings?
- Are you proud to show others the environment you choose to live in?
- Does knowing that you have a lot of stuff represent a sense of security?
- Do you feel that an item might be useful someday if it is not thrown away?
- Do you like to collect things for the sake of collecting them?
- Are you living in clutter because you do not know how to organize yourself and are unwilling to hire someone to help you?
- Do you find that cleaning and organizing are painful tasks?
- Does it make you feel uncomfortable to give away and/or throw away things that come into your life?

- Do you feel that you have to keep heirlooms even if they have no sentimental or monetary value? Do those items fit within your décor? Would you have picked them if you were making the original choice for them to occupy your space?
- Do you find it difficult not to display gifts from family and friends that have no value to you? For instance, are your walls filled with Aunt Tillie's myopic masterpieces where the only redeeming value is that the frames would make good kindling?

The need to hold on to things causes some traders to be unable to change or improve their space. Moving a table or a chair can be threatening to them. These traders are holding on to a way of life because they fear change. The problem is that keeping things in a static system prevents traders from being able to adapt to change and respond with flexibility to ever-changing situations. Once your visual field has remained unchanged for a long period of time, you actually stop seeing what is right in front of you. When that happens, you are no longer emotionally uplifted by your physical environment. But, the simple act of moving an old painting from one wall to another will allow you to suddenly "see" that painting once again. These changes in your physical environment create a sense of newness and excitement, as well as a sense of liberation. People who are unwilling to let go of things feel trapped by the need for sameness. Once things change, they feel a sense of renewal and freedom as long as the change is not radical or uncomfortable. It is small steps like this that will break down the old stifling patterns. As long as these small steps have positive feedback, the result will be continued change because the changes will feel very liberating.

Buy and Hold

For a handful of traders, holding on produces good result in their bottom line. Take Tim, for example. Tim grew up in a family where security was a prized way of life. All assets went toward securing the next stage of life. As a child, Tim saved his money to invest in his college education. In the next stage of life, he saved for his children's education and his retirement. The money was saved in mutual funds until he was able to put sizable money in the stock market. Tim's strategy was similar to Warren Buffet's, "buy 'em and hold 'em." As a result, he was able to retire early. Tim still holds on to everything that comes into his life and he has never wasted money on frivolities. He has never traveled outside the United States, and he only goes to special restaurants on special occasions even though he can well afford to enjoy the fruits of his labor. Some people might look at his life and not envy his choice of personal and material sacrifice, but most of us would envy his financial security.

Contrast Tim with Rex, who enjoyed the process of making money and secured his life as well.

A Story for Everything

Rex was a world traveler who savored and cherished memories of people and places that he had experienced. His home was filled with such interesting and beautiful items that I found myself complementing everything when I visited him. Each comment inspired an interesting story, which filled us both with good feelings. When I visited his office, I viewed an efficient, comfortable, supportive environment for trading. The only papers, equipment and tools in his immediate view were all useful to his daily tasks. The room was filled with light, had plenty of open space, and had an orderly desk, both inside and out. Rex was an exceptional trader whose environment supported good trading results.

Letting Go of Holding On

If you are not happy with your trading results, the clutter that results from holding on could be one of the reasons. To overcome this problem, it is helpful to understand some of the ways that these habits are created. Very often, understanding the roots of the issue make it easier for you to want to overcome it.

- One trader moved so much as a child that he constantly had to let go of meaningful toys and surroundings. As a result, all changes felt uncomfortable to him. So, when he became an adult, he vowed that he would stay in one place and would not let go of anything that had meaning to him, which he gave to most everything.
- As a boy, one trader's parents criticized him for being wasteful and unappreciative if he did not hold on to everything that came into his life. As an adult, he continued to want to be "the good boy" who kept everything.
- One trader was given toys to show that he was loved as a child. When he lost his family in a plane crash, he would not let any of that love go. He continued to fill his life with toys, hoping to feel his family's love.
- One trader lived with his father who had become an alcoholic after his wife died. His father refused to have anything cleaned or changed from the way it was before she passed on. When his father died, this trader took over his parent's possessions. He felt too guilty to change anything or give anything away. Instead, he added his accumulated things to theirs and wondered why he could not focus on his trading.

**When you decide that your past must not equal your future,
make a plan to take action.**

Getting Spacey

- Hire an organizer.
- Make some rules that you will be willing to stick by. Notice, I did not say that you would be comfortable with because your comfort zone is not working if your trading is not working. The key to making the rules is in the questions asked above.
- Hire someone to keep up with the cleaning. This could range from live-in help to someone coming in once every two weeks.
- Make sure that your trading space has only the papers, tools, and equipment necessary to do your job. Store or throw away everything else.
- Make sure that there are places on your desk where you can actually experience the surface of your desk. The more space, the more room for opportunity, flexibility, creativity, expansion, and affluence.
- Have a space for everything and remember to put things in their appropriate place.

Dealing with significant others who cannot let go of things:

- Leave the situation and/or the relationship: if you cannot live with the situation and there is no way to improve it, sometimes this is the only option.
- Compromise on the situation, whenever possible:
- Common space must be kept organized, neat and clean, with chores divided.
- Each person has a place to express his level of comfort in space and clutter.
- Hire someone to clean and or organize.
- Keep your own space organized – by taking responsibility for your own space, you will feel a sense of control and less resentment for the messes made by others.

Conclusion

If you are unable to let go of things in your life, clutter will eventually get in the way of your focus. As a result, your trading results will suffer and it will become costly not to handle the problem. You need not feel guilty that you have difficulty in letting go and remember that not everyone has the skill to stay organized, but this skill can be learned. Hiring someone to handle the problem is far less costly in the long run, than paying for the losses incurred by fuzzy trading.

SUNDAY SPECIAL!
ROASTED CHICKEN

Chapter 6

TRADER HAND-ME-DOWNS

It is difficult to consistently make money at trading if your attitudes and behaviors continually sabotage your efforts. Trading profitably is even more difficult if the attitudes and behaviors are so deeply rooted in your upbringing that you are unaware of them. These sabotaging legacies are the hand-me-downs that prevent traders from following their trading rules and taking the right actions when they need to.

The Resistant Trader

When Marty started trading in the pit, he developed a simple set of trading rules that worked so well that he consistently earned money and was considered a top player by his peers. When the development of Electronic Trading threatened his comfortable lifestyle, Marty decided that he was not going to be left behind. He made the proactive choice to learn to trade using a computer.

At first, Marty thought that he could buy his way to instant success by hiring people to do the hard work for him. He bought top-of-the-line computer and software packages, but was unwilling to learn to use them on his own. Then, he hired tutors who could spoon-feed him through the process, but he hated working with the computer. Using the software was also a nightmare. Each element of learning the software seemed easy enough, but by the time he had reached the end of the lesson, he could not remember the first steps he had learned. Something inside of him was resisting his efforts.

Rather than spending the time and energy to develop his own system, Marty purchased expensive systems from successful traders. Why reinvent the wheel if he could make money from proven systems? Not surprisingly, nothing he did worked. He became convinced that he had been cheated. Eventually, Marty decided to ignore Electronic Trading, return to the floor, and make as much money as he could before he lost his final opportunity. Unfortunately, his failure to succeed off of the floor destroyed his confidence on the floor.

Marty's sad plight is becoming an epidemic among floor traders. The question for most people is: "Should I milk the floor for everything it's worth while the opportunity is still there, or do I learn the new method of trading, so I won't be left behind?" The answer for Marty was to resist the change. Why?

Chicken on Sunday

When Marty lived at home with his family, he could count on pot roast sitting on the table at 6:00 P.M. Tuesday and a roasted chicken at 3:00 P.M. on Sunday. Predictable routine was a part of the ritualistic environment of his family life. Marty's parents had an overwhelming need to maintain the status quo.

His father, Lenny, had worked for the same jewelry store as a diamond cutter for 31 years. Except for a limited amount of Temple activities, Lenny's life was about working, arguing with his wife about how the family should handle themselves, reading, or listening to the news. After surviving an impoverished childhood, Lenny felt that spending money was anathema, even though he could well afford to make life more comfortable for his family. Eating at a restaurant was a waste of money and moving from their small, cramped apartment to one that was more spacious was not considered an option. Lenny was even afraid to take a vacation for fear of missing something. While Marty did not want to be anything like his parents, he did not realize that he already was.

Like Marty, most of us want to take the best of our parents with us and dispose of those parts that we find unattractive. Problems arise from the fact that we are unaware of the influence that the disposed of parts will continue to have on our lives and on our trading.

Uncle Sam

Marty's first attempt to break from of his family confines was a trip to Europe after college. Three days into the trip, Marty found that he was feeling more and more uncomfortable and was eager to go home. Once he returned home from Europe, Marty decided to trade in the pits because he wanted to be like his Uncle Sam, who was a high rolling floor trader who lived life in sharp contrast to Marty's parents. Sam was recognized and welcomed in every high-class restaurant in New York when he entered with a new, beautiful woman on his arm.

After a month of womanizing, Marty sought out Judy, his high school sweetheart, and soon, they were married. Shortly after the wedding, Marty asked Judy to make pot roast on Tuesday and chicken on Sunday. As much as he resisted the ritualistic behavior of his parents, Marty was becoming more and more like them. If you pointed this fact out to him, Marty would emphatically deny it.

A Tug-of-War

Through daily exposure, our parents bequeath to us a set of repeated behaviors that become part of who and what we are. Even if we resent these behaviors and want to change or eliminate them, they create a comfort zone for us in our neurology, which pulls us back to them, especially during times of insecurity. These behaviors form the best and the worst of who we are. Very often, these patterns bring out the best and worst in us at the same time.

Recognizing the existence of these patterns is the first step in determining which parts of these behaviors are serving you and which parts are sabotaging your efforts.

In Marty's case, the consistent, predictable behavior that he learned from his parents provided him with a good, steady marriage and a successful trading career. He discovered that Uncle Sam's life was only good for Uncle Sam. However, when Marty came to the crossroad in his career, he did not know how to handle a radical change because the experience was outside of his comfort zone and behavior patterns.

Keeping the Baby and Throwing out the Bath Water

Below is an exercise designed to help you discover if your family's habitual patterns are blocking the way to your trading success:

1. Identify the patterns in your parents that you do not want to inherit:
   - They are not good at handling their emotions or sharing their feelings
   - They have addictive behaviors (such as alcoholism, gambling, etc.)
   - They have obsessive/compulsive behaviors (such as overcleanliness, overeating, overspending, etc.)
   - Their etiquette skills are crass or low class
   - They are negative or pessimistic
   - They are highly critical and judgmental
   - They complain about everything
   - They do not take care of their health properly
   - They do not feel they are worthy of treating themselves to a happy life style
   - They are not good at handling finances
   - They are gossips
   - They do not support or love their children in an emotionally healthy way
   - They are inflexible in the way they think and they believe

2. Do you feel that any part of your behavior resembles their behavior at any time? If so, what?
3. Ask others who are close to you if they feel that any part of your behavior resembles our parents' behavior at any time?
4. When do you demonstrate these behaviors? What time of day? What is going on in your life at that time? (If it happens in the morning, you may not be getting enough sleep; if after work, you may be overly stressed, etc.)
5. Can you recognize a correlation between when you demonstrate these behaviors and your trading results?

Overcoming these Behavioral Patterns:

The best way to eliminate a behavior you do not want is to replace it with a behavior that you do want.

1. How would you like a new behavior to look?
2. Plan the new behavior(s).
3. Visualize and mentally rehearse the desired behavior.
4. Consciously recognize when you are displaying the negative behavior.
5. Immediately translate it to a positive behavior in visualization or in physical action.

Example:
Your parents lived on their entire income and had no money put away for retirement. Your present life is very stressful because you and your family live beyond your financial means. When times are tough, your family has nothing to fall back upon. This lack of security creates stress between you and your family and adds additional pressure to your trading.

New behaviors to change could include the following:

1. Put back 10% of your income or a specific amount every month for retirement and 10% for rainy days
2. Come to an agreement with each member of the family defining a "rainy day"
3. Pay credit card debt before there is additional spending beyond immediate needs
4. Create a budget so that you can pay off all credit cards thereafter
5. Save for major purchases in advance, so that you will not increase the base of your spending
6. Sign an agreement to spending rules and note the fact that the rules will be referenced when any member of the family asks to change course

If Hand-Me-Down behaviors are not recognizable to you,
or if you cannot deal with them in an effective way,
seek professional help!

In contrast to Marty, Tony is an electronic trader dealing with patterns of inconsistency that were handed down to him by his family.

A View from the Other Side

In direct contrast to Marty, Tony's parents wanted to make sure that he was raised correctly. His mother, Mary, read the child raising experts of the day and tried to follow their advice faithfully. The problem was that Mary read so many conflicting books on child raising that the rules were constantly changing. Tony's early behaviors were largely determined by his mom's latest child book of the month. Tony's dad, who also wanted to do the right thing, listened to and agreed with his wife's assertions. After all, she had two years of college while he was a high school drop out. From these early experiences, Tony learned two behaviors that directly influenced his trading life. He learned flexibility and inconsistency. The flexibility allowed him to be ready and willing to change with the market. But, the inconsistency in his life made him want to use the flavor of the month trading system.

Salvaging the Good from the Bad

Marty eventually identified the negative part of the change resistant behavior that he had picked up from his parents. He had made the same mistake that many traders make when they are trying to trade a new style. He was trying to be an instant top trader without having to put in the effort. Marty was trying to buy success and immediately acquire skills that take months to develop. Dealing with change too quickly sent Marty outside of his comfort zone. By studying his behavior patterns, he gained an appreciation for the consistent, predictable behaviors of his parents and agreed to take on the challenge of Electronic Trading, one small step at a time. Marty and I worked together to change the negative anchors that he had created from his losses. Now, he is back trading successfully on the floor and is feeling better about the prospect of going behind the screen in the future.

Conclusion

Without realizing it, we inherit Hand-Me-Down behaviors and attitudes from our parents that become an integral part of our response to trading dilemmas and personal situations. In the meantime, we fool ourselves into believing that we have left behind the very behaviors and attitudes that we disliked in our parents. When things are going well and our trading is on track, we are not aware of the influence that these legacies have upon us. However, when we are under stress, or have to deal with change, ambiguity or loss, we often find ourselves responding in a way that is counter-productive and self-sabotaging. In other words, we act like the worst in our parents. Sometimes, these patterns reveal themselves in daily cycles, which are dependent upon the way we feel at a given time during the day. The fact that these behaviors follow patterns allows us to identify them and replace them with positive behaviors. Of course, not all of the behaviors and attitudes that we inherit from our parents are negative. Some of these bequests form the very best in us, especially when we need the best strategies to succeed. The important thing is to identify our behavior patterns and decide what is "baby" and what is "bath water." Then, we have the means to save the success strategies and replace the sabotaging ones with new and healthier strategies for trading success.

SECTION 2

Your Mind & Emotions...

DUE YESTERDAY
HASTA LA VISTA!

Chapter 7

SCARED MONEY: EMOTIONS ATTACHED TO MONEY

What does your trading account represent to you and your family? Is it your savings account, your family retirement, the children's education, your next vacation? If it is any of these things or endless others, then you are probably trading with what I call "scared money." In my dictionary, money in trading that is thought of as anything but inventory for your trading business is "scared money." When emotions are attached to trading capital by you or your family members, the likelihood of loss increases because decisions that are charged with emotion will sabotage your trading efforts.

Strike One

Greg called in a panic. He lamented, "I've got to make money! I'll do whatever it takes, but I've got to make money." Because he wanted the consultation as soon as possible, my assistant faxed a copy of our Traders' Evaluation to him immediately so we could find the elements we were dealing with psychologically. We set an appointment for the next day, and by morning, he had faxed not only the completed fourteen page Traders' Evaluation, but also a ten page typewritten analysis of his whole life. My first reaction was to have my assistant call him and inform him that the evaluation took between twenty and thirty minutes, and more time than that would be needed just to read the letter. However, I found myself in the drama of his life while perusing his letter.

In describing himself, Greg told how he had successfully worked his way through medical school and his entry into practice. He was a good medical doctor, but running a business was not his strength, and after four years in practice, he had been forced to file bankruptcy losing all the money he had borrowed to set up his medical practice. Despite the temporary failure, Greg made a good living practicing medicine for an HMO which had an automatic retirement contribution plan. Rather than considering this a retirement fund, Greg saw it as a source of funds to recoup his losses Even with his best intentions, Greg's entrepreneurial spirit continually kept him in financial trouble as he tried various side businesses and multilevel marketing schemes, most of which failed.

Now retired from medicine, Greg wanted to be a futures trader. He read a few books on trading, purchased a trading system from a vendor, and paper-traded the system for a month. With this background, Greg thought that he was ready to trade with real money. He had twenty-five thousand dollars with which to work. Unfortunately, this represented the last of his family's savings and he knew that without additional income, he and his wife were facing the prospect of living a very modest lifestyle. Complicating matters further for him were a variety of health problems, relationship issues, and addictive behaviors.

Greg's Traders' Evaluation showed that he did not have the psychology to support disciplined trading which was something he did not want to hear. At the time, he could not afford to work with me privately to improve his situation, nor could I afford to choose him as a client. However, because of his determination, I wanted to give him some guidance which would prove to be beneficial. I suggested to him that he needed to complete a good trading business plan and offered to provide him with a model of one if he did not know how to set one up. I urged him to complete the plan and explained that it would help him to see the reality of his situation and would give him a direction to proceed. I knew that if he were ever going to turn "scared money" into seed money, he would have to see workable and positive results from this plan.

Strike Two

Travis was a very successful trader at one time in his life. During his first wife's unsuccessful battle with cancer Travis could not follow his trading rules, and in the course of events, lost everything he had. Several years later, he met and married Bonnie, a corporate executive, who loved Travis dearly. She recognized his talent for trading and wanted to help him get back on his trading feet.

With Travis' return to the trading world, he was able to draw on the lessons learned on his first trip toward financial success. He told Bonnie that if she would give him six months to establish himself, he would put the world at her feet. Bonnie made a good income, and she had one hundred thousand dollars in savings which she willingly gave Travis to work with. In the first three months of preparation, he spent forty thousand dollars for computer equipment, software, and start up costs. Bonnie did not object because she totally trusted Travis to use the money wisely.

Then, the time of reckoning came. In the past, Travis considered draw-downs to be an inevitable part of the process of earning money in trading. Now, these same draw-downs represented fear and that fear created failure. Each day he traded, he became more manic-depressive. Bonnie, who was sensitive to his mood swings, also became depressed. This depression eventually turned to fear leading to mistrust and conflict in their relationship. At this point, the pressure on Travis to trade well became so intense that he lost the last of his trading capital in one dramatic trade. This loss not only wiped out his trading money, it left a large debt because it was highly leveraged. A part of Travis wanted to end the day to day emotional roller coaster ride and that part of him sabotaged the best of his efforts.

Many traders fall into the trap of thinking that psychological issues can be overcome with money and technical education. When a trader has established a pattern of being unable to follow his trading rules, the subsequent losses create negative psychological anchors which will in turn, create conflicts sabotaging good trading results and planning.

Home Run

Yosef was left an inheritance by his parents who had escaped from Bulgaria when it was under Communist rule. This young couple's early dream of freedom motivated them to secretly plot an escape by frolicking near the border while wearing bathing suits on a hot summer day. The belongings they carried with them were in a picnic basket. In order to reduce suspicion, they carried no cash or personal memorabilia figuring that if they were stopped their innocence would be apparent. Luckily, the attention of the border guards was drawn by other escape attempts, and they were able to cross the frontier without incident.

Yosef's parents worked long and hard. They saved every penny so that their children could enjoy a more fruitful life than they had. Their escape from Communism into freedom represented the gift of a lifetime for them. Yosef was always encouraged to follow the path of his dreams no matter what the cost, and when he decided that his destiny was to become a trader, he viewed his inheritance as the "seed money" for success rather than "scared money," He saw trading as the opportunity to financial freedom for himself and his family.

Yosef found many hurdles on his pathway. First, he had to find the right trading system. Then, he had to discover the best money management rules to use. And, when he could not follow his trading rules, he realized that he had to handle psychological issues which could have sabotaged his efforts. Once these hurdles were overcome, Yosef was well on his way to financial freedom.

Stories to the Hall of Fame

Everyone has stories to tell which justify the direction their lives have taken. The most compelling of these stories drive people to reach the heights of success or find the depths of failure. We all like to dramatize our stories because drama stirs emotion, and most people are attracted to powerful emotions and feelings. This is especially true for those individuals who appear to suppress their feelings. The choice is between stories that will lead to success or to failure. Yosef could have entered trading with "scared money" rather then "seed money" as he certainly had a good story to justify "scared thinking." The problem remains, you can consciously choose a positive story, but negative anchors from the past can weigh you down.

Here are a few questions to determine if you are trading with "scared money."

1. Is your trading capital free and clear of negative stories and psychological issues?

2. Do the people in your life support your use of the money for trading capital, or do they see it as family money to be used for other purposes?
3. Are you realistic about the results your system can give you after the cost of doing business?
4. Will your projected profit from trading be sufficient to support your present lifestyle?

If your answer to any of these questions is "No," then you are trading with "scared money." You will find it very difficult getting to first base in trading, let alone hitting a home run.

Conclusion

The money you use for trading capital is inventory and seed money for your trading business. The more emotional attachment there is to that money, the higher the probability that you will sabotage your trading results. Handle the psychological conflicts attached to your trading money before you add more hurdles to becoming a trader. Otherwise, you will add unnecessary stress to your life, and risk losing the opportunity to become a successful trader.

Chapter 8

CHARGED WITH GUILT: EMOTIONS AND TRADING

When Jeff placed a trade he was filled with a sense of discomfort. Winning trades brought feelings of great discomfort for him as well as losing trades. These feelings created a great deal of distress for him until he finally sought professional help in dealing with them. Strangely enough, he was unable to put a name to these feelings of discomfort. However, he did know that they were sabotaging his efforts, not only professionally, but in other areas of his life as well.

The Power of Guilt

People plagued with guilt long to find a place where they can unburden themselves of something for which they are deeply ashamed. Very often, they have a longing to change their painful feelings, but they cannot identify the source of their discomfort. For many, transformation of the guilty feelings can take place as a result of voicing them in a psychological setting or confessing them in a religious setting. For others, a payment must be made to relieve themselves of these guilty feelings, such as, doing something for the person they have wronged or giving in some way to a charitable cause. And then, there are individuals who will carry their burden of guilt for the rest of their lives with the result being continuous sabotage of their efforts.

Seeds Which Motivate Guilt

All emotions are motivators, either positive or negative. Feelings of joy and fulfillment can motivate us to share our good fortune with others. Fear can be used as both a positive and negative motivator. For example, it is wise to make children fear something that can harm them such as fire or heights, but it is harmful to a child's psychological stability to motivate them by fear of physical intimidation. Guilt can also be used with positive or negative intentions, but a distinguishing feature about guilt is that people who create these feelings in others are very often doing it unconsciously. It is never a parent's intent to limit the future success of a child, but a pattern of behavior is established at some point in life which becomes a part of the way they present themselves in life.

When the Cause is Elsewhere

What happens when the cause of the guilt that is sabotaging a trader's career is a generational behavior pattern? In far too many cases, this undeserved burden of guilt was given by those who were closest to him for things he did not do or could not do. The guilt is not always fully verbalized because it is often the result of an attempt to gain power and control. Since the persons who are manipulating the guilt have agendas which are often hidden even from themselves, the burden is accepted and rarely questioned by the one who is required to carry it, often a small child. The manipulators are not "bad" people nor are they manipulating through evil intent; instead, they are unconsciously meeting some of their own unmet needs. For example, parents often manipulate their talented, beautiful or brilliant children through guilt because exceptional gifts often make the parents feel inadequate. Or, parents may make their children feel guilty when they enjoy the benefits of success because the parents experienced painful deprivation in their own childhood.

Undeserved Guilt

In Jeff's case, he had spent most of his life feeling guilty without ever verbalizing or identifying his feelings. Yet, as he talked about his life, he had led a fairly upstanding life. In fact, he had devoted much of his time to his family and community. His motives were selfless and his actions were ethical.

As we probed deeper into Jeff's past, he began to talk about his parents and, it became clear that he had sensed early on that his parents did not really love him. This was in contrast to the way they treated his younger brother and sister, who they showered with love and attention. Jeff was left to wonder what he had done to lose their love. When he was twelve, he overheard an argument between his parents. In anger, his mother told his father that she was sick of being reminded that she had gotten pregnant and that they had to get married. Furthermore, she was just as miserable about being stuck with him as he was with her.

Interestingly enough, Jeff said that he had forgotten all about that conversation. When asked what he thought his mother had meant by her remark, Jeff appeared to be confused. On some level, Jeff had known from that moment his parents blamed him for forcing them to live together. This was why they did not love him and this was the reason that Jeff felt guilty and unworthy of success. It also explained why they had treated the younger siblings differently because they blamed them for nothing.

You Make Me Sick

Anne was a highly intelligent and capable trader. She was in a terrible slump after suffering a bad case of bronchitis last year. Although she had recovered physically, she was worried because she felt depressed about trading and was close to giving up her career. What was going wrong?

When Anne was a child, she had suffered from asthma. Often, her attacks were so life-threatening, that her parents lived with the constant threat of her death hanging over their heads. This very real hazard forced them to micromanage their daughter's health, leaving them little emotional room to feel joy or hope. A simple cold often turned into bronchitis, which developed into pneumonia and then into a life-threatening asthma attack. When Anne became sick, her parents felt fear and anger. They were angry at themselves, at the doctors, and at the little girl who made their lives so miserable. Anne felt guilty for getting sick and bringing her parents so much pain.

Eventually, Anne outgrew her asthma. But, her recent bout with bronchitis rekindled her old feelings of guilt. Both of Anne's parents had died in their early fifties of heart and stress related illnesses. Anne interpreted this fact to mean that she had brought them both to an early death.

Smothered With Guilt

Todd's case is one of my most significant cases of trader self-sabotage, because it has such a familiar ring for many of the traders with whom I have worked.

To meet Todd, you would never guess that he burned with internal fires of self-accusation. He was always the life of the party, a friend ready to help out in times of need, and the first person to celebrate with you when things were going well. But, Todd had another side that was a nuisance to his life, especially his trading.

To understand where this pattern originated, we have to go to the beginning when Todd's parents emigrated from Czechoslovakia. Todd's mother was from a caring family that did not know how to show its affection. Then, she married a man who was very much in love with her, but he did not demonstrate the kind of affection that made her feel loved. So, when her only son, Todd, arrived, she smothered him with affection, and when her affection was not returned in kind by him, she made him feel guilty. In her mind, she was showering him with love, but in reality, she was expressing an insatiable need to be loved. No matter how much Todd professed his love, it was never enough to satisfy her. In the end, he always felt guilty for failing and because of this he felt undeserving.

This guilt permeated all aspects of Todd's life. In business it meant that his goals would not be realized because no matter how he tried, he would sabotage himself in some way. In his personal relationships, he would run from a woman if she initially showed she cared a great deal for him. If he cared for a woman, and she didn't return his affection in kind, he would become obsessed with trying to win her. The cycle of sabotage would repeat itself if she showed she cared too much for him, as he would then want out.

Enter trading. When Todd became a trader, he followed the steps to become a successful trader, but he couldn't follow his rules. Following his rules meant that he would become successful which was not okay, because part of him felt unworthy for any great success. It was too difficult for Todd to admit to these limitations, because he felt too vulnerable expressing any perceived weakness. As a result, he attempted to understand the source of his psychological problems on his own. But, even when he understood the source of his limitations and self-sabotage he could not transform the child perception in him.

Cultural Guilt

Another source of this undeserved guilt is cultural. Certain religions and cultures instill guilt in their members as a form of wide-spread control and/or moral authority. Although the political and social motivations for this guilt-control have their roots in historical conditions, applied to the late twentieth century and early twenty-first century, the long arm of history continues to guide the thinking and humble the emotional development of hundreds of millions of people. In parts of the Middle East when a loved one passes on, immediate family members are expected to wear black for years, conform to a set of rigid rules, and not show any sign of enjoyment. For a trader, this could mean that he would never again be able to earn a good living from trading because it would make him feel good, and it would not be appropriate for him to feel good. This has been the case of a few traders that I have spoken with while in this business.

Regardless of the source of the undeserved guilt, the result is the same for traders: they feel that they do not deserve the successes they achieve. When you don't feel deserving, you will create situations in your life that will sabotage your efforts.

Diffusing the Charge

If you are burdened with guilt like the traders depicted in this article, there is a way out of the cycle of self-sabotage where you have been stuck:

1. The first step to take to diffuse the charge of guilt from others is to recognize that sabotage is affecting your results and that guilt might be the cause. The source of the guilt must be identified before taking the next step.

2. Once the source has been identified, you must reframe your perception of the intent of the one who originally wanted to invoke guilt from you. This means that you see the person who is provoking guilty feelings as not having bad intention. See them as victims of others, or see what is missing in them which results in their need to make you feel guilty. Usually, people who want to invoke guilt do so out of a sense of powerlessness. When you begin to realize that their need to control is because they feel out of control themselves, then, you will be able to transform your feelings about their intentions. Realize, most people learn to use guilt to control others because they were once its unwilling victim. When you can reframe the intentions of your controller, you can also feel less anger toward him or her and yourself. People rarely use guilt consciously to hurt or control.

3. If the feeling of guilt comes from doing something wrong or hurting someone, you

can do or say something to that other person which will make you feel that you have paid the price of your actions. If this is not possible, then do some charitable service in their name.

Conclusion

Guilt can be a positive motivator in your life if it stimulates you to change negative behaviors or to atone for past transgressions. But, if you have been charged for crimes you never committed and are unaware that you are carrying this burden of guilt, you will find yourself sabotaging your trading. This guilt, left to do its work on your unconscious mind, will erode your self-esteem, making you feel that you do not deserve to succeed professionally or personally. It will help you to create more and more reasons to feel unworthy, so that the original guilt will be hidden by a string of failures and transgressions. The escape is to identify and target the source of the guilt, and reframe your perceptions of its originator. Once you truly see the person who charged you with guilt for the limited individual that he is, and not the venal, power-hungry and wounding authority, the charges will be dropped and you will be free to succeed.

VOILA!

Chapter 9

DISCONNECTED:
HOW MIND CHATTER DISRUPTS FOCUS

The "E" Word

Rudy had been a floor trader in the S&P pit for many years and knew that he would earn a steady income from floor trading because he always had. Then, one day, Rudy began to hear about electronic trading. His colleagues on the floor did not seem too concerned about the stories at first until the subject was headline news almost daily.

Rudy wanted to be proactive and prepare to trade electronically. He acquired the necessary equipment and split time between trading on the floor and trading from his office. His trading was profitable on the floor while he lost his profits trading from the computer. Soon, he was losing his confidence and started to question even his abilities to trade on the floor. His internal chatter caused by his fear grew louder and more insistent. For the first time in his trading career, his results were flat for the year. To make things worse, he realized that he would have to relearn how to trade if he were going to survive.

Rudy's story is rapidly becoming an epidemic among some of the best traders on the floor. A trader having to start over with electronic trading is like returning to square one in Monopoly when you're almost at Boardwalk and then giving up the property acquired along the way.

When Rudy and his fellow traders begin to fear that they will not be able to learn to trade electronically, they lose their state of connectedness with their trading. Their thoughts are filled with busy signals and the lines to their unconscious intelligence, which once fed them with correct signals for trading, are now disconnected.

The State of Connectedness

The state of connectedness allows a trader to focus on following rules exactly and interpreting intuition clearly, thus allowing them to take signals at the right time. If the state of connectedness is important to good trading, what is it and how can you achieve it?

To answer these questions, I would like to tell you about a recent encounter with a Jain Priest visiting from India. In the course of conversation, he asked me, "Do you ever feel alone?" I answered, "Yes, when I disconnect myself from Universal Consciousness." (Other people might say God, a prophet, or saint.) We continued to discuss how the conscious state of mind is an illusion and that what is real is a state of this connectedness with all that is. This state can be compared to the instructions given to Luke Skywalker in the movie, Star Wars, to "Let the Force be with you." When Luke allowed negative feelings to be part of the moment when he was fighting the Dark Side, he lost his power against evil. When he was connected with the strength of good, evil was no match for him. In order to gain the strength of the universe, Luke had to be in the "Now Moment," which is the state of connectedness.

Soon after my meeting with the Jain Priest, I was in the process of mourning the loss of a dear friend. In the midst of my grief, I recalled the conversation with the Jain Priest and said to myself, "How can I have a connectedness with Universal Consciousness when I feel so sad?" Then I remembered the "Now Moment" and realized that I was feeding into my sorrow. I had been replaying conversations and moments with my friend and, therefore, was living in the past. I had also been focusing on moments that would never occur, therefore, I was living in the future. This is not to say that you should not mourn the loss of a friend. But, you will continue to increase your uncomfortable feelings when you create stories that make you feel bad. We prolong our feelings by feeding our minds with stories of the past and the future.

In a trading situation, when you think about losses in the past or the possibility of losses in the future, you will feel uncertain about your choices. This creates the conflict of wanting to take the trade, on the one hand, and the fear of being wrong or of losing money, on the other hand. Conflict leads to indecision. In the meantime, you have become disconnected from your trading state of mind, the "Now Moment." To be in the "Now Moment" and to stay in it, a trader must continue to focus only on the signal and not on superfluous chatter.

In Over his Head

Pat was a "Now Moment" trader until he overextended himself with material things. He was a good steady trader with a comfortable life style. Pat was not what you would call a physically attractive man and did not have a way with women. When Gloria entered his life and paid attention to him, Pat began to blossom. Gloria was an attractive, self-confident, out-going woman and Pat wanted to impress her. He read every book he could find about capturing a woman's heart. It worked. While Gloria did not require Pat to shower her with material things to maintain the relationship, he was so happy and flattered by her attention that he wanted to please her. Gloria found herself in a lavish home with a new Mercedes and an enormous diamond ring.

Pat was in debt over his head. His mind was now occupied with the chatter of fear that kept him from being able to do what he did best: trade in the moment. Pat was not only afraid to lose money, but was afraid not to make a lot more money, as well.

Getting Off-track

A person can spend years studying and practicing the right things to do to keep on the health and prosperity track of life only to be derailed in an instant. Hopefully, education will at least make you recognize when you are off course so that you can return to the right track quickly. Unfortunately, even the most educated person, when faced with challenging or distracting moments can find himself mired in them. This is the mind's way of telling you that you need time out. When you are faced with a big distraction, you must stop, get out of any risky position, allow sufficient time for the feelings to disperse, regroup by making a plan for handling the situation, take action, and then return to trading when all is settled down. Here are some examples of what I would call more intense moments that need immediate attention:

- Your spouse has just asked for a divorce
- A member of your family has just passed away
- You have just become aware that one of your children is taking drugs
- Your secretary just announced she is having a baby and it is yours
- A bomb has just exploded in your building
- A tree fell on your house during a hurricane

There are distractions that are not quite so dramatic, which can also pull you away from being focused. These distractions are annoyances that can play over in your mind until they grab your full attention. The way to handle these distractions is to first recognize negative self-talk and notice how you are feeding into it. Then, give yourself advice and take that advice as if you were your own coach. Examples of what I would call medium-size distractions are:

- Your broker of 15 years has just announced he is going to retire
- A big customer has decided to pull out his money
- Your in-laws have just announced they are going to stay another week
- You overheard your son say in prayer, "Please make daddy love me the way Joey's daddy loves him."

There are those smaller distractions that can be equally damaging in taking you off track. When these mini-distractions occur, it is time for a mini-break. Get up from your desk while taking a few deep breaths on your way to drink a glass of water. It would be good to find humor in the distraction if you can. If time allows, you can take immediate action, then complete that action; if not, make an agreement with yourself about the action you will take and when you plan to take it. It is very important that you follow the agreement with yourself. If you do not, you will not take yourself seriously the next time. This will result in not having a strategy for overcoming distractions. Here are some examples of minor annoyances that can be attention grabbers:

- You just received a newsletter in which your mentor is taking a market position opposite to your own.
- Your wife just called for the third time. This time, she is crying because they killed off her favorite soap star. You realize that she is really calling for attention.
- The sandwich shop is out of your favorite sandwich, which you were looking forward to having for lunch.
- It is the beginning of the day and a friend has just dumped all of his problems on you.
- You cannot find your favorite pen that you have had for the last 10 years.

When getting back into trading, take at least a minute to refocus your mind by clearing it of all thoughts. When you can focus on no thoughts for five minutes, you will have a tool, which will enable you to be ready to follow your rules and stick to them in any crisis. First, you must practice on the easier distractions before this strategy will work on the more challenging ones.

The Hook

Why do we get hooked into thoughts which disconnect us from focusing on the task at hand? There are many reasons which are justifiable on the grounds that we are rational human beings:

- Concern for the welfare of others
- Protecting ourselves from harm
- Overcoming a loss

Low Blow

Alan, who was a consistently good trader for many years, suddenly began to lose focus. The cause of his problem was that he was avoiding asking his wife a difficult question the answer to which he already knew. His wife, Prisi, had become more and more involved with her female friends, particularly her friend, Glenda. When Alan finally confronted Prisi and asked if there was a romantic relationship between them, she confirmed his fears. Prisi said that she did not want her lifestyle to change and could not understand why they could not go on just as they had always done. She explained to Alan that he could not give any wife his full attention because he was married to his trading. Prisi was a good homemaker in every way and Alan had been happy up to that point. Furthermore, since she had her friends, he had more time to do the things he wanted to do. Alan was filled with conflicting feelings of confusion, guilt, and anger. On the one hand, he did not want to lose Prisi and knew that she was right; but on the ther hand, he could not stand knowing that she was not romantically interested in him alone. Totally confused, he sought out counseling, but in the meantime, he was completely disconnected from good trading.

While Alan's mind was still filled with chatter, he came to a careful and painful, but final, decision. Before he could return to trading with confidence, he would have to divorce Prisi. By this time, Alan had nearly lost everything, including the confidence in his manhood and his ability to earn a living at trading. We worked together until he was able to reconnect with his trading. Now, he has recouped his losses and is back on the road to good trading.

Boxed in Chatter

Alan's story is dramatic, but a lesser distraction from the "Now Moment" can be nearly as damaging to your results as a trader if allowed to capture your attention or persist long enough:

- Not taking care of your physical, emotional and mental self
- Avoiding the fact that you do not have the skill or method to be a profitable trader
- Having old stories being replayed in your mind because you have found completion with them in the past

Telly worked so many years at becoming a trader that he did not want to face the fact that, in all those years, he was not doing what was necessary to be a successful businessman in trading. His father's words from his childhood kept repeating in his mind, "You're a bum. You'll never amount to anything." His father, a successful businessman, told Telly as an adult, "If I ran my business the way you run yours, I'd be broke." As the result of his father's verbal attacks, Telly was unable to hear the good advice his father eventually did offer. In the meantime, the voices from his past prevented Telly from being able to connect with the "Now Moment" and benefit from information available to him.

Conclusion

When your mind is occupied by chatter that has nothing to do with the "Now Moment," you are disconnected from the part of you which guides you in making the right decisions in your trading. Regardless of the reason for the chatter, the result is the same: taking an entry signal while disconnected is a reliable indicator of failure in the future. The remedy is finding a resolution for the chatter and bringing it to a stop. The first step is simply to listen to what is being said in your mind. Then, make a commitment to take action - to right the wrong, to do the thing you are avoiding, to confront the problem, to get counseling, to bite the bullet. Once the internal chatter has stopped, you will be reconnected and ready to listen to your inner signals once again.

Chapter 10

EVENING THE SCORE

"What's fair is fair," or as Robert DeNiro said in "The Untouchables," "You hurt me and I'm gonna hurt you." The temptation to get even when we feel that we have been wronged brings out the worst in all of us. Certainly, when a trader feels the pang of loss, a part of him wants to get even with the markets. However, when a person acts out of revenge to regain his losses, this retaliation results in greater loss. Typically, a trader will take greater risks to overcome the losses creating a vicious circle of greater losses and more psychological pain.

Daddy Dearest

Charlie grew up in a home where Dad made all of the final decisions. Even when choices were made that should not have involved his input, such as deciding what food to order at a restaurant or what clothes to wear Dad always introduced his unwavering opinion. If Charlie made a choice that was agreeable to his father, he was never acknowledged with a self-confidence-building anchor such as "you chose well." If, on the other hand, Charlie's choice did not please his father, he was chastised and punished for making "a stupid choice." As a result of this bad parenting, Charlie built up a great deal of frustration and anger, which accumulated because he was not allowed to express negative feelings. Charlie dreamed of getting even with his dad one day for creating his angry feelings.

As a teenager, Charlie defiantly made choices that were harmful to himself and others. When he was caught, his father punished him severely by taking away something meaningful to him. Charlie wanted to attract the approval of his father, but his father did not have the ability to give positive feedback. Instead, Charlie's actions continued to attract coarse words from his father, which further diminished his sense of self-value. Despite and because of his father's Draconian treatment, Charlie graduated from college in the top 10% of his class.

After college, Charlie built a family of his own and became a businessman and an equities trader. However, the pain from his past took its toll on Charlie's relationships. While he did not want to be like his father, Charlie silently resented his family members making their own decisions. He responded by rendering vengeful punishments, which did not appear on the surface to be connected with the choices they were making. Charlie did not confine his accumulated wrath to his family members. He extended it to his colleagues and anyone else who happened to step into his path. Eventually, his wife and children divorced themselves from him. Charlie had succeeded in creating a lonely life for himself where people either left him or he left them first out of fear of being abandoned.

As a trader, Charlie created rigid rules to follow because it was not okay to "be stupid" and have losses. When inevitable losses occurred, he wanted to get back at the markets, which represented his father taking things away from him. When Charlie contained his rage, it led to depression and sabotaging his trading rules. If he vented his rage, he would create more losses by taking more risk.

Loop the Loop

So, how do you get out of the loop of self-destructive behavior caused by your parents' negative programming? Below is a simple exercise for those of you whose pattern of getting even with the market is sporadic and not complicated with other issues.

1. Recognize the patterns of behavior that you or other people find unattractive about your parents.
2. Are any of these same patterns showing up in your own behavior? (Sometimes we don't recognized these patterns in ourselves and it takes an outside observer to point them out to us. Ask people you trust to give you an honest assessment of their experience of your behavior.)
3. Recognize offshoots of behaviors that result from mimicking your parent's negative behaviors.
4. How would you describe the feeling that you get when you have a loss in the markets?
5. In what part of your body do you feel that feeling?
6. What are you saying to yourself when you are experiencing a loss? Whose voice is it? Yours or your parents? Whose expression is it? Yours or your parents?
7. What is the truth about the behavior and what you say to yourself? Examples:

What you say and do	**The truth**
I am stupid.	I have above average intelligence.
This is a bad choice.	This is a rule – my system creates 45% losses.
I'm going to take back my money.	Getting even will create more losses.

8. Visualize yourself with the consequences of thinking negative thoughts on a long-term basis. (Make sure that your pictures are vivid enough to create a strong negative

feeling.) Develop a still black and white picture representing this negative visualization and store it in the back of your mind for a moment.

9. Visualize yourself with the consequences of following rules that work, creating even more intense feelings. (Make sure in this visualization that you see the rewards that come as a result of good thoughts and actions.) Develop a color picture representing this positive outcome for your life and store it in the front of your head for a second.
10. Now, bring out both pictures and set them along side one another making the color picture brighter, larger, and more appealing. Diminish the black and white picture until it is the size of a postage stamp and put a black slash through it from top left to bottom right with a circle around it.
11. Whenever you are tempted to get even with the markets, bring out these two symbols and pick the obvious choice. The more you make a choice of the right symbol, the more good choices will feel like the natural action to take.

Unfortunately, Charlie's issues were too deep-seated for this exercise alone. They were intertwined with other issues that he also had to overcome. For Charlie, private counseling was necessary to achieve the success he wanted in trading and life.

Revenge is a double edge sword in a battle that no one wins.

The Blame Game

No one wants to believe that he is vengeful and almost everyone who is vengeful justifies his actions with a collection of evidence. Rodney was no exception. As the owner of a money management firm inherited from his father, Rodney was the decision-maker on long-term investments for the company. Although his ability to run a tight ship was good for the company's bottom line, Rodney's destructive pattern of vengeful behavior toward family and colleagues when he was under pressure was not. Even though he was aware that his behavior was devastating to the significant people in his life, he continued to create the very conditions that triggered his negative responses.

When his life was out of balance, Rodney became a vengeful person. Nevertheless, he would take on too many responsibilities and refused to delegate tasks that others could easily have performed. Rodney knew how to create a daily plan but was not good at looking at the big picture. The result was that Rodney was continually caught in last minute crunches. Compounding this problem, he underestimated the time necessary to complete tasks, making him late for appointments and adding to the stress of his life.

Rodney's company took on a new fund with foreign investors requiring client entertainment, meetings, and never-ending paper work. Rodney's schedule was already a ten-hour day. He often slept only 4 hours and worked 7-day weeks. Meals were replaced with a chocolate bar downed with diet cola. The normal family contribution of time became a major burden to him. Rodney viewed cordial greetings in the office as a dreaded waste of time. Making matters worse, he would not consider assistance because it would cost too much money. Why? Because Rodney viewed training an assistant as a waste of time when he could accomplish what had to be done in half the time.

By over-taxing his mind and body, Rodney's focus was off balance. He lost his normal good judgment in making trading decisions, resulting in a major loss. This loss made him more angry and vengeful, resulting in further losses. In his unresourceful state, he would not consider how he had set up the climate for a series of major losses. Aware that he had made trading errors, Rodney could not face others also knowing it. He had to point the finger of responsibility away from himself, blaming everyone for the loss, including his family. The carnage from his finger pointing resulted in the dismissal of his secretary, a trader, and one of his brokers. He held a meeting with his employees where he listed all of their mistakes. While he felt justified in pointing out their mistakes, he did not take responsibility for creating the pressure cooker environment leading to his own mistakes, as well as theirs.

Tough Love

Rodney's wife called me to relate her husband's problem and see if I had anything in my bag of tricks that would help. She decided to seek me out after a few of his colleagues had met privately with her to discuss the Rodney's behavior. I told her that he needed to call me seeking help himself, but I could give her some useful strategies in the meantime.

To Rodney's surprise, his wife called a meeting at his office including the attendance of his children. Each person in the room presented his grievances regarding Rodney's behavior. They all threatened to leave him if he did not get help. What finally motivated Rodney to seek help, however, was when his five-year-old daughter announced that she and her dolly were leaving him, too, because he was "a grumpy daddy with an ugly face when he got mad."

Biting Off What You Can Chew

After transforming the issues that led to Rodney's revenge problems, we put together a big picture plan that included realistic time management. One of his agreements was to encourage the significant people in his life to hand him notes with wake-up calls to his increasing stress levels. These notes would say things like, "time for lunch," or "perhaps a walk would feel good." His response to these requests would be a "thank you," followed by taking an appropriate action to reduce his stress. Rodney also agreed not to add anything to his schedule without taking something else out and check with his wife or secretary to make sure he was not setting himself up again for overwhelming stress and resulting frustration. As a result of this concerted family strategy, Rodney kept his life in balance and eliminated the impetus for vengeful behavior.

Conclusion

There is no such thing as a winning outcome for someone trying to even the score. This is especially true for traders who are trying to get even for their losses. Revenge adds to their existing problems and leads to the repetition of more revenge. The result of this pattern is increasing losses, not only in the market, but in the rest of their lives, too. The first step in freeing yourself from the revenge loop is to become conscious of the pattern of revenge feelings and behavior. Visualize the negative consequences of the negative thinking that leads to revenge, and then visualize the positive patterns of thinking and behavior that lead to following your trading rules. By focusing on the rewards of staying on course and following through on executing a big picture plan, you are more likely not to fall into the trap of needing to even the score.

Chapter 11

THE NIGHT/DAY MARES OF TRADERS

If trading is a high-stakes game of skill, psychology, and chance played on a multi-dimensional board, then none of the dimensions can be ignored. Yet, one influential dimension is consistently overlooked because it is assumed that it is under control or has little effect. The dimension in question is our dream world. This world includes our dreams from sleep as well as our waking hours. Unwittingly, many of traders have been trading from a very powerful part of their dream world - their nightmares.

"I have the same nightmare at least once a month. I enter a trade against my signals and better judgment and it goes against me. Then, I'm powerless to stop the carnage. Before it's over, I've lost everything. When I wake up, my heart is pounding and I feel an overwhelming sense of being out of control. For the rest of the day, my trading is worthless. I might as well have stayed in bed." Robert was anxious to find a way to stop this recurring nightmare. "Why am I doing this to myself?" he asked.

Robert's experience is not an unusual one for traders. Trading nightmares play an influential role in the lives of many traders, successful and unsuccessful. Traders take the images of these nightmares to the trading floor or to the office where they haunt them. Then, these nightmares sabotage a trader's performance all through the day by constraining his ability to think positively and objectively.

Often, a trader wakes to the sense that he has had a nightmare, but cannot remember the details. He trades all day with a feeling of "heaviness" or "dread," that he cannot define, almost like a lingering taste in his mouth. Often, some unrelated event will spark the memory of the nightmare so that it can be remembered completely.

How Bad Can It Be?

How can the memory of a trading nightmare cause so much damage? The human brain cannot distinguish between an image that is remembered repeatedly in vivid detail with an intense feeling from an event that is actually occurring in reality. The body responds to the imagined event with similar physiological responses as it does to the actual event. People who watch frightening movies produce heightened levels of stress hormones and their muscles react in the fight or flight response of someone who is actually being pursued. This physiological effect also happens when a person is plagued by the vivid memory of a frightening nightmare. As he relives the images of the nightmare, his body will tense up and he will produce a heightened level of stress hormones. These physiological responses will affect his trading, making him less able to respond objectively to his experience.

But, it gets worse. The repeated images of a serious mistake in judgment causing failure and loss get buried deeply in the unconscious mind and begin to direct the trader's action in the very direction he fears the most. The reason for this is our human goal orientation. Even if we do not acknowledge it on a conscious level, the deeply etched image of failure becomes the subconscious goal.

Another problem for traders is that our minds formulate a perception of reality and disregard evidence to the contrary. The unconscious mind does not care if the image of trading failure comes from an unreal nightmare. With enough repetition, the unconscious will accept the images of failure and loss as reality and disregard any pictures contradicting that view. The net result is that a bad trading nightmare can sabotage trading decisions, creating the potential for the very disaster that the dream foretells.

Daymares

The same dream experiences bothering your sleep can occur in the waking hours, too. Take for example, Jeff, who creates his own nightmares by clearly visualizing the same type of trading horror story as Robert. The difference is that Jeff appears to be awake when he is dreaming. Although he is sitting upright and his eyes are open, Jeff's mind is operating at the Alpha level. This Alpha level of consciousness is just below the Beta state of high brain activity which we call wakefulness. The Alpha state of mind is the level of "high focus" or "flow" where enormously creative and productive work is accomplished. It is also the state in which daydreams occur.

Instead of being in focus, Jeff's mind is plagued by a clear vision of the devastation caused by his next trade. To heighten the trauma, Jeff repeats to himself such phrases as, "I'm losing everything" and "How could I do such a stupid thing?" Jeff recreates these negative stories over and over again. Naturally, these daymares sabotage his trading results in much the same way that the nightmares sabotage Robert's trading.

In Jeff's case, the negative results are more pronounced because of the self-talk which accompanies his daymares. All vividly imagined pictures which come with a strong emotional content are significantly strengthened by a voice track, which lends interpretation to the picture.

Night and Day

The effective difference between nightmares and daymares is small. Although taking place in different time frames, their causes can be the same physiological triggers. For example, both nightmares and daymares are caused by an increased production of stress hormones or a significant drop in blood sugar levels. The psychological triggers of daymares can be easier to identify at the time, but nightmares can have psychological causes as well.

Even if these dreams arise from a physiological cause, the underlying fears, which are expressed through them, are the same. If a trader does not harbor unconscious fears about trading, the trading nightmare nor daymare will likely not bother him. Instead, his nightmares would be about IRS audits and losing his hair. Regardless of the causes, for a trader, the subject matter and the emotional and physical outcomes are essentially the same.

A nightmare and a daymare consist of metaphors that have a negative outcome playing in our head. The outcome is always a loss of something. Sometimes the loss is real and tangible, such as the loss of life, money, position, or possessions. But, more often, the loss has to do with the loss of control either of oneself or of a situation resulting in fear. These feelings spill over into whatever we do robbing self-confidence and unconsciously directing us to the very self-destructive behaviors we fear.

A nightmare starts in the subconscious and often wakes us to consciousness in a state of anxiety. In a daymare, negative thoughts are chosen and dwelt upon until the negative details of the story are combined and anxious feelings are created. Of course, people do not realize that they are making the choice to think the negative thoughts. Feeling instead that their thoughts have a life of their own and come into their consciousness unbidden. This notion is a great challenge to overcome when counseling a trader who is creating daymares. How can you stop the flow of powerful, negative thoughts from creating the daymare images?

Watching in Slow Motion

Have you ever had the experience of sending your arm into motion to hit a nail knowing that you would be hitting your finger instead? Or heading your car into a stationary object, knowing you are heading for an accident? Yet, in either case, you continued in the same path. Traders tell me that they can see losses coming in a position but they go ahead and keep trading. They feel paralyzed to move. It is true that a part of the trader who continues this self-destructive path wants to lose - for any number of reasons. One of those reasons is that it feels comfortable. In the case of the traders who have had these trading nightmares, they have been performing a mental rehearsal of this self-destructive trade so many times that it feels right and comfortable for their physiology.

The Fear of Thinking Positively

One of the major reasons that traders create these negative stories is that they are afraid to think in positive terms. Sometimes this fear results from a childhood where family members were told that it is not okay to think positively. Parents may fear that positive thinking will bring negative results. This fear is a natural, but erroneous conclusion from a previous experience when positive thinking resulted in a negative outcome. From that time on, positive thinking could be considered a jinx.

In addition to superstition, a fear of thinking positively can come from religious beliefs and low self-esteem. Some religions caution their members to avoid thinking positively. It is considered to be ego-driven and a sign of independence from church authority. Low self-esteem can also create the fear of thinking positively. If you believe that you are not worthy of a positive outcome, you could fear the consequences of thinking better of yourself than you deserved.

Nightmares as Emotional Escape Valves

Our dreams are the outlets for the emotions that we are uncomfortable expressing. Traders who bottle up their negative emotions are at risk of releasing these emotions into their dreams, which turns them into torrents of negative feelings. One trader had dreams in which he was desperately trying to escape from a particular room. The problem was that he was paralyzed and there was no escape. He did not realize that escape from the room would not solve his problem. He needed to escape from was the terrible feelings associated with being out of control. This trader was dealing with a well of unexpressed painful emotion from his childhood. He had never been in the company of anyone he trusted enough to allow those feelings to be expressed. Instead, they were coming out in his dreams.

The Physical Causes of Nightmares and Daymares

Positive thinking requires more energy than negative thinking. When traders are physically and/or mentally exhausted, they seem to find it easier to imagine the darkest results than any positive outcome. The condition of physical exhaustion can result in low adrenal and immune system function. At night, low adrenal function causes your adrenals to fail to alert the liver to release glycogen into the blood stream as the blood sugar levels drop during the night. Nightmares which seem to go on and on result from low blood sugar, which is the reason people often have nightmares at the end of their sleep cycle when blood sugar levels are at the lowest of the day.

How do people get low blood sugar? From poor diet, dieting, and excessive sugar in the diet, which causes the body to produce too much insulin. High sugar intake leads ultimately to low blood sugar. When this happens, all of the negative scenarios come out and take over your unconscious mind.

Another cause of nightmares is illness. Fever creates nightmares as the brain is over-heated. In addition, respiratory congestion can create nightmares. When you are sleeping and having difficulty breathing, fears of being unable to breathe can emerge. The fear of being helpless and out of control can become very real at this time.

A bad day at the trading desk can leave a trader feeling exhausted and anxious. Instead of getting to bed early, he may stay up late, watching television and drinking beer to relax. Unfortunately, the combination of stress hormones from the day and alcohol will affect his adrenal function, causing a drop in his blood sugar. The result could be a bad night of frightening trading dreams.

Other Causes

Ongoing anxiety about trading or money will create repeating images of loss and/or failure in a trader's mind. Those images will creep into his nighttime dreams and daytime reveries. Conversations and thoughts centering on fears and trading problems before going to sleep are another cause of bad dreams for a trader. Watching the news before going to bed can trigger anxiety, which is expressed through dreams. The same can be said for daymares. Focusing on alarming stories in the news or other negative thoughts can create fertile ground for trading daymares. Watching violent movies or reading violent books can also inspire bad dreams. And finally, traumatic experiences from the past can create bad dreams. Although these dreams originate from different experiences, the trader's mind will transfer the anxiety from them to the most pressing concern: trading.

Turning Around Nightmares and Daymares

If it is too late for prevention and you find yourself stuck in bad trading dreams, the most effective self-help strategy for dealing with them is to neutralize them. This involves a three-step process. The first is to recognize the effect these bad dreams have on your trading. This step will give you the motivation to proceed. Then, learn to identify the particular dream that is bothering you. Finally, go over and over the dream in your head ending it with a positive outcome. Once you have done this enough to change the images in your mind, the nightmare will be turned into a pleasant dream.

Conclusion

Our bad trading dreams, whether they come in the night or the day, can have a subtle or profound impact on our trading. They silently undermine our goals and our ability to focus and make good decisions. At the same time, they can guide us unconsciously to the very ends we fear the most. The phrase, "it's just a dream" is often repeated out of ignorance and should be replaced by the old Greek phrase "the net of the sleeper catches fish." Dreams can create reality and a wise trader pays attention and takes action when his dreams start catching man-eating sharks.

HOUSTON, I THINK WE HAVE A PROBLEM!

Chapter 12

THE EXPLOSIVE TRADER

When a trader buries emotions because he does not know how to express himself appropriately when discomfort is felt, these emotions fester, waiting to erupt. Once the sum of these unexpressed feelings reaches a critical mass, a single, insignificant annoyance is enough to release them in an eruption of inappropriate anger. The result is there go the profits. In other words, this volcanic eruption of anger creates "the move that breaks the traders account."

Doing the Dental Grind

The only indication that Ben's normally sweet disposition was harboring unexpressed emotions is the grinding of his teeth. When Ben was a child, his parents did not allow him to display anger or negative feelings in the home. Although he did not really enjoy participating in athletics, Ben used physical activity to release these negative feelings. As a result, he was often benched for aggressive behavior. In college, Ben suffered a knee injury providing him an excuse for not doing any type of exercise. Now, his sport of choice is playing armchair quarterback with the remote control. Now, without physical activities to buffer his anger, at times Ben exhibits an erratic, explosive personality. As a trader, he sabotages his account each fall and spring season with major, weeklong eruptions, coinciding with the beginning of school and tax time. These pyroclastic blasts reduce what should be incredible annual profits to average profits. He manages to handle the small eruptions without too much damage to his trading account. However, the bi-yearly eruptions diminish his profits to roughly half of what they should be.

These eruptions are devastating on his relationships, too. Ben's wife and children take cover as soon as Dad begins to grind his teeth. Despite the fear and loathing that these outbursts create in Ben's family, his wife has no interest in leaving him. She and the children have come to see these eruptions as "normal, the way things are." Of course, she has effectively cut off most intimate relations with Ben because she cannot trust him emotionally. In addition, she rarely includes him in her social life for fear that he will humiliate her publicly. Ben thinks that the demand of caring for their family is the reason that his wife has little time or energy for intimacy. Plus, he has been so absorbed in his work that he does not miss the lack of a social life.

It is difficult to believe that people tolerate such incredibly obvious demonstrations of negative behavior, yet many people do. Equally strange is the fact that traders spend so much time, money, and effort perfecting their trading systems but are unwilling to do anything about the psychological handicaps that destroys their profits. These losses are merely accepted as part of the cost of trading.

Dampening a Fit

When I first started working with people on emotional issues that were damaging their well being, a woman with debilitating seizures came to me for help. Using my training in Neuro-Linguistic Programming, I asked her to detail the exact events and feelings leading up to her seizures, tracing the build-up of the seizures backward to the point of no return. By altering her behavioral choices, she was able to prevent most of the potential seizures from occurring.

This same process can be used to ward off potential volcanic emotional eruptions. Each eruption is preceded by a build-up of choices made over time. Each choice results in an emotional response. If these responses are not expressed appropriately at the time they arise, they will accumulate. However, if you find the point where the choices you make can lead to an inevitable eruption, you can head off the emotional pyroclastics. But, first you have to identify the issues leading up to that point and the emotions that you are feeling and why.

Storing the Ammunition

How many small upsets do you have to accumulate before you can justify a major blow up? One way to find out is to begin to notice your behavior patterns. Ask yourself:

- Do I explode in periodic, emotional eruptions which leave me feeling deeply upset, angry, depressed, ashamed, and/or alone and which clearly upset the people around me?
- Do I store up stories to excuse my emotional eruptions and blame everyone but myself for the blow up?
- Does it make me even angrier when my behavior is pointed out? Then, later, do I feel badly about myself?
- Do I make choices to get even with others and justify my behavior as appropriate?
- Do I damage myself or the people around me when my negative actions play themselves out?
- Do I experience losses as a result of my eruptions? Do others incur losses from these eruptions, as well?

Many of the traders with whom I have worked have had a problem with volcanic eruptions. The nature of trading is such that it creates strong, potentially destructive emotions. Both winning and losing create strong emotions: fear, panic, anger, depression, joy, greed, pleasure, and anticipation. The lack of losses or wins can create strong emotions, as well: frustration, boredom, and helplessness. The potential for emotional build-up and subsequent eruptions becomes an occupational hazard, especially if a trader is whipsawed by windfall profits and devastating losses or a steady stream of small losses.

Formula for Handling Eruptions

With behavior modification, you can work on issues of anger by yourself. Here is a formula that can help eliminate emotional outbursts:

1. The first step in correcting a problem is acknowledging it. After answering the questions, you should know whether you have a problem with holding back emotions and demonstrating anger inappropriately to minor situations. Do you? Examples of inappropriate temper outbursts would be getting overly angry at traffic jams, at toys in your path, or at insignificant unfulfilled expectations.

2. Make sure your diet is balanced with protein, carbohydrates, and fats. The best proteins are low in fat, while the best carbohydrates are fruits and vegetable and the best fats are olive oil or canola oil. To start your day well when you have no time to make a breakfast, try a soy protein drink high in antioxidants that you can get from your local health food store. You can add fruit such as a banana, or some berries to flavor it up. Save the egg breakfasts for the weekends. And yes, breakfast is a must.

   If you do not have time for a balanced lunch, carry a balanced protein bar with you. Have some raw nuts and a piece of fruit as an afternoon snack and stay away from caffeine beverages. Drink lots of water or herbal tea.

   For dinner, have a balance of protein, carbohydrates and oil. For dinner, you need real food. Keep away from snacking on carbohydrates that are sugar or white flour based in the evening.

3. If your exercise is limited because of an injury, do whatever you can to increase your heart rate. There are videotapes on Tai Chi, Chi Quong, and breathing exercises for almost all exercise limiting conditions. If you can walk briskly, do so. It is one of the best exercises to maintain health and equilibrium. Purchase a treadmill to eliminate the excuse for not exercising on bad weather days. Listen to tapes, watch the news or a movie, or read a book while walking outside or on the treadmill if you do not enjoy this activity.

4. Notice minor annoyances when they occur and rate them on a scale of one to ten – ten being the worst. Split yourself into two personalities: your critical self and your positive self. Have a conversation with your two selves that would sound like this:

- State the level of upset: "This is a seven annoyance." This is your negative self talking.

- State why you are upset: "I am upset because I thought I was going to the game with my friends and now my wife announces that she has to take our daughter to her recital and expects me to stay home with our baby son. I want to enjoy the game with my friends and not be a babysitter to my son. I could insist that my wife and daughter stay home and disappoint them while I go and enjoy the game. My wife should have planned her activities in a way that I would not have to be inconvenienced." Again, this is the negative self.

- State possible positive options: "We could find a babysitter – I could invite someone over to watch the game with me on television – I could rent a video, read a book, or work on my computer." This is your positive side coming out.

- State the big picture about this situation: "My wife explored all of the options. The recital is important to my daughter. I chose to have children and one of the trade-off in benefiting from all of the joys in having children is inconvenience and sacrifice. I can make my wife and child feel uncomfortable and feel like being taken advantage of and not appreciated. Or, I can see my wife and child enjoy a wonderful experience and know that I made it possible while I create a serendipitous evening of enjoyment with my son." Again, positive side.

- Write down all of the major blow ups in your life and the price you and others had to pay because of that blow up such as: The time you cancelled the family vacation when you were angry with your wife. It broke down trust between you and your family and this resulted in the family not wanting to plan anything with you. Or, the time you doubled up on your trade to get even with the markets and it increased your losses. Here, your negative and positive sides are talking together.

- On a scale of one to ten, decide if the issue of your babysitting is worth fighting over in the big picture of life or if this is something you can let go of and choose a different way of thinking. It's a ten if it is worth the fight because the cost is too great on your side. For example: you have Super Bowl tickets and you get to have dinner with the players. In this case, you will fight your fight. If not, let go and find a way to enjoy your evening.

- Keep a log of the things that upset you. Go over them yourself or with the significant other people in your life to come up with a way of minimizing situations in which you would be upset or decide on better ways of interpreting these situations.

Sabotaging this Process

The damaging effects of volcanic outbursts can ruin a potentially great trading career. But, these outbursts can be corrected, neutralized, or eliminated by following these strategies. However, while these new good behavioral choices will work for some of you, others will have issues which will sabotage the process from the very beginning. Some traders might find that this process works well for a while, but then they slip back into old patterns. If you sabotage your efforts for change, figure out what the cost is to you and to the significant people in your life. If the cost is too great, take action.

Conclusion

People who explode with emotionally eruptive behavior often think that it is normal for them. They also believe that others should accept them for who they are and not try to change them. Volatile behavior is not healthy for relationships and not healthy for trading decisions. Healthy, sensible choices can make a difference. The strategies outlined above can help if you are able and willing to take the time and make the commitment to create changes in your behavior. If you cannot do this by yourself, seek help in turning your active volcano into a dormant one; you will become a happier, more successful trader.

I'M FINE! PERFECTLY FINE!

Chapter 13

THE PASSIVE TRADER

Over the course of five years, Ed had applied his training in math, science, and engineering to create a profitable trading system - which he could not put to use. Why?

Several years ago, Ed attended a three-day seminar that I presented. Judging from his questions and feedback for the first two days at the seminar, I thought of him as an ideal student who was receiving maximum benefit from the seminar. Was I ever wrong! As it turned out, Ed presented me with the greatest challenge of all the traders at the seminar.

At breakfast on third day, Ed presented me a letter detailing how inconsiderate I was towards the needs of the group. First, I did not keep the schedule of breaks and lunch, running over and keeping everyone late. He was unhappy with the fact that I did not serve something for vegetarians on breaks and was also unhappy that the group chose a steak house for one lunch and a seafood restaurant for the second lunch. He also resented the fact that he had not been told in advance that the course required homework and socializing with other participants was necessary to get the work done.

Surprised and grateful for the feedback, I asked the hotel to bring fruit for the breaks and suggested a vegetarian lunch for the group on the third day. Ed was given the responsibility for alerting me at an appropriate place for breaks. I announced to the group that while homework was a part of the seminar, it was OK if anyone preferred not do it. Still, Ed was consumed with anger and frustration from the two previous days and continued to look for things to criticize. I received a letter complaining about the air conditioning being set too high and other environmental discomforts he had experienced well after the seminar had ended.

Then, I understood Ed and the problems he was having in his trading. He was a passive trader.

Whatever Happened to Passivity?

In the 1970's, one of the fashions in pop psychology was passive/aggressive/assertive behavior. Classes on assertive behavior and support groups for passive people sprung up around the country in the major metropolitan areas. Public consciousness was raised to recognize the fact that assertive behavior could get you what you wanted without doing harm to yourself or others, while passive and aggressive behavior resulted in self-destructive patterns that created poor results and unhappy relationships.

Like all trends, the focus on passive behavior was replaced with the newest psychological issues: sexual abuse, bi-polar behavior and attention deficit disorders, to name a few. Although all of these issues are important in understanding the human condition, they, too, are being replaced in the public debate with other, more timely psychological issues with exotic new names that lead to other self-destructive behaviors. But, the fact that certain psychological issues are no longer in vogue does not mean that their diagnosed effects have ceased to influence our lives. In fact, I have recently encountered a significant number of passive traders, although Ed gave one of the best demonstrations of this behavior. The effects of passivity on a trader's performance are like roots of a tree. Spreading out in every direction, under the surface until there is no place else to go except pop right out of the ground.

What is Passivity?

The passive person believes that he is powerless to have his needs, his feelings, and his wants understood and met. Furthermore, he usually believes that he is not really worthy of having his needs, feelings, and wants met. Since he does not have the power to meet his needs, he expects and demands others to meet them. After a childhood of feeling unworthy and unable to have his needs met, a passive person begins to lose the ability to verbalize his needs as they occur, or verbalizes them after the fact. Even more disturbing for a passive person is the fact that he often loses the ability to identify his needs, how he feels, and what he actually wants in a particular situation.

In Ed's case, he was identifying his needs after the fact, but was not revealing to himself or to me his real need: he was not getting the individual attention that he desired. During the first day of the seminar, I gave Ed a great deal of individual attention. He was not happy when he felt I abandoned him to pay attention to the needs of others in the group. He actually wanted the seminar to be a private consultation.

Here are some of the issues that relate to passivity and the costs these issues have for traders:

1. **Control Issues**
   A passive child is often raised in a highly protective environment where he is never allowed to do for himself. The child is overly dependent upon his parents, who like to have and maintain control. The message is: "You can't do it for yourself. I'll do it for you." Later on, this child looks to others to do things that he should be doing

for himself. The problem is that he does not believe that he is able to do things for himself. Although this attitude is inappropriate in an adult, it can still exist under the surface.

The Cost: In my experience, traders who feel they are not in control of their lives have a great need to control the markets. This need leads to all manner of trading problems, unrealistic expectations, and frustration.

2. **The Mind-Reader Connection**
As a result of this dependent relationship, the focus of a passive person is on the other person. The all-powerful other person who can meet his needs becomes the source of tremendous tension for the passive person. Since the passive person cannot verbalize his needs, he expects the other person to mind-read his needs, his feelings, and his desires. Since there are very few people who are mind-readers and even fewer who want the responsibility of having to mind-read someone else's needs, the passive person is nearly always being disappointed, which is usually translated into anger. So, the passive person tends to build up a lot of anger at others. In fact, the predominant emotional state of a passive person is anger or frustration. Beneath the pleasant, pleasing exterior is often a very irritated person.

The Cost: A passive trader is, by definition, out of touch with his own needs, wants and feelings and this lack of awareness is extremely dangerous for a trader. He is liable to undermine his own well being, while waiting for someone to take care of him. He will fail to plan for his goals because he will be unable to formulate them. Or if he formulates them, he won't believe he should really be able to reach them.

3. **The Aggression Trap**
The flip side of passivity is aggression. This relationship becomes very clear when you watch a passive person build up so much anger over time until he finally releases all of his frustration and rage in an irrational act of aggression and/or revenge.

A class on passive behavior was given to pre-release inmates at a prison in North Carolina who had been imprisoned for murder, armed robbery, and other violent acts. At the end of the class, nearly all of these inmates approached the instructors to say that they had realized how passive they had been all of their lives.

The Cost: A passive trader is likely to build up anger and frustration and seek an aggressive outlet for these pent-up feelings by getting back at the markets.

Ralph was a passive trader who threw his computer across the room in a fit of rage. He was unable to salvage his computer and lost considerable time not to mention the expense of replacing his expensive computer. This episode was not his only act of aggression in the throes of anger and frustration.

4. **Hurting Themselves and Others**
   Because a passive person will not speak up for his needs, feelings, or wants, he sacrifices himself for the needs, wants, and feelings of others.

   The Cost: A passive trader will have difficulty maintaining a happy personal life. His relationships with others must always bring him tension and frustration unless he is as lucky as Ed was to find a mate who was willing and able to intuit and anticipate his needs. Many passive traders feel thwarted and misunderstood by the significant others in their lives. Since they cannot stick up for their needs, they are often put upon, or feel that way. This anger poisons their relationships, eroding the emotional support they need to trade well.

In the case of Ed, the passive trader, he was suffering from not having his nutritional needs satisfied and would not speak up. The result was that he hurt himself. When the passive person absorbs too much frustration and anger from not having his needs addressed, he explodes into aggressive behavior, thus hurting others by trampling on their needs, wants, and feelings. Either set of responses is inappropriate, unbalanced, and unskillful.

5. **Low Self-Esteem**
   Although the passive person can be a high-achiever, he will still have a very poor self-image. At heart, passive people do not believe they are worthy. Usually this belief comes from the criticism, rejection, control, and dependency-issues from relationships with his parents, teachers, and important people in his life. The childhood of a passive person is often filled with overt or subtle messages that they cannot have what they want. Eventually, they often believe that they cannot have what they want because they do not deserve it.

   The Cost: Harold, a passive trader with low self-esteem, was unable to utilize the potential of his system because he continually sabotaged his results. It turned out that Harold's passivity was based on a deeply held belief that he was unworthy of having anything good in life. His parents had told him this repeatedly whenever he asked for anything that required more effort or money from them. As a result, he was unable to create wealth for himself as a trader.

6. **The Victim Complex**
   A passive adult fails to take responsibility for expressing his needs, wants, and feelings. Instead, he lays the responsibility onto the shoulders of those around him. Then, when he discovers that others cannot mind-read what he is thinking, he becomes angry. He sees everyone around him as the cause of his own unhappiness. Hence, he is always the victim. This posture is not simply unappealing and non-responsible, it is a great handicap for someone who wants to reach their greatest potential and enjoy the fruits of a happy life.

   The Cost: A passive trader is unable to take full responsibility for the things that happen to him. Unhappy events, such as losses, are always the result of someone else's behaviors. This failure to take responsibility means that a trader cannot take a hard look at his own methods and actions in order to improve them.

In addition, a passive trader who feels like a victim, at the mercy of the people and forces around him, finds it difficult to be proactive. Instead, he tends to react to situations because he feels powerless and needs to wait to see what others do to him or for him. To be successful, a trader needs to take a proactive posture towards the influences around him. He needs to feel that he is responsible, in control of his life, and able to take charge. With this psychology behind him, he is able to plan, to anticipate, and to take action.

7. **Emotional Swings**
   A passive adult is at the mercy of his emotions because he veers between sadness at not being able to get what he wants and anger because he feels victimized. Unfortunately, he is rarely able to get a handle on these states because he does not understand where these feelings are coming from.

   The Cost: Because a passive trader is out of touch with his feelings, he is unable to identify them and is more likely to be at their mercy. Unfortunately, emotion can undermine any trading system no matter how good it is.

8. **The Undisciplined Adult**
   One of the by-products of passivity is the inability to maintain the balanced life that leads to discipline. It is difficult to be disciplined when you do not feel responsible for your well-being, when you are waiting for others to determine your needs and provide for them, and when you do not even know what it is you want.

   The Cost: A passive trader has difficulty maintaining his self-discipline. Discipline arises from a high level of self-value, from a deep passion for trading, from a set of goals, and from a healthy psychology. A passive trader has difficulty developing the plan that is needed to create the goals and business plan for a successful trading business. He finds it difficult to identify his needs and so setting goals is a complicated task for him. In addition, his lack of self-worth makes it hard for him to stick to a plan that would ultimately bring him success.

There are so many more areas of trading that are affected by passivity that I cannot list them all. Nevertheless, it should be clear from the preceding list that passivity can be the cause of many self-destructive patterns in trading.

Conclusion

A life-long pattern of taking the passive road is a difficult one to give up. However, it is possible when a person is able to admit that he has passive behaviors and is willing to give up the belief that there is nothing that he can do about it. For a trader, this position is a very destructive one. The underlying attitudes and beliefs that characterize passivity make it very difficult for a trader to reach his full earnings potential. If he has a successful run, he is more likely than not to sabotage his results from feelings of unworthiness. As difficult as it is to face the problem, the cost is much higher than the cure.

CISCO SYSTEMS

Chapter 14

THE PROUD TRADER

Has your pride, the very quality that has inspired you to reach farther, try harder, and refuse to accept mediocrity, nearly cost you your business? If you are like Martin, a trader with a once solid career, you serve both as the master and the slave of your pride. When we fail to consciously choose which of these relationships we are going to have with our pride, we can place our trading at great risk.

The Call Before the Fall

For the past decade, Martin had been trading exceptionally well. After a long preparation period that was devoted to the development and testing of his system, Martin moved into trading in a smooth and successful transition from his former career as a top-level computer programmer. While learning the business of trading, he discovered that he possessed qualities such as patience, self-discipline, courage, and the ability to control his fear and greed that he never knew he had.

The result of Martin's growth as a trader was the creation of a level of comfort for himself and his family that brought him pleasure and pride. He moved his family into an enormous house in a very exclusive neighborhood. His wife joined the most select clubs and his children attended an expensive private school, took countless private lessons, and wore the designer-label clothing that brought them acceptance into even the most popular circles.

The material symbols of success were nice, but Martin had established a growing reputation in his ever-widening circle of influence as a trader with a nearly perfect track record of significant profits year after year. He was beginning to experience the heady sensation of being recognized and deferred to when he attended conferences and seminars. His opinion was sought and his ego was massaged. Life was good and Martin was a happy man.

Then, the Trouble Began

As Martin began to enjoy more of the perquisites of his success, he spent less time doing his homework. In fact, his focus on trading was continually diluted by his undivided attention to his reputation. In the midst of this, he made a serious mistake in his trading and sustained a significant loss. Emotionally unprepared to handle loss, Martin's reaction was one of shock and dismay. All of the genuine confidence that he had exuded for years seemed to vanish suddenly. Rather than feeling confident, Martin was scared while pretending to still feel confident. This unsettled emotional state eroded his trading and he experienced a string of losses. Suddenly, he was in great danger of ending the year with a significant loss. In order to return to sound financial footing, he and his family would have to do some temporary belt-tightening, which coincidentally would occur at the holidays, when they tended to shower themselves with expensive gifts, trips, and entertainment.

These year-end losses would also mean that he was off of his perch as the trader with something to crow about. Now that his trading record was becoming open to comment, he would have to admit publicly that he had done badly.

Martin was having a problem with his pride. He had begun to believe in his own invulnerability. He had also begun to feel that the privileges and comforts that he supplied to his family were so important to their sense of self that he could not withdraw them without losing face. The fear that he was feeling was new for Martin. He had never faced the prospect of having to swallow his pride and take a step backward, even temporarily.

Stepping Backward

But, stepping backward was exactly what Martin did. Instead of recouping his losses and rebuilding, Martin maintained the illusion that everything was going well. He dug in deeper financially to spare his wife and children the embarrassment of doing things on the cheap. The truth of the matter was that Martin could not face the embarrassment for himself.

As Martin took money from savings and then resorted to using his good credit, he began to worry. He would awaken in the middle of the night with anxiety attacks that would leave him shaken. The following day, he would be off his feed and his trading would suffer. As a result, he made more and more mistakes. Facing catastrophe, he fell apart. His wife, Anne, was so absorbed in her social activities and in chauffeuring their children from one activity to another that she had failed to notice the change in Martin's outgoing nature. When Martin collapsed emotionally, she was shocked and frightened, but she was able to take charge and insist that he seek help.

That was when Martin called.

Pride and Prejudice

Most people cannot reach high levels of personal achievement without high self-values. The self-confidence and self-esteem that give impetus to our goals are based, in large part, upon our pride in what we are and what we have accomplished in the past. Very few individuals are capable of attaining their goals out of a sense of shame or failure. So, pride in what is worthy in ourselves is a valuable asset.

Pride also allows us to live healthier lives. We take care of ourselves because we take pride in our appearance and strength. Our resulting good health, in turn, allows us to achieve more and reinforces our sense of pride. This self-reinforcing system spirals upward, making our lives better and better.

If this form of pride is so wholesome and supportive, how does it become such a destructive force for traders?

The process of pride becoming a liability for a trader rather than an asset is usually a very slow and innocent one. As a trader builds his business, he devotes enormous energy and time to the perfection of his craft. Eventually, if his commitment is strong enough, he will begin to reap the rewards of his efforts. If he began the journey with a sense of self-worth, his pride justifiably will increase through his awareness of the enormous difficulties that he faced and the skills that it took to overcome them. He will take further pride in the visible signs of his success. He begins to hear the voices of others telling him how smart, how successful, and how worthy he is. At this point, our trader will begin to believe that he is special.

The danger is that a successful trader will begin to believe what he hears. If he internalizes the voices around him like Martin, he will tell himself that he is invulnerable and deserves to succeed. His self-esteem, once linked to his positive qualities of character and the goals that he has achieved is now linked to his sense of superiority and entitlement from his feeling of invulnerability. This transformation is so subtle that the trader is unaware of it until he makes a misstep and must deal with the consequences. Then, the great danger is that he cannot or will not admit that he might be wrong and stays on a path that is completely wrong. He continues the downward spiral because his pride will not allow him to admit that he is imperfect. Disbelief is followed by anger. How could this be happening to me?

The High and the Mighty

The process of pride overtaking talent and success has strong parallels to problems that many high-profile performers and athletes develop when they acquire a large public following and are paid vast sums of money. The pride-driven misbehavior that occurs in these pampered public figures is played out for all to see in the newspapers and on television magazine shows. Instances of this problem abound ranging from the actor who insists upon total artistic control over an expensive film project that bombs to the overpaid athlete who assaults the umpire for making a call against him. The result of pride-driven self-destructive behavior in celebrities is often the loss of the public adoration that sustains their success. Suddenly, the air rushes out of the balloon and they land with a painful thump. At this point, actions coupled with a little luck determine whether they are able to rebuild their healthy sense of pride and make a chastened comeback to public acceptance.

Putting the Air Back in the Balloon

With luck, a trader whose career takes a nosedive due to excessive pride is also able to make a comeback. Actually, luck has almost nothing to do with it. In Martin's case, he needed to take the plunge and admit to a supportive listener what had happened. The more he detailed the chain of events, the more relief he began to feel and the more responsibility he was able to take for what had occurred. Eventually, he began to put the entire situation into perspective:

- He was not his reputation, but a human being
- He did not have to be perfect
- His family would and could be happy with less
- His value as a human being was not a function of his bottom line
- He was a valuable, capable, and worthy human being
- It was OK to lose and to make mistakes because these experiences were opportunities to learn and grow
- All traders, no matter how great they are, have losses and draw-downs

Martin had to undo the damage that his string of losses had inflicted to his confidence. Left alone, these feelings will continue to sabotage his trading results and he will be unable to trade profitably. Once he was able to overcome his negative associations with trading, Martin began to focus on trading instead of the distracting emotions and thoughts that had plagued him. Strangely, Martin announced that he was feeling more proud of himself than he had ever felt before. But this time, he was aware of the flip side of pride and was able to guard against the feelings of invulnerability.

Conclusion

It is not enough to be proud of your trading skills and accomplishments. You must be able to keep that pride in balance with the awareness that losses do occur and have no relation to your worthiness. Healthy pride in your self-discipline, courage, insights, hard work, and accomplishments that result will keep you on the road. This pride keeps the focus on the process and not on the end result. And finally, it is important to listen to your own inner voice instead of the voices that come to you from the outside. Too often they come your way with an agenda that is not one that you would choose for yourself.

SECTION 3
Your Choices...

YELLOW BRICK HIGHWAY
1ST LIGHT - 1 MILE
YELLOW BRICK AVE.
YELLOW BRICK PLACE
FOLLOW THE YEL
BRI ROA
YELLOW BRICK DRIVE

Chapter 15

PATHWAYS TO SUCCESS: MAKING RIGHT DECISIONS

The Yellow Brick Road to Success

If someone that you trusted offered to show you the yellow brick road of trading success, would you travel it? Of course, you would. However, things would be a little more complicated than that even in the best of all possible worlds. Instead of facing a single road, it is more likely that you would be led to a major intersection where each road leads to success of one kind or another. Complicating your decision further, each path, with its unique focus, has its own success guru cheering you on with all kinds of evidence proving that his or her path is the right one to choose. Under these circumstances, would you be able to recognize the right path for you? Well, let's find out.

Picture yourself standing before three yellow brick roads leading to the land called Las Vegas, where it is said that a great wizard named Jack will grant you whatever you want. Which road will you take? Before you make a decision, let's start at the beginning of our story.

Don Becoming a Trader

Don presented himself as plain and withdrawn. He was a below average student with little motivation to succeed at anything in life. One day, as he observed the drama playing out loudly before him on a school outing to the Kansas City Board of Trade, Don suddenly knew that his destiny was to become a floor trader. Initially, his friends and family humored him when he let his desire be known. As his interest persisted, these people became hostile and unsupportive. As a result, Don decided that he was only going to share his enthusiasm with his dog, Toto.

Don began receiving volumes of mail from people who wanted to sell him their trading products and services. One day, he received a brochure advertising a trading conference in Las Vegas. He wanted to attend, but his parents refused and listed many reasons his dream was impossible. As the conference date approached, Don became more and more determined, until he found himself on a bus headed straight for the sparkle of the Las Vegas lights. Once he and Toto reached Las Vegas and the casino doors, he was met with a firm "No" as they tried to enter. He picked Toto up and said, "Toto, I don't think we're in Kansas anymore."

Meeting the Scarecrow

As Don sat on a step outside of the casino in a state of depression, he found himself talking to a wiry, bifocaled man with a gentle face named Crawford. His caring manner gave Don the courage to tell him about his dream to be a trader. As the conversation continued, he found out that Crawford also was going to attend the conference, mainly to hear a market wizard called Jack. Crawford told Don, "The only pathway to success in the trading business is knowledge and you have come to the right place to obtain that knowledge." His new friend would help direct him to find the knowledge that he would need to succeed in trading.

Like Crawford, many people believe that knowledge is the only true pathway to success. Certainly, that is true of people who come to America from "the old country" and live their lives for their children's success. These people might not have finished high school themselves, but they are often responsible for giving their children the monetary resources to achieve great academic success.

Let's look at Charlie who was one of these second generation kids. His parents were not going to let him play frivolously. When he made straight "A's," his parents wanted to know why they were not "A+." Charlie went on to be a successful equity trader, but his successes were never enough to satisfy him. Although he had achieved monetary success as a result of his intellect, he was not able to enjoy this success. The problem with the knowledge path to success is that eventually it fails to create appreciation for its own rewards.

Meeting Tin Man

Don's new friend, Crawford, took him in the side door to the convention center and helped him go through registration. Over the continental breakfast served before the introductory session, a well groomed man introduced himself as Rusty. He, also, came to see the wizard. In conversation, he told Don of the importance of creating the right image for himself and others. "If you act as if you're successful and people think you are, then you'll begin to believe it yourself," he said. "Image is everything in life."

Many success books of today emphasize the importance of dressing the part of success. Successful people look good and surround themselves with status symbols. The problem with emphasizing things and the outer shell of a human being is that one learns the shallowness of the path. Success is limited to what you can see and buy. Eventually, the golden path will lose its luster.

When Samson was a young man, he told me that he wanted to be a millionaire by the age of thirty. Since he had no plans to go to college, I suggested that he become a salesman. His motivations were to own a Ferrari, a Rolex watch, to wear Armani suits and to escort beautiful women to the top night clubs. As a broker, Samson made his first million by the age of twenty eight and acquired all of the things which defined success for him. With his material collection, however, came bleeding ulcers, migraine headaches and heart tremors. Now, at thirty five, Samson looks like an unhealthy man of fifty. He has no close friends, no wife and no family, but, he is successful - - at making money, that is.

Recently, a television news magazine featured an article about an ordinary-looking woman who spent her life idealizing Barbie, the girl's doll with the perfect face, blond hair and hopelessly perfect body. After experiencing some painful rejections as a plain-Jane, she set out to prove how shallow the world was by demonstrating that looks are the pathway to success. Thirty-some operations later, she reached her goal: she looked like Barbie. The new face and body did bring her a successful profession, a tremendous amount of public attention, and a rich man of substance whom she is planning to marry. The funny thing is that this once cynical lady now cherishes the feelings in her relationship. Especially significant is the comment from her man that he fell in love with her eyes, which are the only part of her body that came with the original package. Like Rusty, this woman was wading in the shallow end of the pool until she found something of substance which gave meaning to the quest for success.

Meeting the Lion

Don and his two new friends wanted a good seat at the conference, so they entered the meeting room early. Upon finding a chair, Don found himself seated by a man who introduced himself as Leo. Soon, the four of them were discussing their dreams of successful trading and the wizards they had come to see. This conversation prompted Leo to talk about the importance of character in the trading profession and how people succumb to greed and lose themselves in the process. Leo, the lion-hearted trader, was committed to the ideals of personal character. "Without a strong character and a good heart, success is an empty shell," he said. The only problem with Leo's path to success is that it sometimes takes the by-pass and misses the destination to success in the material world altogether. Strict adherence to Leo's path can leave the traveler unaware of the other factors that are required for success to occur.

Leo explained to Don that at the turn of the century, most of the books on success were about the importance of a person's character. It was not until World War I that success books began to focus on personality and cloning strategies such as dressing for success and acting as if you are already successful. Before World War I, American's assumed that success would inevitably result from these elements of character: hard work, honesty, integrity, modesty, keeping your word, maintaining financial frugality, morality, and religious devotion, etc.

Gerard's experience epitomized Leo's ideal path to success. Gerard grew up in a small Southern community where everyone was a neighbor and friend. People who were selfless, courageous and of good moral character were considered the pillars of the community. Taking these values to Chicago, Gerard was respected and liked by his fellow brokers and clients. He would only work from the highest level of integrity and everyone trusted him. While he was greatly admired, Gerard did not educate himself beyond high school, and he placed little importance on how he groomed himself. The result was that he was left behind on the path to financial success.

Meeting the Wizard

Finally, Jack the Wizard appeared. He was a well-groomed man, wearing signs of success. He spoke clearly and simply. Talking about the importance of a basic understanding of the markets, he emphasized that you could never get enough education and the importance of ethics and high moral values. As Jack spoke, Don's new friends looked at him, happy to see that they had each given him a necessary piece of the trading success puzzle. Don was not confined to one yellow brick road to success. For an abundant life, he needed the package deal.

Conclusion

While there are many paths to success and many interpretations of what success is, you are not limited to only one type of success. The people who enjoy all forms of success surround themselves with the benefits of education, high principles, and monetary rewards by pre-planning a wish list and attaching completed goals to the acquisition of new toys.

PAWN
OPEN
OLD SYSTEMS

Chapter 16

NO RETURN ON DEPOSITS: MAKING RIGHT CHOICES

Are you burnt out and washed up? Do you feel like you have been hung out on the line to dry? Or does it seem that you are headed in that direction? Even the most successful of trading careers can end up with nothing. Perhaps you are reading this while saying to yourself, "This can't happen to me. I've got everything covered." Perhaps you do. But just in case you don't, here are some warning signs to look for or you could wind up with "no returns."

What's It All About, Ralphie?

"Where did it all start?" Ralph wondered. He had done everything according to his parents' master plan, or so it seemed. They were proud of him when he earned his engineering degree, married the right girl, and put those three grandchildren on their laps. And he was ambitious, all right. He was the top salesman for the engineering firm where he worked. There were drawbacks, of course, his work required him to be on the road five days a week, but that was merely a price he paid for success. He had delivered the big diamond, the Rolex, the house with the pool, and the expensive, private schools for the kids. So, why was his wife always angry with him? Okay, there was the blonde in Des Moines and that redhead in Tucson. But, there was no way his wife could be aware of them, or was she? And why should his drinking and smoking bother anyone? A guy's got to have an outlet for the tension, right?

Ralph got religion when he discovered the commodities markets. All of his activity adjusted to accommodate the demands of trading. He asked for a desk job at his company and was home every night to live by the computer doing his research until that day that he was ready to go into full time trading. Ralph was a natural! He did everything by the book and, as a result, his income doubled. Of course, he had to have the bigger house, the yacht, some cocaine lines for his ten minute evening break at the pool and...oh yes, his brand new shiny, twenty-year-younger, trophy bride.

The divorce took two years to be finalized. In the process, Ralph lost most of his toys, his wife of twenty years, and the respect of his children. The alimony and child support payments made it impossible for him to maintain his rich life style. But, the biggest financial burden was his new bride whose expensive tastes resulted from his training. While Ralph continued to work hard at his trading, he paid for his new wife to get her law degree. The increased stress from the added financial burdens eventually became too much for him. His trading fell apart and he began to emotionally unravel when he could not meet his many obligations. When he began living off of his trading account, Ralph's life was on a fast downhill slide. The final results were a double bypass operation, diabetes, and a severe case of hemorrhoids. When his new bride discovered that he was not the fun-loving person she had married, she left him for a younger man. Presently, Ralph is living in a modest apartment with his income from a few real estate investments and wondering what life is all about.

While this story sounds like it comes straight out of *Soap Opera Digest*, the only part that is not true is Ralph's name. You may even think that you know the real character, because his story, with a few modifications, has become a fairly common one among traders.

Camino Real

The characters in the play, *Camino Real*, by Tennessee Williams, have much in common with the traders I have met who have come to the end of their careers with no returns. Each of the characters in this play lived his or her life to the fullest without considering the consequences; for example, Margarite Guitier, lived her life as a femme fatale and became just a withering flower; Jacques Casanova, lived his life as one of the great bon vivants, but faced the same end; and Don Quixote who took daily walks down Camino Real with only his memories of the quest.

Williams placed all of his characters on a street whose name can represent either the road to riches or the end of the line, depending upon its pronunciation. The implication of this double meaning is that a shift in perspective can change an individual's entire reality. Had these same characters been able to shift their perspectives and see the consequences of their actions, rather than living in a dream world, they would have wound up on the road to riches instead of at the end of the line. This is the lesson for traders, as well.

The question to ask yourself is, "Do you see yourself on the road to riches or is the path you are traveling taking you to the end of the line?" The road you are on was determined by the choices you made at each step of the way. Each of us has made some very good choices and some very bad choices in our life's journey. If we are self-disciplined and guided by good information and a set of positive values, ethics and goals, we will make many more life-rewarding choices than life-depleting ones.

When you know the facts of life, you are more likely going to make better choices along the way, right?

The Facts of Life

- If you want to work for someone, most established companies want young people with experience, energy and enthusiasm, and are less likely to want to hire people who have gone out and tried business for themselves.
- If you want to work for yourself and be an entrepreneur, it takes discipline, capital, and the ability to handle risk and be a self-starter.
- Very few people can successfully maintain a trading career when they are under a tremendous amount of stress.
- Women and men who have developed themselves intellectually and have acquired substantial resources want to be with their counterparts.
- If you continuously borrow on the your body's energy reserves without making deposits back into those reserves, you will pay the price in the loss of your body's ability to function at its optimal capacity. This loss in vitality and health can cost you everything that is important to you.

When you live life on the edge with no thought of the ultimate consequences of negative action, there will be a price to pay. So, watch out for the warning signs.

The Warning Signs

- Broken Agreements
- Not having a plan - not following the plan
- Not having the right resources
- Neglecting loved ones
- Addictive behaviors
- Excessive stress
- Poor maintenance of body parts
- Avoidance of psychological issues
- Not giving enough quality time to all important areas of your life

With Three You Get Solitaire

Jeff had it all: all of the trappings and all of the warning signs. Naturally, his family did not understand him. When you look through healthy eyes, it is difficult to understand addictions. It was difficult for his wife and parents to watch their loved-one depressed in the morning after being on a high in the evening, only to see him behave rationally after adding Prozac to the mix. But one could argue that Jeff's bankroll was getting very healthy. At thirty-five years of age, Jeff could handle it. But it is important to note that each body has its breaking point and each mind has its point of no return. When you get older, it takes longer to recover. However, some people do not get a second chance. It is amazing how a small fortune can be wiped out in a very short period of time. Medical bills or a lavish lifestyle have proven to be good at rapid withdrawals.

What will Jeff have to show when he is wheeling his I.V. down the corridor into the game room to play Solitaire?

Depositing Into the Right Account

Occasionally, I have the opportunity to help someone reverse this process of endless withdrawals and begin making deposits into their life account. This reversal happened with Ivan, the boy genius. For Ivan, everything came too soon, too fast. Reality struck one day when he called me to say that he was falling to pieces. Ivan's facade of "energy personified" combined with his exceptional trading results had placed him in the position of managing millions. Unfortunately, Ivan was not ready to handle the responsibility physically or emotionally.

Fortunately, Ivan is in his twenties and motivated to change. We put him on a regimen of healthful living. Ivan's colleagues now have respect for him and, more importantly, he has respect for himself. While the transition from his old habits and choices was difficult, Ivan finds it easier to reach his destination now with people who support him on his new healthy course in life.

Here is a successful strategy for putting deposits back into your life account to bring the balance high enough that large, emergency withdrawals will not close your account:

Keep a daily log of good and bad choices. Then begin to make better choices and watch your account grow.

Counting your Healthy Deposits

- What are you doing to relieve stress on a daily basis?
- How is your relationship with yourself and others?
- How many supportive and positive relationships do you have in your life?
- Do you make good choices in food and beverages?
- What are the choices you make for the thoughts you have?
- How do you exercise your body to keep it flexible and strong?
- What information do you add to your brain every day to keep it mentally agile?
- What keeps you motivated and excited to participate every day of the week?
- How have you handled the issues of the past to make them resources instead of baggage?
- How do you spiritually expand to make your life more enriched?
- What philanthropic things have you done lately to support your prosperity consciousness?
- What rewards have you given yourself lately that make you feel like you have accomplished something special and what rewards do you have to look forward to?
- What decisions have you made lately that will have a positive effect on the future?

Denials for Bigger Rewards

When people learn how to deny themselves temptation and immediate gratification for long-term rewards, they make deposits into their life accounts. The net results of these deposits are easy to calculate compared to the net results for the withdrawals that are made by those who do not say "no" to themselves. In your own life, you can see the comparable account statements. For example, did you ever track those kids who were hanging out on street corners while your nose was in the books? Or how about the ones who dropped out of school to explore an early adulthood while you were going to college? Then there were those early pregnancies, and experiments with drugs while you were enjoying family outings. Later on, there were choices of business deals you elected not to participate in because they looked a bit shaky or illegal. You said "no," when everyone else was cheating on his wife. You could have been one of the millions who plunged into the markets without a business plan, but you did not. Instead, you chose to take the professional approach.

You could have been like the others taking on too many material responsibilities when you were not ready. You chose security first as you added and appreciated each step to achieving comfortable affluence. You could have chosen to overly stress yourself and your family in order to have more material comforts. But you decided to balance your time and enjoy each part of your life.

There is a saying, "The one who dies with the most toys wins." This saying can only be true if you enjoy your toys along the way.

Conclusion

Life offers us many opportunities for failure and success. Many of these opportunities for success are available to us by knowing that certain choices are more likely to make deposits into our account and provide for a comfortable and fruitful life while other choices are more likely to make withdrawals and lead us in a less favorable direction. It is important to look at the probable number of years we have in this life and make the best choices for life as a whole. Make the choices for yourself that you would for a dear friend if he were to ask you what direction to take. While solitaire is an absorbing game for some, it's a lonely one without a payoff. So, make sure it is the game you want to play.

Chapter 17

MAKING CHOICES YOUR OWN

When a trader has difficult or unacceptable choices thrust upon him, he can react in a number of predictable and destructive ways. Resistance to making a decision is the most common reaction, followed by avoidance and refusal to accept responsibility for the choice. Any one of these reactions can deal a blow to your trading.

Between a Rock and a Hard Place

Jeff was an angry and bitter man. When his business partner, Mel, suddenly disappeared, Jeff discovered that he had left the partnership with crushing debt and obligations. While Jeff was busy trading their clients' accounts, Mel was responsible for company promotion and sales, as well as managing the firm's business accounts. Although Jeff believed that Mel was abusing the company's money by purchasing the most expensive office furniture and equipment, he ignored the situation because he was so busy trading their investors' money. Furthermore, he loved Mel's choices in décor and justified the extravagance as a means of presenting the best company image possible. But, the bottom line was that Jeff wanted to believe he could trust his partner.

What Jeff did not realize was that Mel's spending and abuse of company funds went far beyond office furniture and equipment. Jeff discovered much too late that Mel spent large amounts of money entertaining potential customers that did not exist, and reimbursed himself petty cash expenses on lavish items that filled his home. The final outrage, however, was the quiet siphoning of the firm's money into foreign bank accounts.

The enormous debts that Mel left in his wake forced Jeff to make a choice between two terrible alternatives. Jeff could declare bankruptcy, avoid paying the debt, and destroy his credit and credibility or he could accept responsibility, pay the deficit, and preserve his credit and good name. However, this second alternative would mean that he and his family would spend the next five years living at a subsistence level with no guarantee that Jeff would be able to salvage the business when everything was finally completed.

Jeff chose to pay the debts, but he hated everything about his life from that moment on. Because he felt pushed into the decision, he resisted the changes that he was forced to make. The new and smaller home his family relocated to was a source of constant irritation and disappointment. His new and less expensive office was "inconvenient and depressing." The fact that he was required to do all of the business' paperwork himself created additional frustration. Suddenly, Jeff began suffering periods of depression that were frequently punctuated by outbursts of rage.

In the meantime, Jeff's trading suffered along with his relationships with his investors and his family.

Coulda, Woulda, Shoulda

In hindsight, we can see how a different scenario "coulda" played out better if we "woulda" made better choices in our thinking and actions. Very often, we get caught up in the mental turmoil of knowing that we "shoulda" made those better choices while we are still feeling bitter and resistant about accepting choices that are not our own. In other words, we are not taking responsibility for our decisions. We do not own them. The decisions own us and we are angry about the fact and self-destructive as a result.

Rose Colored First Choice

Let's say that instead of being "forced" into bankruptcy, Jeff chose bankruptcy, thereby relieving himself of the obligation to pay all the company's debts. Since he "chose" this option, he would feel emotionally empowered to deal with the situation in a proactive manner. So, his first step would be to meet with his family to decide how everyone would pitch in and make it a family project to rebuild. The resulting plan would enlist everyone's participation at the level of his or her ability. Each person would come up with ways to enjoy the process of downsizing and making the best of the situation. When people are asked to find the best way to handle a situation, they feel good about their choices because they own them.

At dinner, each family member would report on his or her progress and receive accolades for their progress and innovative ideas. They would reward themselves with family fun that would not necessarily involve spending money. Special times create special feelings. When people gather and share the best of themselves, good feelings result. Settings for special times could be a walk in the park, a picnic by the lake, playing games, a celebration of life on a non-holiday, etc.

A Different Point of View

In the movie *Life is Good*, Roberto Benigni, a famous Italian movie star, played a father who created a unique fantasy for his son in order to handle the horrors of life in a Nazi concentration camp. He told his son that whatever happened was part of a big game in which one received points and the winner would get a Grand Prize. This game spared his son the experience of the horrors around them. Eventually, his son realized the truth, but what his father had done for him was the greatest prize of all - the knowledge, at the core of his being that his father loved him.

The message in this movie is the fact that we choose our own reality by the choices we make in our thoughts. Our thoughts create our feelings and these feelings, in turn, direct our actions, all of which determines our reality. Of course, you could create scenarios that command bad feelings and win the debate, but lose the war for your state of mind. The fact remains that we choose to think our thoughts and feel our feelings, regardless of whether or not we want to take responsibility for them and own our choices.

Second Rosy Choice

Suppose that instead of filing bankruptcy, Jeff chose the second option of paying off the debts. However, this time he took responsibility for making the decision instead of resisting his choice and viewing it as a burden to overcome. Since Jeff was making this his choice, he would set up a family meeting to develop a family plan. In addition to the family plan, Jeff would put together a business plan that would not only pay off all of his bills, but would make a profit for both himself and his clients. He would meet with his creditors and present his business plan to show them how he planned to make his business work and pay them back. Most creditors would support his efforts and appreciate his honesty and his workable plan to pay them back. Jeff could ask his friends to help him in establishing a good credit reference to set up a new office.

Since the right working environment supports success, Jeff would be better served by surrounding himself with friendly people and successful businesses. This is available in the form of a one-room office space with a common reception area and back-up staff to assist him part-time.

Jeff would also need to meet his investors and tell them that he was moving to a new office. Due to his partner's decision to enter a new line of work, he would not require as large a space. He should make it clear that while he is moving, he will not trade since one of his rules is that he will not trade during a stressful time. Clear focus is important to decision making and he should emphasize that he is dedicated to only giving the best of himself when investing their money.

Now, Jeff has created a workable plan with the support of the people involved in these difficult circumstances. If he does not succeed, at least everyone will know that he gave it his best effort.

By taking responsibility for his choices, Jeff could have taken control of the situation and himself. Instead, by resisting and failing to take responsibility, he actually put himself under pressure, risked losing the good will of those around him and created a negative state of mind that impaired his trading.

Point of Focus

I recently saw an old movie where a young, married couple moved into an attic apartment. They had no money and could afford nothing better. The young wife promptly began to decorate their space using whatever resources she could find. Using orange crates, cement blocks, discarded items, and hand-me-downs, she turned that little attic into a charming, lovely little place that was eminently livable. She chose to enjoy the process of transforming their humble apartment into a love nest. Her young husband, on the other hand, was unhappy with their situation because he was embarrassed because he could not give her a better lifestyle. One day, in the midst of a rampage about how little they had, she held a dollar bill up to his eyes. "What do you see?" she asked. "Money," he replied. Then, she had him hold the dollar as far from his eyes as possible. "What do you see now?" she asked him. "Everything," he replied. "That's right," she said. "When you look at this room, all you see is money, and when I look at it, I see everything."

This principle applies to traders as well: If you focus on the limitations of your choices, you will see only problems. If you focus on ways to make the best of your limited choices, you will have everything.

Instant Zillionaire

When Ron decided to become a trader, he attended a conference where he could meet all the gurus of the trading industry. "Wow!" he thought, "These guys are just handing me the answers on a silver platter." Now, all Ron had to do was to choose one of the gurus, buy the recommended software and equipment, subscribe to a few newsletters and just let the experts make the trading decisions for him. Ron was sure that he was well on his way to becoming an instant zillionaire. It is instructive here that Ron would choose to listen only to the people who were telling him where to place the trades and not to the people at the conference who were saying you have to make your own choices. By the way, Ron did not become a zillionaire. He did, however, become a computer salesman. Like other naïve new traders, Ron thought that he would not have to take responsibility for making his own choices.

Choosing Your Own Reality

How to choose

1. Carefully weigh all of your options, regardless of whether it seems like you are forced to make a choice or if you are facing many possible paths.
2. Write down every choice that is available to you including those that you would not consider.
3. Ask family members, business associates, and others who have made similar choices what options they feel you have. It is important to write down all suggestions without prejudging them.
4. Play each suggestion out on paper, in your mind, and with others. Look at each choice, first, as a devil's advocate, and then through rose-colored glasses.
5. Make a choice, compose a winning plan based on that choice, and then elicit everyone's cooperation and help.
6. Follow the plan, making adjustments along the way to improve on the plan.

Conclusion

Traders are often faced with choices that they do not like or want to make. If they resist the choices, they will cut themselves off from their own creativity and problem-solving abilities. In addition, they risk alienating the very people whose help they need to bring about a successful outcome. And, of course, their trading suffers. By owning their choices, traders can positively influence the direction of the outcome. Choices they originally did not want to make can become choices that lead to a way out of trouble, that rebuild self-esteem and important relationships, and ultimately, create profits.

56

Chapter 18

THE STAGNANT TRADER

Mediocrity, according to Sammy Davis, Jr., is a curse. When you are at the bottom of the heap, you have nothing to lose and when you are at the top, you usually know how to stay there. But, when you are somewhere in the middle, you are afraid of losing what you have. So, you avoid taking the risks needed for growth.

He was right. Mediocrity is a curse, especially for traders.

Many traders earn a consistent, solid living from their trading activities and are rightfully comfortable with their level of success. After all, being average in the difficult and highly competitive business of trading is a significant achievement. On the other hand, should these average traders consider themselves successful when they are capable of achieving much more than they demonstrate?

The answer lies in how the trader feels about his achievement. For example, take two students achieving the same grade. For one student, the "B" he earned is the result of hard work and steady progress, while the other student did not have to break a sweat to achieve his grade. Which student is successful? The answer is the student who feels proud of his accomplishment. Surprisingly, it could be both of them.

Stagnating in Small Town, USA

Steve was born and raised in a small Mid-western city, attended a local college, dated a local girl, and managed his family's business. In his spare time, he traded equities. While growing up, Steve longed to leave his provincial world for the big world "out there" filled with its opportunities and new discoveries. However, like the protagonist in the movie, "It's a Wonderful Life," when he tried to explore beyond his safe haven, it seemed that something or someone pulled him back. His family and girlfriend, sensing that he wanted to break free, feared losing him to the city. As Steve's interest in trading grew, so did his level of performance. When he took an opportunity to attend a trading seminar in Chicago, the moment arrived for Steve to take flight.

At the seminar, Steve met a money manager who offered him a position managing a portion of his portfolio. If Steve's performance remained consistent, he would triple his income. Accepting this position required that Steve leave his family business and move to Chicago. Returning home, Steve announced his decision to move to Chicago and settled his accounts. He hoped that everyone would wish him well. He proposed marriage to his girlfriend, thinking that she would be eager to marry him and move to Chicago. To his surprise and disappointment, she refused his proposal and went into depression because of his decision. Compounding his disappointment, his family reacted negatively to it as well.

Undaunted, Steve moved to Chicago. Once he was there, he began to meet the exciting people of his imagination. These new friends included a beautiful woman with a level of education, self-confidence, and experience that dazzled him. However, Steve's dream was not quite reality. Calls from home continually kept tugging at his sleeve. His father became ill and his mother asked him to come home temporarily to care for the business during his father's recovery. Steve returned home—permanently.

Ten years later, if you asked Steve publicly about his decision to return, he would tell you that it was the best choice. Alone, however, he would tell you that he capitulated. He gave up his dream of the excitement of the city because he was afraid to take the risks involved. He was afraid that he was minor league material being "called up" to the major leagues to fail. So, he used family obligations as an excuse. In the city, he was no one. In Small Town, USA, he was a leader of the community, and a success to everyone but himself.

After a bright future, Steve was stagnating.

What is Stagnation?

Stagnation is the lack of movement. When something is stagnant, it is immobile, passive, asleep. When water does not move, it becomes brackish and foul like a swamp. Interestingly, we are primarily made of water. In fact, wherever there is a lack of movement in our world, things seem to go bad. The lack of movement for humans is especially damaging. In our physical selves, movement is essential. Muscles atrophy when they are not exercised. Our hearts lose function and our endocrine systems break down after long periods of inactivity. Many studies have directly linked the level of activity to our longevity.

It is equally important to keep our emotional parts moving. When we are stuck in certain emotional patterns, we become sick in spirit. In order to keep healing ourselves from the daily assaults on our psyches, we need to keep in motion.

And, finally, it is vital that we keep moving mentally. As our muscles atrophy from lack of use, our minds also atrophy from lack of exercise. We must keep our minds stimulated and growing just to stay even with the processes of decay.

Traders stagnate when they stop educating themselves about trading and the markets. When a trader stops doing research and comes to a point where trading becomes so routine that there is no longer any joy in the process, he will stagnate. When a trader stops the movement toward growth and stops developing as a human being, his life begins to wind down.

Movement and Change

When things move, they change. Constant and steady change is essential to the appreciation of our lives. Without it, we become stagnant. When things cease to change, we stop seeing them. If you never change the furniture in your living quarters, you will stop seeing it and you will stop enjoying it, as well. When people do not change their physical appearance or the way they adorn themselves, the people around them stop appreciating their physical value.

When we stop seeing things in our lives, we fail to give to our senses the specific details that stimulate them and create feelings that make us feel that we are alive. And so, we stagnate. The need for sensorial stimulation is one of the reasons that travel makes us feel so alive. We are actually seeing new things for the first time and are unable to discount anything. This sensorial stimulation makes us feel truly fulfilled.

Under the Surface - Decline and Decay

But isn't it our goal to have things to idle along nicely without change? Isn't this the stability that makes successful trading possible? If stability is a goal for traders, then what is the difference between stability and stagnation? On the surface, the two look identical because the surface looks calm, almost serene.

Stability looks calm on the surface, but the processes under the surface are in dynamic motion to keep the surface calm. Stability requires constant change and adaptation to keep the processes of life going on at an optimum pitch. Stability requires you to be prepared for anything. In other words, stability requires growth and that growth indicates change.

On the other hand, stagnation looks calm on the surface, but there is no positive change in process beneath the serene surface. Deep down the system is in decline and decay. Slowly, the processes that are maintaining the system are in decline because they are not in motion and no growth is taking place. As the gradual decline leads to decay, the system loses its flexibility and its ability to adapt and respond to challenges. Eventually, the system will fail.

Stagnant Standing

A floor trader who had been making nearly $500,000 a year began to stagnate. He felt that he did not need to do any more than he was doing to keep his life and career at current levels. Slowly, his health began to change and his level of vitality eased downward. As his physical stamina declined, his mental acuity began to lose its luster. Since he put no energy into maintaining his family, he was surprised when his wife asked for a divorce and his children did not seem to mind. Then, electronic trading overtook him and he did not know where to turn.

Spiraling Downward

Although the surface looks calm, stable traders have achieved a state of homeostasis where all of their parts are in smoothly running, dynamic action. This adaptive process keeps the system in perfect running order anticipating future changes. Stagnant traders are riding on past success leaving things to run as they always have without preparing for coming challenges. Meanwhile, stagnant traders are imperceptibly losing ground without realizing it because:

1. Muscles atrophy in their physical, emotional and mental selves
2. Flexibility is lost in the ability to deal with change
3. Defenses deteriorate and complacency takes ovcr putting them at the mercy of change and crisis
4. Passion and the feeling of joy are lost
5. The basic upkeep of the system falls slowly into disrepair

Movement out of Movement: A Blessing or a Curse?

Movement is necessary to get a trader out of stagnation, but movement for the sake of movement can be very dangerous. I have counseled far too many traders who have put everything at risk, often losing it all, because of the need for movement in their lives. However, unexpected dramatic movements sometimes are a result of stagnation and neglect in areas of a trader's life left for another day. When these movements occur, they often arrive as a major time of reckoning. Examples of this type of dramatic movement would be divorce, bankruptcy, loss of employment, a major loss in the market, or a major medical problem.

Sometimes these unexpected movements can be destructive and beneficial at the same time. They can serve as a wake-up call that catapults an individual out of complacency and stagnation. For example:

1. Divorce can be a wake-up call showing you that you can be more than you previously have been and that better relationships are available for you elsewhere. I counseled a trader who was overweight, frumpy, and unaware of her physical self when her husband left her. Months later, she had slimmed down to a fashionable size 7, had

new make-up, a new hairstyle, and a new wardrobe. She was stunning and having a wonderful time.

2. Getting fired from a job can light up your career with a wake-up call to do better, find a better job, or look for a better opportunity. When a trader was pushed out of a long-term partnership, he soon discovered that instead of being devastated by the loss, he was earning three times his previous income in his own business.

3. A major loss in the markets for a trader can serve as a wake-up call to recognize the deficiencies in his system, lack of self-discipline, or a money management problem. A major improvement in any of these areas is a benefit to a trading career.

4. A major loss can cause a trader to take better care of his health. When a floor trader was knocked off the floor because of a major loss, he was shocked and depressed. However, as he began to learn to trade on his own, he discovered that his back pain, which had grown severe as a floor trader, had improved dramatically now that he was in a better situation to take care of himself.

Enjoying the Process

Why do traders settle for mediocrity and stagnation rather than face down the challenge to be the best they can be? Perhaps it is because they have not found a strategy for reaching their goals that brings them lasting pleasure, so they give up on success as a goal. The old adage, "success is a trip, not a destination" does not provide the same emotional impact as the symbols of success—money, toys, status, education, or moments of recognition. Without these milestones and the feelings that come with them, most of us do not feel that we are successful. Human beings are goal-oriented creatures. Without goals and the achievement of those goals, we tend to feel as though we are drifting aimlessly. Unfortunately, when we reach the milestones that define success, the feelings that result from reaching them do not last very long. Eventually, we stop feeling successful. Instead, we could begin to feel that, despite our obvious success, we are not successful at all. Therefore, in order to feel that way again, we need to raise the bar and redefine success. This process leaves us emotionally with moments of grandeur followed by long spells of feeling dispirited, needing to achieve more to have that feeling of success again.

This natural process of resetting the bar to feel the feelings of success makes enjoying the process a nice, but meaningless concept for many traders.

A Strategy for Coping with Stagnation

Although Steve settled for a mediocre life, he still longed for the high emotional states that were part of the very successes he was unwilling to strive to achieve. The result was stagnation. Steve could not accept stagnation any more than he could fight for what he wanted. To solve his dilemma, Steve had two choices. He could learn to love the process of his life or he could learn to create those feelings when he needed them.

In my experience with the traders who achieve the next level of success, their progress is not based on material things, but on self-discovery and the expansion of the inner self. Interestingly, those traders who are looking for spiritual growth invariably receive the other rewards as a by-product.

Conclusion

A trader who stops growing and changing is a trader who is beginning to stagnate. A lack of movement in his life means that he will eventually lose the ability to respond to change and challenge. He will not be able to attain new levels of success because he has set the bar too low. In his own mind, he will no longer be successful. While he stagnates, a trader's life may look like he is maintaining stability on the surface, but stability is a peaceful surface supported by dynamic change, growth, and activity.

Chapter 19

TO LEAVE OR NOT TO LEAVE

To leave or to not leave is truly the question for many traders. Nearly every month over the past six years, I have fielded at least one call from a desperate trader faced with this monumental decision. Most of the time, the trader is trying to decide whether or not to leave his or her spouse. Frequently, children are hanging in the balance of the decision. Often, there is a third person waiting in the wings for the decision to be made. At other times, the trader is considering leaving a partnership or a long-term job or even his trading career.

Regardless of the specific circumstances, the decision to leave or to stay is so important to a trader that it will affect all aspects of his or her life, especially in trading. One of the axioms of my field is that successful trading over the long haul requires a foundation of stability based upon emotional well being, supportive relationships, and financial soundness. Few experiences can topple your trading edifice as quickly as a major personal upheaval such as a divorce.

Since the decision to go or not to go has such profound effects upon trading, it is very important that the trader understand the implications of his decision and receives support in making the necessary adjustments to his or her life. Without this support, traders often spend months, if not years, floundering in their trading as well as the other areas of their lives.

The Devil or the Deep Blue Sea

Mel married the woman of his parents' dreams. Shelly came from the right family and the right religion. She had the right education, the right looks, and the right social and economic goals. She was a good homemaker and a loving mother to the three, small children who came into their lives. The problem was that Mel did not love her and probably never did. Although Shelly was a nice and decent person, she was limited in her ability to cope with the circumstances of Mel's occupation as a trader. The insecurity of his income drove her to make probing inquiries each night about his trading that day. Mel found her pointed questions and constant criticism to be intrusive and irritating at best, and harmful to his trading, at worst. They constantly bickered about this issue to the point that they had little else to talk about. On the other hand, Mel did love his children very much. Unfortunately, Shelly's passive nature kept her from disciplining the children during the day. Consequently, after a hard day at his computer terminal, the unreasonable amount of unruliness from the children made Mel irritable and impatient.

To make matters worse, Shelly had little interest in the trading world or any of the other passions in Mel's life. What held Shelly's interest were the children, her social life at the country club, and her family and friends. Although Mel was a brilliant math and science student, Shelly was an intellectual dilettante who attended a good school in order to catch the right husband. What she had in mind was a doctor or lawyer. Since Mel had been studying pre-med at the time they met, Shelly had unrealized expectations of his career path. Even though Mel was making more money than he would have made in medicine, Shelly was always worried that his income could disappear in a single bad day of trading. Ironically, her fears were potentially creating the very thing that she wanted least. In the meantime, Shelly used Mel's income to compete in the material one-upmanship that characterized her social life. No matter what possessions they had, it was never enough to satisfy her voracious need for social acceptance and status.

Kate was the sales rep for the company that sold Mel his new computer system and she fit his dreams. She could empathize with him about erratic income as a commissioned salesperson and when she walked into Mel's office, the chemistry drew sparks. In fact, the two had so much in common that they could talk for hours and never tire of each other. Kate had a keen sense of humor and possessed intellectual gifts that made Mel feel alive. Before long, Mel began to resent Shelly for depriving him of the woman he really loved. He dreaded arriving at home in the evening and the strain of holding his conflicting feelings in check was taking a toll on his trading results.

Because Kate knew that Mel was married, she refused to enter into an intimate relationship with him. Kate did not want to feel responsible for causing the break-up of Mel's family, regardless of the emptiness and unhappiness that plagued him. In fact, she was so uncomfortable about their friendship that she seriously considered ending it in spite of her own longings for him. This fact drove Mel nearly out of his mind.

It was at this point that Mel called for help. What should he do? If he left Shelly, how could he live with himself? If he didn't leave her, how could he go on?

Making the Decision

Mel wanted an immediate answer, but I needed to ask more questions. The answer to the question of whether to go or not to go is inside the person who is asking it. Mel's decision to go or stay had three options, each of which had pros and cons.

1. **Mel could stay where he was and allow the situation to stay the way it was.**

   PROS: If Mel stayed and did not do anything to improve or change the situation, he would not have to upset any of his applecarts. His trading would not be drastically interrupted. In the meantime, his children would not suffer the loss of their father and all of the other problems that are associated with divorce. He would not feel guilt about leaving and he would not suffer the economic consequences of divorce.

   CONS: If Mel stayed and didn't change anything, he would be miserable knowing that he had given up a chance to be with the one person who was "perfect for him." Inside, he would begin to feel dead. His irritation at his wife and children would increase and he would find himself exploding at them. Eventually, he would find himself in the same position again. All of the aggravation would most likely lead to losses in the market because he was not working to get the rewards that earning money for trading brings. This is breeding ground for self-sabotage in trading profits.

2. **Mel could leave Shelly and live with Kate.**

   PROS: If Mel left, he would have the opportunity to live the emotional life of his dreams. This was a very big pro for Mel. He would no longer have to listen to his wife's complaints and fears, nor would he have to put up with all of the noise and confusion created in his home by his disruptive children.

   CONS: Mel would feel extremely guilty if he left his children. He would also feel guilty for not having tried to work on his marriage. He would face the condemnation of his family and friends. His trading would take a big hit while he made the transition to his new life. It is possible that once Mel actually lived with Kate, he would find that she had issues that were as uncomfortable to confront as Shelly. He would also pay the economic costs of divorce, which would go on for many years.

3. **Mel could try to make the best of the situation and do what he could to improve it.**

   PROS: If he and Shelly went for counseling, it is possible that their life together could greatly improve. Mel would grow through the counseling, if nothing else positive came from it. His relationship with his children would improve. If counseling did not help the marriage, he could possibly find the emotional support he needed outside of their marriage, thus taking the pressure off the marriage. Mel's trading would not be interrupted.

   CONS: He would not have Kate, or if he did, it would have to be a discreet relationship that was not fulfilling. There was also the risk that his efforts would not produce positive results and he could lose both Kate and his family. He would go through the financial pains of divorce, which would probably have a bad effect on his trading.

As you can see, the decision could only come from Mel. He would have to live with the effects of his decision and each one held the potential for disaster. Mel would have to decide which benefits he wanted the most and which tradeoffs he could bear the most easily. For Mel, each alternative had nearly equal consequences when he weighed the pros and cons.

The trick to making the decision to stay or to leave comes down to these same alternatives. The pros and cons will be unique to each individual situation, although Mel's pros and cons are similar to many of those people who are considering leaving a marriage.

Mel's Decision

After carefully considering his alternatives with their pros and cons, Mel decided to leave Shelley and become a part-time dad. He concluded that the social and economic costs of divorce were far outweighed by the potential benefits of his life with Kate. In addition, he was willing to take the potential damage to his trading. This was a difficult choice in the short run, but Mel has since developed excellent relationships with both Kate and Shelly, who has since married a doctor. The children have learned that there is a different set of discipline rules at their dad's house and he greatly enjoys their visits. A benefit for Shelly is that she gets to enjoy more time for her country club activities. And, Mel's trading is consistent and better than ever.

It is important to remember that each trader will look at this decision and give different weight to each of the pros and cons. For that reason, Mel ultimately had to make his own decision. It could have had a disastrous outcome, but fortunately, it worked out for everyone.

Leaving the Partner

Over the years, I have had quite a few calls from traders who were preparing to leave their partnerships. Steven had been in partnership for four years with one of his long-time trading associates. The two men decided that they could bring complementary talents to a partnership that would make more for each of them than they could make working separately. In fact, that is what happened. Their partnership was extremely profitable. The problem was that Steven could not tolerate some of the personal habits and attitudes of his partner. His partner was a decent and talented fellow but lacked certain social skills. Steven was very particular about the way things should be done and became increasingly intolerant of his partner.

We framed the pros and cons of the same three alternatives:

1. Steven could stay and change nothing.
2. Steven could leave.
3. Steven could attempt to make the best of the situation and do what he could to improve it.

Steven's Decision

Steven took Option Number Three and decided to stay in the situation while doing what he could to improve it. For Steven, the prospect of losing significant income, starting over again, and finding a new, talented and trustworthy partner far outweighed his personal considerations. His first step, and the most risky part of his decision, was to sit down with his partner and relate candidly what was bothering him. The third alternative does not work if you are unwilling to communicate the problem to those involved. If his partner had taken umbrage, Steven would have had an uphill battle to salvage both the relationship and partnership. However, to Steven's relief, his partner was more than willing to work on the things that were bothering Steven. The surprise in all of this was that, once the door was open, the partner was able to tell Steven about some things that were seriously bothering him, as well. The result was that the partnership became even more successful.

Leaving Kenny

Sometimes, the situation that must be left is not a marriage or partnership, but a troubled child. Kenny was a nineteen-year old whose life was completely out of control. His father, Richard, came to me for help, along with his wife. Richard was having trouble trading because he was so upset with Kenny. This bright and talented son had failed his way through school and was well on his way to becoming a career criminal. His father had caught him selling drugs after his recent release from a court-mandated program. Richard and his wife had tried therapies of all kinds including tough-love therapy, residential treatment, Outward Bound, and scare-tactic incarcerations. Nothing had worked. In the last week, they had come to believe that their own safety was in danger of compromise. While high on drugs, Kenny had threatened to harm them if they did not give him money.

Richard and his wife had reached the end of their rope. The only option they could see was "leaving" Kenny. That meant telling Kenny that he could not come home until he had straightened out his life. This option was almost too painful for them to consider until this most recent threatening episode. They clearly understood the short list of three options available to them, which was a modification of Mel's list:

1. **Let things go on as they were.**
   If they selected this option, chances were that Kenny would wind up in jail after having escalated his destructive path, possibly harming them.

2. **Let Kenny go.**
   With this option, Kenny would have to recover on his own and possibly not make it, in which case, they would feel terrible guilt. On the other hand, their lives would less likely be in danger and they would be able to live in relative peace.

3. **Let Kenny stay with them and try to improve the situation through any means available.**
   Unfortunately, this alternative had already been tried and failed.

Richard's Decision

For some people, regardless of all considerations, the decision to let go has to be made because the emotional and physical toll is too great. If everything has been done to improve the situation, and the current and potential damage to them is too great to bear, then leaving is the right option. My job was to help Richard and his wife come to terms with their decision to let Kenny go. They needed a great deal of support, so I put them in touch with a local support group that could help them through the transition period and the next few years. Once they made their decision, it was clear that they began to experience a new sense of relief, freedom, and determination. The process was difficult but necessary. Eventually, Richard and his wife were able to reconcile their feelings of guilt with the fact that Kenny was on the path he had chosen for himself. Kenny did wind up in jail, dried out from drugs, and felt remorse for his earlier behavior. Richard corresponded with Kenny and they eventually began to build a new relationship.

Conclusion

When traders come to a crossroad in their lives and they need to decide whether to stay or to leave, they usually have three alternatives:

1. Stay and keep things as they are
2. Leave
3. Stay and try to make the best of the situation

Weighing the pros and cons is different for each individual, but it is the only way to see the consequences of each decision as they are weighted by our own set of values and needs.

The important thing is to make a decision and know why you are making it. Then, you must also be willing to live with the consequences of the decision. Once you decide, you will find that you are able to take action. Taking action and making decisions empowers us and gives new energy to cope with the consequences of our decisions. On the other hand, the act of not making a decision produces stress for the trader, which translates into poorer trading results. Consequently, it is better in this case to make the decision to stay than not to make any decision at all.

If you are faced with a go or stay decision, you will need support either in making the decision or in living with it. Do not hesitate to ask for support from those closest to you, from support groups, from professional counselors, and even, if you choose to stay and improve the situation, from the people involved.

TAKE
TRADE
DO NOT
TRADE

Chapter 20

SHOULD I TRADE TODAY?

If you honestly answered this question every day and traded only on your peak performance days, your annual gross income would exceed anything you have ever produced. Assuming, of course, that you have and are following a good trading plan. The chances are that most of you do not want to ask this question because you will trade regardless of the answer. The objective of this short question and answer session is to minimize your risk and maximize your potential for taking successful action. The way to accomplish this is to follow your trading system faithfully, which should require that you trade only when you are in a peak state of physical and emotional readiness.

Self-Deception

Neil lies to himself about his ability to trade on the days that he should be putting himself on the bench. The resulting trading sessions usually incur losses that require significant time for him to recover lost trading momentum.

What Neil wants to know is why he persists in trading when he should know better. Since Neil is not the only trader who trades in self-deception, it is important to understand why this happens and what a trader can do to prevent it.

Bad Trading Days

Let's face it, we all have good days and bad days. But, traders are not like stage actors who have to perform despite wracking fevers, sprained ankles, and broken hearts. While an actor's career depends upon his showing up and giving his best performance for a paying audience every day. A trader simply cannot rely on memory and rehearsal to make it through days when he feels bad because the play of the market is never the same from moment to moment. In an instant of miscalculation, emotional weakness, or lack of focus, a trader can suffer a crippling loss with long-term consequences. These lapses are most likely to occur, not when you are at the top of your form, but when you are off your feed.

At the very least, there will be days when you simply did not get enough sleep, missed taking your allergy medicine, or are coming down with a cold. While these conditions are physical and moderate, they have a definite and measurable effect on your ability to think and take action: your brain is not as quick, your perceptions are dulled, your reaction-time is longer and your decisions are not first-rate.

While they are not actually sick or in pain, there are also a fair number of traders who are never at their physical peak. These traders are the ones who hit the bars after work, abuse drugs, eat unhealthy diets, and either over-exercise or are permanently adhered to the sofa cushions. Banking on their youth and strong constitutions, they may not have really bad days, but they will not trade to their full potential even if they are showing good performance.

If moderate physical changes can have a significant impact on your trading edge, imagine the profound impact of severe physical challenges! I have worked with traders who are trying to make major trading decisions on days when they are suffering from migraine headaches, severe back pain, unrelenting arthritic pain, injury or post-operative recuperation. A handful of traders can actually use their pain to enhance their focus and can trade better as a result. These traders are the exception. For most of us mortals, severe pain and discomfort drain off energy, focus, and commitment to our self-disciplines. It gets harder and harder to follow your system when you are trying to survive physically.

When Everything Goes Wrong

Not all bad trading days result from physical consequences. Emotional and personal factors can also be the cause of potentially disastrous trading days. Traders facing a personal crisis such as a divorce, a death in the family, or the loss of a close friend should not be trading. Over the past several years, I have repeatedly cautioned traders who were going through a personal crisis to stop trading. Marital conflict is one of the most common causes for bad trading days. A trader who has just decided to leave his wife and family or is in the middle of a stressful divorce is often looking at months of bad trading days. It is difficult to convince such a trader that he can afford to stop trading. Unfortunately, his trading often becomes very costly during this time.

Another common cause of bad trading days is taking a major loss in the markets. At that point, fear and low self-esteem can cause a trader to make mistakes or take too many risks in order to make up for the losses or to get back at the markets.

When Everything Goes Right

On the other hand, a reason for not trading can be the day after a major win in the markets when a trader can be too emotionally over-charged with ego and greed to make good decisions. When everything goes right and everything seems wonderful and happy, a trader can experience a tremendous drain on his focus and attention. The reasons could be when a new baby is on the way, a family reunion is being planned, a wedding is in the works, when you are blissfully in love or lust, or when you are building a new house.

Filtering Reality

What makes a day unfit for trading is when a trader's emotional or physical condition filters out the information normally received in making good trading decisions. The result is that trading rules are not followed. Once normal perceptions are altered, reactions, regardless of how good or bad they are, will not match normal, good decisions.

Neurologists studying how the human brain perceives reality are discovering that each brain's perception of reality has far less to do with the thing perceived than with the individual's genetic predisposition, past experiences, and preconceived notions. As a result, we see things in a predetermined and limited way. Nevertheless, those perceptions are our very own perception, ones that we understand and can use. If these perceptions are changed because the normally filtered information is distorted by emotional or physical disruptions, we will not behave in our normal patterns – hence, sabotaged rules.

How to Decide

So, you are convinced that it is a good idea to ask yourself each day whether you should go to bat today or sit on the sidelines and wait out the game. But, how do you make the decision? Based on what criteria? Below is a list of questions that could be helpful in making the decision. Each day is different so that one question might be relevant today, but not tomorrow.

Jim, one of my clients, copied this list, changed some questions to make them more relevant to his own life, added some questions, and pasted it on his bathroom mirror. Each morning before he finished shaving, he reviewed the list. To his surprise, Jim found that he could not get through the list without disqualifying himself at least one day a week. When he went through his divorce, he kept himself on the bench for over a month. Then, Jim put a list up in his office by his computer. During a trading day, he would check the list if he felt he was losing energy or was feeling out of sorts. If he failed his test, he would pack it up for the day rather than trade himself into a hole. By the way, Jim's trading improved beyond his highest goals. When he gave himself permission to not trade when he was off his form, he found that he had more energy, enthusiasm, and focus when he returned to trading. As a result, his drawdowns were lessened and he was able to pick better trades to enter and ride to their end-game.

Here is the list that I have developed. If a question strikes you as not useful to your situation, simply eliminate it and add your own. At the very least, find one or two that work for you and make them a part of your daily routine.

1. On a scale of one to ten, with one being the most awful and ten being the most energetic and healthy, how do I feel today:
    a. Physically?
    b. Mentally?
    c. Emotionally?
    (Anything lower than a 6 cannot be described as a peak performance day.)

2. Is there something on my mind that has me concerned, distressed, upset, angry, panicked or feeling very guilty, so that I can't seem to stop thinking about it?

3. Did I just have a major win in the market? One that has me over the top? (If yes, read your business plan and tighten up on your risk if you have a rollercoaster issue of losing after major wins.)

4. Did I just have a major loss in the market? One that has major implications for me? (If yes, ask yourself, did I follow my rules? If yes, pat yourself on the back. If not, ask yourself what lesson have I learned? Then pat yourself on the back for deciding to not make that mistake again.)

5. Did I just win in the markets by <u>not</u> following my rules? If so, realize that you are either going to have to change your rules, or accept the fact that it was a mistake and not to repeat that behavior again.

6. Did a major event happen in my life recently, either positively or negatively? (If so, notice how that event has affected your energy and emotions. Pull back from the day's trading if your behavior is different from what it normally is.)

7. Have I been experiencing a series of losses in the market? (If yes, take time for a periodic review of your business plan and make sure you are aware of any changes in the market. Adjust your plan to accommodate any changes.)

8. Did I break my good routines yesterday? This can include failing to take care of yourself such as your exercise routine, your eating disciplines, overdoing alcohol, not sleeping, etc. (Consider anything above a four as a day to stay on the bench.)

9. Could I concentrate on a game of chess (use your favorite game of strategy and concentration) right now in order to beat an opponent as good as I am at my very best? (If not, you're not good enough to compete with the big boys in the market today.)

10. Did I wake up feeling that I needed four more hours of sleep? (If your morning routine includes a good breakfast protein dish, exercise, and meditation, you can leave the house feeling fully energized. This is not an issue, but you need to question whether you can willingly risk the family money if you leave the house exhausted.)

11. It is 11:00 in the morning or 2:00 in the afternoon. Would you give anything to close your eyes for a while? To lie down for a minute? (If so, you should not be trading. The early afternoon period after lunch and until about 3:00 pm is considered to be a biological clock time in which it is almost impossible to learn anything. The body wants to shut down and if you are not feeling physically and mentally fit and alert, you should shut down – at least temporarily.)

During the trading day, if anything happens that would bring you to the negative part of any of the above situations, you might have to quit at that point in the trading day and not wait until the next day.

No Shame in Not Trading

So, you see the kind of questions that you should be asking yourself: what is your mental and physical preparation for the day? Once you review this list, you might find yourself saying, "Okay, maybe I'm not at my best today, but so what? I trade when I'm feeling bad and I usually manage to get through the day without a catastrophe. If I waited to trade when I felt wonderful, I'd never trade. This is a lot of hooey." If you find yourself responding this way, you will have a lot of company. I have seen countless traders who are convinced that they can trade regardless of how they feel. But, I wish you could see them after they decide that they are going to sideline themselves on those low-energy days. Once a trader takes control of his trading on this new level, he finds that he trades better than ever before. It is only after trying this strategy that traders are able to honestly look at their performance and see the strain on their trading from the long-term habit of trading when unfit. If you force yourself through the first rough day, are you doing any better the second day?

There is no shame in not trading when you should not be trading. This concept is one that you should cozy up to if your goal is to reach the next level of trading mastery and success. And by the way, those traders who have the discipline to take themselves out of the game when they are not up to par have fewer days they have to do so because they figure out ways to prevent occurrences. The shame is in doing something that you are not prepared to do while putting yourself and your capital at risk. I have never heard a trader have to apologize to the ones he loves for staying out of the market because he was not in shape to trade that day. However, I have heard many ashamed traders have to explain the reverse to their families.

Getting in Shape to Trade

The best way to insure that you can answer the question of whether or not you should trade today is to be disciplined. The routines of self-discipline that address your physical and emotional well being are your best defense against bad trading days. They are also the means to insure that you follow your trading disciplines, as well. If you find yourself answering the checklist in the negative column, chances are good that you have been breaking your disciplines. Your disciplines may not be able to protect you from some of the major shocks in life such as divorce or death of someone close to you, but they can give you the strength to weather these shocks and return to your trading sooner.

Conclusion

Because successful, long-term trading requires you to be at your peak each day that you trade, there will be many days when you should not be trading. Unlike many professions in which you can coast through your bad days, a bad day in trading can mean the end of a career at worst and unexpected losses at best. Simply by asking yourself honestly each day whether or not you should be trading and keeping yourself out of the game if your answer is "No" can vastly improve your trading results.

SECTION 4
Your Habits...

DREAM HOUSE
PSYCHO-LOGICAL BALANCE
MANAGE FUNDS
DIVERS
HAVE RULES
TEST RULES
FOLLOW RULES

Chapter 21

THE HABITS OF SUCCESS

Habits shape our lives. What we do every day is what we build on and if the habits we develop are good ones, we will have a strong foundation. If the habits we develop are poor ones, we will find that when we go to the bank on that inevitable, rainy day, there is nothing in our account.

A good case in point for the power of personal habits is Mike Tyson, the great heavyweight boxer. In the heat of his title match with Evander Hollifield, when he was under a great deal of pressure, Tyson did something that shocked the sports world. He brutally bit his opponent's ear. The question everyone asked was "How could he do such a thing?" But, the answer is really quite a simple one. The habits of thought and behavior, which characterized Mike Tyson's life, directed his behavior when he was no longer under conscious control in the ring. In other words, Tyson did what he was habitually programmed to do.

If you doubt the power of your daily habits, consider the occurrence of a year later. After having his boxing license suspended for a year, Mike Tyson and his attorney appeared before the sanctioning board, which would determine his professional future. Apparently, there were board members who were not satisfied with Tyson's sincerity in his apology for what he had done. After an hour of questioning about whether he was really sorry for the assault on Hollifield, Tyson snapped. Unused to and unable to control his temper or his language, Tyson resorted to his previous pattern of verbal assault. In four letter words, he issued a volley of invectives at the board that his lawyer was unable to stop in time. The story was headline news.

Here is the moral to Mike Tyson's story: If you use profane language habitually whenever you are upset in any way, will you be able to control yourself and refrain from using it in the most important and stressful moments of your life? Apparently not. The reason a person resorts to habitual behavior under stress is that the unconscious mind takes control at these stressful times. Actions become involuntary when the unconscious mind takes control just like when you blink your eyes or gasp in surprise. This is why someone can make bad choices even when an entire future hinges upon a choice or decision.

Crossing the Line into Sabotage

If you develop a skill for boxing while developing a habit for violence, it is easy to cross the line and sabotage your skill with your bad habit. This is true for any skill, which has a sabotaging habit that can take over when stress builds. The reason is that the conscious mind is limited in its capacity to handle quantities of information at the same time. When the conscious mind becomes overloaded with information, the unconscious mind takes over and executes the pattern, which is appropriate to the situation based upon learned behavior. In Tyson's case, a violent act was appropriate when he was angry.

Let's suppose that you are an investor who has developed a successful trading method, which, if followed, would return a good profit. Unfortunately, you have a habit of not taking action when you doubt yourself and your abilities. When you mix these two factors with a stressful day, you have the recipe to take no action on a good entry signal.

The Overnight Wonders

In the music and entertainment business, the public is constantly introduced to "overnight wonders." This phenom of the moment is usually a young, unknown performer who bursts upon the scene and is instantly exploited by the industry and its media outlets until the public tires of him or her. Then, the overnight wonder becomes an overnight has-been. The truth is that there are no overnight wonders. The great majority of these unknowns have been practicing their skills and performing in obscurity since they were children. Years of long practices, self-discipline, and performance-level expectations are responsible for their "instant" success - in other words, their habits of success.

Identifying Your Foibles

Most of us would rather sweep our habits under the rug, rather than go through the effort required to change them. People will live with all kinds of discomfort and excuses rather than tackle the self-sabotage that keeps them from living their best selves. Many people will recognize the need to change only when it is brought to their attention in a serious way, for example, when it hits them in their pocket book. Often in a relationship where one partner finally says, "I can't put up with you anymore," the other person responds, "Why didn't you say something before?" The truth is, he never heard the message that was being sent in a million different ways until it was too late.

A trader recently called me and confided that he had lost over seventy thousand dollars last year and even more the previous year. I recommended that he take my *Trader's Evaluation* to identify his problem. From the evaluation, we discovered many things, the most prominent being that he was afraid of success. His fear contributed to his habit of not following his rules. This was a complex habit that originated from issues that he experienced when he was a child. He could not change this habit although he had read every book on the subject of how to overcome his problem, because he was unable to consciously change the habit. Reading books on making changes helped him to understand his problem, but did not make it any easier for him to change his behavior.

Simple habits can be changed by the conscious repetition of a new behavior. Highly destructive habits, however, are usually based on complex issues, which are hard to change unless you first change them unconsciously. To make this happen, you have to be in an unconscious state and be directed by someone who knows what he is doing. Our trader who was not following his rules has deep-seated issues, which are directing his self-sabotaging habit. Unless he is willing to deal with these unconscious issues in a way that will actually reach them, he will either get hit so badly financially that he will get out of the game or he will decide to do whatever it takes to make the changes

Making Changes

Are you willing to continue to let your habits get in the way of getting the best and being the best you can be? If so, just continue doing what you are doing and put up with the consequences. If not, then start becoming aware of yourself.

Ask yourself:

- What do I do, say, or think in private that I do not want to demonstrate in public, but has been revealed on occasion?
- What behaviors take over when I am in a stressful situation that cause me to lose in business or create disharmony with my relationships in some way?
- What do other people say about me that I have been ignoring?
- What are the patterns that repeat themselves which hold me back from reaching my goals?

Consciously Changing Habits

Steps to change:

- Ask yourself: How would my behavior look if I were to change it to support me rather than sabotage me?

- Ask yourself: How would I feel about that change of behavior?

- If this new habit feels comfortable, take the next step (if not, seek help or keep things the way they are).

- During quiet moments, visualize yourself performing one new habit. (If you try to change too many things at once, you are more likely to give up because it will feel like too much work.) This visualization will give your unconscious mind a model of the new pattern you want it to follow.

- When stress is the cause of your bad habit erupting, visualize a time when the habit surfaced inappropriately. - What were you doing just before this occurred? Continue to ask yourself the question until you discover the point of "no return." This is the point at which you cannot help but to do the unwanted habit.

  Example: A woman who had seizures remembered a time she was late for an appointment and arrived so stressed she had a seizure. I asked her what happened before that and she said, "My husband could not find his keys, the kids needed their lunches prepared for school, and I was low on gas."

- Head off the stress points "at the pass" by being pro-active in making choices.

  Example: For the woman with seizures, she should have a key hook by the door and remind her husband to put his keys there when he does not do it automatically. Eventually that should become a pattern for him. Make the kids' lunches the evening before. And, always refill the gas tank when it's half-full, unless she's late for an appointment.

- When habits are a way of life, for example when you curse out loud or to yourself, devote part of the day to making the changes by saying "Stop." Repeat your message to yourself or others in a more eloquent and gentle way.

- Very often a habit is an unwanted emotion, such as fear. As a result of this fear, you might not have the discipline necessary to follow the tasks you wish to complete.

  These types of habits very often are coupled with major psychological issues and conflicts, which are better handled by working with a professional. This is especially true if there is a high cost to keeping the habit, as in the case of the trader that cannot follow his trading rules and keeps losing money. Another example would be an important relationship that is at stake unless the habit is changed.

- Reward yourself every time you perform the good new habit until it is firmly established. This reward system links the good, wanted habit with a pleasurable outcome and makes it more likely that you will repeat it.

- Add a penalty to a bad habit. For example, in a drafting class many years ago, each time a student dropped an instrument, he was fined a quarter. At first, you could hear pencils and fine instruments dropping every few minutes. After several weeks, you never heard another instrument drop again.

If you want to make an attempt at changing the habit yourself, use the above strategies of visualization, stress reduction, and consciously changing the habit.

The Daily Habits of Success

If you are aware of your sabotaging habits, you are halfway to accomplishing your goals. You may be surprised to discover, however, that many people can identify their sabotaging habits, but have no clear idea of the habits that support success. Therefore, the following is a general list of the habits of success, which I have seen in the most successful people with whom I have worked:

- Motivating yourself every day regardless of how you feel
- Planning
- Following up on your plan
- Having fun in the process
- Balancing all areas of your life
- Loving yourself and appreciating your efforts
- Acknowledging the efforts of the people around you
- Being thankful for what you have
- Prosperity consciousness - which involves giving away a portion of what you have
- Taking care of yourself every day physically, emotionally, mentally, and spiritually

Conclusion

Our successes in life are rarely the result of luck. They are more likely to be the result of good habits, which support success. Those "instant successes" who are lucky enough to be "discovered" usually arrive on the scene after long years of paying their dues and practicing their skills daily - in other words, practicing the habits of success. On the other hand, our losses and failures are often the result of our bad habits. These negative and sabotaging habits will surface when we are under stress and our behavior becomes automatic. At that point, we will resort to our everyday behaviors. At the very moment we need to be at our best, we may find that we are guided by the actions that we never think about and would not want to display in public.

Changing simple, bad habits into good habits can be accomplished by using the strategies listed in this article. Changing complex bad habits can be easy, but usually cannot be done alone. These deeply destructive habits that come with a high price tag are often the result of complex issues in your unconscious. Changing these complex habits usually requires professional help and needs to be tackled before they take you, as in the case of Mike Tyson, out of the game.

Chapter 22

TRUST: THE HEART OF DISCIPLINE

Your ability to trust yourself will determine your ability to be disciplined in trading. Without trust there is no dependable relationship between you and yourself, between you and another person, or between you and your faith in your ability to follow your own trading rules. All of these relationships exist, whether you are consciously aware of them or not, because your conscious and unconscious mind divide up into parts, which have different and often competing roles and belief systems.

The Four Elements of Trust

In order to gain long-term trust, four elements must be present. The first element is inner security. The foundation of inner security starts when you are in the womb. Infants must know that their basic needs are being met: they must feel that they are safe in their environment, that their need for nourishment and comforts will be met, and that they are loved, wanted and accepted. As children develop, they must be able to test their environment, encounter reasonable limits and feel that their individuality is acknowledged. They must know that they can make choices that will be accepted by their parents and that they will have the freedom to make other choices that will be learning experiences. Children must be encouraged to have skills and abilities and be praised for their efforts. In addition, children must feel that they are attractive to others as well as to themselves. And finally, children must have the feeling of belonging in a family, in a community and among their peers. This is the social and psychological mix that creates a sense of security in each of us.

Too many of the people with whom I work did not feel loved as a child even though they recognize the fact now that their parents loved them. But, being aware that they were loved does not change the insecurity in their inner child. Many of my clients were criticized and did not feel their choices were acceptable to their parents. Now, as adults, these individuals question their choices and punish themselves with sabotaged efforts when they make choices that are different from what their parents would have wanted.

Just by having this first element of feeling secure a person can go out into the world trusting himself and other people. When the harsh reality of life sets in, he may learn that three other elements are necessary for long-term trust.

The Second Element

The second element in creating self-trust is knowledge. Many people call me and say, "I'm ready to trade because I just finished reading a couple of books about trading." Recently, a wannabe trader called to say that he had just quit his job and thought he would be able to support a family of four with his trading profits. He had taken a few real trades and felt he was ready. The only resources his family had was their $25,000 savings account which he planned to use for his trading capital.

Unfortunately, there are many people who enter trading believing that they don't have to have an extremely good education to become a successful trader. I know that a person is ready, educationally, to trade when he says, "I've read almost everything in trading that is out there. I have a business plan and a system that is back-tested which I believe will be profitable." Assuming what he says is true, the only thing needed for his success is whether he has the inner security to trade. Education builds trust in your ability

The Third Element

The third element necessary to build trust is evidence. For a trader, the evidence he needs is evidence that he:

1. has successfully developed skills and abilities in the past.
2. has carried through on goals he has set for himself.
3. has created the probability of making money by back-testing.
4. will make money, when he develops a system or methodology as a trader through study and training.

Successful back-testing gives a trader the confidence to believe that the probabilities of making money are in his favor. There are some people who skip this step and are successful for a period of time. The trouble comes when a drawdown occurs. If a trader has failed to back-test and develop trust that his system will produce results over time, he will develop negative emotional anchors during a drawdown and lose trust in his trading and his system. Traders who see me when they are going through this kind of mistrust are directed back to the basics.

The Fourth Element

The fourth element in building trust is the experience of repeated success in real-time trading. While it is true that "nothing builds confidence like success itself," I would add, "nothing will topple a person faster from success in a negative environment than the absence of the first two elements, inner security and knowledge."

I enjoy working with traders who experience a setback because of personal issues or because they have not adjusted their system to changing markets. It is easy to direct them to even greater success because they have already experienced success through their own study and self-discipline.

If you would like to measure the level of trust you have for yourself and for others, all you have to do is look at your day-to-day behaviors. They will also indicate whether or not you have the discipline necessary to become a good trader. Here is a quiz that will give you an idea of the level of trust you have in yourself and others through your daily behaviors. It will also give you insight into some of the behaviors you would have to change to build trust.

The Self-Trust Quiz:

1. Do you have a pattern of always being late (15 minutes, half an hour, etc?)
2. Do you break or miss many of your appointments?
3. Do you make commitments to yourself and break them such as:
   - starting diets and breaking them soon into the diet?
   - starting exercise regimes and breaking them?
   - creating budgets and breaking them?
   - setting deadlines and breaking them?
   - promising to stop a negative behavior (smoking, drinking, gambling, etc), and then breaking the promise as soon as you are tempted?
   - buying self-help programs and giving up shortly into the program?
4. Do you fail to follow through with plans and promises to yourself and others?
5. Do you borrow money and then not pay it back?
6. Do you break the promises you make with your children?
7. Have you betrayed your marriage vows?
8. Do you break serious traffic laws without thinking about it?
9. Do you justify breaking rules at work or in other settings in your life?
10. Do you believe that, "Rules are meant to be broken?"

If you can truthfully answer NO to these questions, you are well on the way to becoming a disciplined trader or investor. However, if you give your unconscious mind the message that it is okay to break the rules, it will be okay with your unconscious mind to support you in breaking trading rules.

Breaking trading rules is like trading without a system.

The Proof of the Pudding

The training we give to our children is often a perfect reflection of our own training because that is usually the only model we have and the one we unconsciously use. If that model is a good one, then we are doing well by our children. But, if that model is filled with recrimination, rejection, promise-breaking, or any combination of a host of negative factors, we will do our children a great deal of harm. For that reason, it is important to look at the model we have for raising children in light of our own experiences and feelings as children as well as our own observations now as adults. If we put a little more time into the training of our children when they are young, they will require less from us when they are teenagers - and their children will benefit, likewise. It is the greatest gift you can give to both your children and your grandchildren.

The "I'm Sorry" Trader

Josh had been an outstanding trader. Not only was he very intelligent with an impressive background in mathematics and finance, he had devoted himself to learning as much about trading as anyone I have ever met. The problems, however, became evident with our first meeting. Josh had called asking for help, desperate and pleading for an immediate appointment. By rearranging my schedule, I was able to free up an entire weekend for private consulting. Josh didn't arrive until Saturday night, however. He had missed his flight and was unable to get one until the following day. When he arrived, he was clearly chagrined. "I am so sorry," he said sincerely. By rearranging my Monday schedule, I was able to accommodate Josh. However, because this rescheduling caused me a great deal of inconvenience, I was determined not to let it happen again.

An important part of Josh's consulting work was the fulfillment of certain assignments. However, after learning about Josh's childhood, I was concerned that Josh would never complete these assignments according to our agreements. One of the most painful memories of Josh's childhood were the countless times his parents promised Josh and his sisters that they would take the children out and be good to them only to break their promises. Josh and his sisters learned that their parents' word really didn't mean anything.

As much as Josh hated the fact that his parents never kept their agreements, he had unconsciously adopted their model of behavior for himself. Josh was rarely on time for anything (except for a movie, because he hated to miss the beginning.) He made promises to his wife and his two small children, which he never kept and never remembered making until he came home to find them, hurt and disappointed. Then, he would tell them how sorry he was. As he talked, Josh remembered that his parents had always said that they were sorry to him when he was young and how he had grown to distrust them. But, the realization came too late. His wife had already left with the two children and moved in with her parents, calling Josh "heartless and irresponsible."

"How can I be irresponsible?" he demanded. "I made nearly a quarter of a million dollars last year. I gave them everything they wanted." True, but his net had slipped precipitously in the last seven months. His trading was going badly, a problem he attributed to a changing market, a system which had outgrown its usefulness, and the stress of dealing with his wife. These were all good answers. The problem was that they were not the real ones.

At first, Josh was unaware of any personal responsibility for his recent troubles. In fact, he refused to see that anything he said or did could affect his trading. However, eventually, Josh was able to see that he could no longer trust his system or his trading because he could not trust himself. Neither could his wife and children.

Attracting the Snake Oil Salesmen- He Doth Protest too Much

Have you ever thought that you were carrying a sign on your back that said "all snake oil salesmen hit on me" because you attract so many people who are untrustworthy? If your earliest family interactions resulted in mistrust, you will spend the rest of your life looking for the people you can trust. But how can you recognize a trustworthy person? If you were unable to trust the people closest to you, you will find it difficult to distinguish between those who can and cannot be trusted. For that reason, you are more likely than most people to be conned by manipulative and dishonest people who, sensing your weakness, assure you that they are worthy of your trust. However, a person who is trustworthy will never think to say, "you can trust me," because trust is not an issue with them. With trustworthy people, their whole life is about trust, so they don't have to say those words. To say those words means that there is a part of you that thinks in terms of mistrust. An exception to this rule would be a person who has been deeply betrayed. In that case, trust can be an issue without it being a sign of manipulation.

Dishonest people are always going to try to convince you that they are honest. This can also be true when you are dealing with yourself. Many people deceive themselves into thinking that they are honest people even though their actions prove otherwise. They justify their actions to themselves and others. If you were to ask them, they would probably tell you that they hold trust as a very important value. For example, Saddam Hussein portrays himself as an honorable man, despite the fact that he has been caught in a pattern of deceit in his political dealings.

Protecting You from Yourself

While you are avoiding the slings and arrows from the outside world, are you also protecting yourself from the slings and arrows that you are directing toward yourself? If you are living by the principle that not following rules or distorting rules is okay, the sign you're wearing for snake oil salesmen was placed there by yourself.

Making Rules that You Can Live by

Is it ever okay to break your trading rules? The answer is NO, NEVER!!! If you have anticipated all contingencies, you will have a rule for everything, so you won't be breaking rules. You'll be following the contingencies. For example, if you say, "I'm going on a diet and I'm never going to eat anything fattening," suddenly you will have an overwhelming urge to eat a piece of chocolate cake. However, if you will make the rule about going on a diet to include a periodic slice of chocolate cake as part of the diet, then you will not be breaking your rules. The result is that you will stay on your diet.

The same principle of creating rules you can live by applies to your trading. Your rules must cover special conditions and exceptions. When they are part of your rules, you will find it not only possible, but easy to stay within your rules at all times. The message that you then send to your unconscious mind is that you can be trusted.

What Do You Do if You're Not Trustworthy?

Basically, you start by keeping your agreements. This may sound easy, but it is not. If you are unable to trust yourself to keep even small agreements because of a pattern of broken agreements, this could present a challenge. It is essential that you must keep all your agreements. For that reason, if you want to send your unconscious the right message, you need to make only those agreements which are very easy to keep and which you have a strong desire to keep. They may be things which you want to do so that you know you won't break them. You may develop back-up systems so that you can't forget. The important thing is to do this one step at a time. Don't overwhelm yourself with agreements. The danger would be that you would slip up and then fall off the wagon as soon as you fail once.

Each time you keep an agreement, acknowledge your achievement and reward yourself. Give yourself a verbal pat on the back. You may even have a special treat you give yourself each day for keeping all of your promises, agreements and rules. After a month of keeping each and every agreement and then rewarding yourself, you will have established a strong pattern of self-trust. From that point, trading discipline is no longer a problem.

Conclusion

Self-trust is the backbone of trading discipline. If you can trust yourself to do what you say you are going to do, you can follow your own trading rules. However, if you have been raised in an environment which neither nurtures and supports you nor provides you with a model for keeping agreements, you will develop trust issues that will continually undermine your ability to trust yourself and those around you. You will find it difficult to keep agreements with yourself and others. This problem will spill over to your trading so that you will not be able to follow your trading rules. The slow, steady process of making small agreements which are easy to keep and then forcing yourself to keep each one, one after another, is an effective strategy for building self-trust and a successful trading career.

Chapter 23

ENVIRONMENTAL SUPPORT

You cannot hide from a negative trading environment. As much as you try to ignore it, a negative trading environment will affect you and your performance. Keep in mind however, that what is negative for one trader is normal and comfortable for another. What is a negative trading environment? My definition is one that, if it were removed or altered, would improve your performance.

Organization

One of the most obvious causes of a negative trading environment is disorganization. Disorganization causes your environment to fill up with clutter and the more cluttered your environment, the more distractions you will have from your trading. The mind can only handle approximately 7 to 10 bits of sensorial information at one time. The attention grabbers that result from disorganization create stress, and stress creates sabotage.

Reasons for Disorganization:

Not enough time
Taking the time to keep things in place might feel like it is more work, but it will save time in the long run. After organizing your environment, get in the habit of putting things back in a certain place whenever you are through using them.

Don't know how to organize

1. Handle papers the fewest number of times by using Post-It notes for the next task with its required completion time. Keep these papers by date or time order.
2. Know which modality (visual, kinesthetic, auditory) you are the most comfortable using:

- Do you find things by color coordination? Do you keep things within visual range, in staggered files or every tab on one side?
- Do you have a feeling about where things should be in a stack of papers? Do you use the floor as an extension of your desk?
- Do you feel organized when you have everything on a computer?
- Would it be better to remind yourself with a tape recorder or hear what is necessary for you to do from a secretary? Do you prefer hearing a signal from your computer when to take a trade?
- Do you need someone to come behind you every day and reorganize you?

3. Schedule a commitment to yourself to go though all of your materials on a regular basis and discard everything that does not support your work.

Not enough places to put things

1. Hire a professional organizer to create the best use of wall space and floor.
2. Go to a office supply store or space saver type of company to see what options you have available.

Too much paperwork

1. As you receive unwanted mail, send out a standard letter requesting to be taken off of their list.
2. Keep everything off of your desk if it does not have to do with your daily activity. In the evening, discard it or attach an action Post-It note to it.

Inefficient flow of information

Write down a flow chart of all incoming information and how and when you will handle it and ask people to support this flow. If you do not know how to organize this flow ask someone who does.

Work Environment

Your work environment should be quiet and non-intrusive so that you can stay focused on your trading. Here are some of the major causes of distraction in this area:

Too much noise
You might consider using ear plugs, relaxing music on ear phones or changing the environment.

Input is distracting
When other traders or the media are giving their opinions, you must change how you view them. See them as saboteurs to your system.

Distracting calls

Use an answering machine for all calls except those necessary for you to receive. Tell others that your trading hours are sacred and you will not take any calls unless it is an emergency.

People

The most distracting part of your work environment are the people who interact with you, whether you want them to or not. You need to put strategies into place in order to take control of these walking/talking distractions.

Colleagues

Choose to relate only to people who are positive and uplifting and communicate in a way that is supportive of good feelings. Let people know exactly what you want and need in communication. If they do not give you what you want and you cannot remove them from your life, let them know that you do not talk to people during trading hours.

Your significant other

1. Explain what you need for good trading results.
2. Behave badly when you do not get the cooperation you need and extremely positive when you do. Unless your love is masochistic she/he should get the message.
3. Take time to listen patiently and enthusiastically to everything the other person has to say and feed back to them by paraphrasing what they just said to you. Then they will know that you have been listening and that the message has been received. If your significant other continues to say the same thing over and over again, it's because you are not "getting it" in the way she/he needs you to get it.
4. Make sure that special time is given during the day/week where you are giving full attention to the other person. If you don't, this person will always be pushing for more time.

Children

1. Each child needs a certain amount of individual attention. Label this time of focused attention as "special time" with you alone, so your child can look forward to it.
2. When children act up, tell them that you need a hug. Children try to get your attention by doing things that you do not want them to do. After the hug, ask them to do what you want them to do and give them a reason that makes sense to them.

Pets and other family members
Pets love routine and they need to be trained if you want them to leave you alone when you need to focus. Putting a little time each day into training them will free up your time to focus on your trading. Just like your pets, the people in your life like to know what to expect. When you are consistent with communication and commitments, they will distract you less.

Troubled relationships
If you are involved in a separation or divorce, or in a relationship which is filled with conflict or pain, these relationships will often intrude into your trading environment. Phone calls from lawyers or anger-filled calls from an ex-spouse can destroy your focus for the rest of the trading day.

1. Maintain a separate telephone line for your trading and let your personal line pick up the messages.
2. Lock your door to your trading office and put a sign on the door saying please do not disturb unless there is an emergency. If anyone knocks at the door, go breathlessly to the door and say in a panic, "What's happening?" This may sound somewhat dramatic, but they will get the message.
3. Seek outside counseling to help resolve the problems in the relationship.
4. Meditate each day to reduce the stress and keep you calm as you go handle the situation.

Physical Setting

Not every physical setting is conducive to trading. Some are too cold and sterile while others are too comfortable and tempting. For example, if you can see a pool from your trading window that is surrounded by a bevy of bathing beauties, you may have a hard time focusing on your trading. Or if your office is situated in an office building with a wonderful top floor bar which serves terrific meals and is the meeting place for some of your buddies, you may be tempted to spend too much time in said bar. Or you may find that your home office is so near the kitchen and the large screen TV in the family room that you are spending your trading time watching Cinemax while munching snacks.

On the other hand, the physical setting can be too heated, too air-conditioned, too polluted by chemicals in the carpet and furniture, or too uncomfortable in some way that makes your trading difficult.

1. If you are too distracted in your present office, move to one that is more conducive to your trading
2. If you can't move, change what you can to make your environment more conducive.

Commitments

The commitments that are a negative part of your trading environment are the activities you have agreed to do during your trading hours, which do not directly support your trading, or after trading hours, which take energy and focus away from your trading. These trading interruptions can be as major as mentoring a young trader or helping to put together a major trading conference or providing frequent updates for investors. Or they can be as small as making a daily call to check on your mother or leaving fifteen minutes early each day to pick up your daughter from school. The problem develops for your trading when these commitments interrupt the flow of your trading or sap emotional energy.

Individually, commitments can be innocent time catchers. But, as their number piles up, the total can be significant enough to create a trading environment in which you are never in the trading flow. If you are overwhelmed by your commitments, the problem may not just be that you have difficulty saying no. You may be using your commitments to prevent you from making a total commitment to your trading

1. Only make commitments that you know you can keep.
2. Set a limit on the number of commitments and the time they will involve.
3. Tie your commitments to your goals and values. Don't make commitments to things you think you should do but which subtract from the things you want to and must do.
4. Limit commitments to non-trading hours completely or as much as possible.

Conclusion

If your trading environment supports your trading by providing you with the level of comfort, quiet, organization and lack of other distractions you need to concentrate on your trading, you will have one of the essential ingredients for your success. But, if your environment is not supportive and is filled with distractions, you will need to take action. No matter how great your system is and your commitment to success, you cannot succeed if you are trading with a fraction of your focus.

Chapter 24

CREATING PROSPERITY

What is the key to creating prosperity? Prosperity consciousness is the answer. This state of mind comes from a sense of abundance, which comes in turn from feeling that you have something to share with others. The more generous you can be, the more you will maintain prosperity consciousness. However, you can only be generous to the extent of the resources you have. Think of all the resources that a person can accumulate, such as knowledge, wisdom, talent, energy, love, joy, friendship, and material things. Generosity is the key to prosperity consciousness and prosperity consciousness is the key to a high performance. Maintaining a high-performance state is what enables professional traders to be constant in their performance, which results in prosperity.

The Ultimate Trading Goal

The vast majority of traders and investors with whom I have worked have said that one of their ultimate goals was to have more abundance so they could give more generously. I tell my clients that if they want to reach that state quickly, they have to believe they are prosperous and become a giver from that moment onward.

One of my clients commented that his goal was to support children in their education. I explained to him that, if he really wanted to do so, he should start immediately. He decided that he was willing and able to begin by helping one child. He also agreed to give away a percentage of increased income. With just a small percentage of his increased income over the next two years, he was able to support the education of twenty children!

Patterns of Prosperity

Regardless of what your goals are, your unconscious mind will support you in reaching them. Your goals will then be reflected in the choices you make in your actions and thought patterns. For example, if you think of yourself as lacking and unable to be generous, these thoughts will be reflected in your behavior. On the other hand, by becoming consciously aware of the resources you have and sharing them lovingly with others, you will choose actions that are in alignment with these feelings and thoughts. Generous behavior creates a state of mind in which prosperity thrives.

Trader Scrooge

Recently, a trader named Dwight told me that he did not believe in sending cards or giving gifts, nor in celebrating just because of tradition. Not surprisingly, he was also a man who disconnected himself from family and had only few distant friendships. In addition, this disconnected man was neither generous to others nor to himself. There were, however, two things Dwight did want. He wanted to accumulate wealth and he wanted to find love.

This unhappy trader was unable to grasp the idea that wealth is not limited to the money that you accumulate, but includes the emotional contributions you make to your community and those around you. These are the contributions Dwight has to make before he can find the love and happiness he desires. Further, he did not understand that love starts by loving yourself; he was out for what he could get, not what he could give. Even if he did accumulate money through his skills as a trader, without establishing a pattern of love, celebration and generosity, he would never enjoy his accumulation of assets.

Generosity breeds support systems around you. Without a support system, people skate on very thin ice. Regardless of how firm that ice appears to be, the smallest stress can lead an unsuspecting skater to plunge through the surface. If Dwight failed to create strong ties to those around him, who would come to his rescue when he needed it? This situation is especially true for traders who require a great deal of support from those around him to be able to handle the stress and demands of trading.

Prosperity Personified

In contrast to Dwight, Antonio personified prosperity. He was born in the tenements of New York City where he had to share his bed with roaches and occasionally other unpleasant critters. His parents came from Sicily with only the clothes on their back and big dreams of the possibilities from the new promised land. Mario, Antonio's father, was happy to find work in a cigar factory, while his mom, Maria, was ingenious at creating a joyous home for them by building furniture out of orange crates, bricks and various other remnants that she was able to collect. Without any material means, Antonio's mother nevertheless filled their home with joy and love. Through their front door, Antonio remembered smelling his mom's garlic laced tomato sauce in the hallways and hearing her Neapolitan songs. He felt an abundance of wealth in this atmosphere of love. Maria and Mario always had something for guests to enjoy, if only kindness. This atmosphere made a lifetime impression on Mario. He learned that there was always something to give of great value.

Maria became a tailor, eventually owning her own business. In the meantime, Mario owned the neighborhood candy store. Antonio started a paper route and later helped in the family businesses. After college, Antonio became interested in the markets. His family's pattern of generosity and love established the patterns that defined Antonio as a person. He always found time to help his classmates in school and those less fortunate. In addition, he shared his material wealth. Antonio was a little league coach, a big brother and a mentor to several new traders. As a result, his life is full of abundance. He is surrounded by a loving family including his wife and children, as well as many close friends and colleagues. He also happens to have a large bank account. But one of his greatest joy continues to be smelling his mother's tomato sauce, while she hums her Neapolitan songs. His dad, while now enjoying the good life, talks about the value of every step he took from the time he left Sicily.

Generosity Begins with Giving to Yourself

Even Mother Teresa had to acquire the skills and knowledge required to be a great leader. Later on, she learned that she must take care of her own health and well being before she could give to others. Doctors spend years studying and training in order to save people's lives. Performers and athletes exhaustively train for brief moments of performance. All leaders and shakers of the world put time, energy and resources to work before becoming great philanthropists. But those who can be generous along the way find they can enjoy the process more and can get there quicker because prosperity consciousness creates and supports a state of excellence.

Early in his career, a trader often works 16-hour days. This extreme effort is likely to cause the demise of his family and friendships because people find it easier to support a young doctor or minister who will eventually save lives and souls than a neophyte trader in whose activity they neither understand nor believe. For a trader to be successful enough to contribute to the world, he must devote considerable time and energy to be skilled. The big challenge he faces is:

Traders are looked on as gamblers if they don't earn money,
and as greed mongers if they do.

For this reason, family and friends seldom support traders on their way to success. Not many people look at the value traders supply to our economy by bringing liquidity to the markets. Often, traders themselves don't feel that they are valuable. It is hard for them to feel valuable while they are betting on squiggle lines and counting their profits. Thus, as the spiritual leader saves souls, the doctor heals and the performer dazzles the trader gives by allowing us to maintain a liquid economy. And when he does not feel this satisfaction through what he does as a trader, he can get this satisfaction by giving from the abundance he has created.

Creating Magnetic Prosperity Consciousness

Think of those generous moments of your life when you selflessly gave and every part of you was part of the giving. The special gift. The time you took out for a friend. The knowledge you shared. Remember how you replayed the moment over in your mind and, with each replay, how it made you feel. Seeing or knowing the delight and joy of the recipient of your generosity added to what I call "Magnetic Prosperity Consciousness." What you were feeling was a high level of the same energy that brings about top performance. Top performance is giving the best of yourself. Habitual patterns of random kindness and generosity lead to habitual levels of this high performance state of mind. And, this is a main ingredient necessary in maintaining success in trading.

- A person who is generous is a person who has high self-values. This is an essential ingredient for becoming a risk taker. Generosity gives you the confidence to assume responsibility for your actions. The worthiness you feel by being generous empowers you with a sense of being capable and deserving. What value does knowledge, wisdom, love and joy have if you cannot share them with others?

- What would life be like if we all did not participate in exchanging materially to enjoy a healthy economy?

- Of what importance has time if it is not used to make a positive difference to the world and yourself?

- What a burden would it be if everyone could not share control and responsibility?

- What would life be without those who are willing to give parts of their being to those who want to continue to live?

Traders who lack these feelings and qualities usually have success issues and, therefore, sabotage their efforts to keep their profits.

The Principle of Tithing

Religions have always taught the importance of giving a tenth of your resources to the religious organization from which you get your spiritual nourishment. While your generosity supports the structure that supports you, you are also taught that your generosity comes back to you if given with love and without expectation. While spiritual love is the highest and most powerful form of energy, all energy attracts similar energy. This is the very energy that creates opportunity. Another way of looking at this is that your neurological response to a feeling of joy is top performance and top performance brings about opportunity.

What are some of the actions you can take today to create these opportunities?

- Recognize your resources by listing your talents, abilities, and skills as well as your material possessions.

- Note all of the ways you give these resources without expecting compensation.

- Ask yourself how you can use these resources to be even more generous in your life without creating a hardship to yourself or others.

- Make a commitment to develop specific new resources now within a predetermined time frame.

- Make a commitment to increase your generosity through sharing more of your resources as you become more affluent.

Conclusion

If you want to experience exceptional prosperity while having a joyous life, you must have prosperity consciousness. While it is true that a trader must attain the knowledge and skills to become successful in his field, if he is to maintain success and enjoy the process, he must choose to be generous along the way. This mind set will maintain his level of excellence which is necessary for top performance.

BUY!
ON THIS DAY
F.J. Torres
DOCTOR
of
ECONOMICS
90 DAY TREND
TAO of TRADE
TRADER'S ENCYCLOPEDIA
BEST KEPT SECRETS

Chapter 25

USING YOUR INTELLIGENCE

Do You Have the Intelligence to be a Master Trader?

Before you answer that question, you should also consider whether you also have the right kind of intelligence, as well...

For a long time, the general public believed that there was only one kind of intelligence because that is what the psychologists and educators who developed and administered tests for intelligence wanted us to believe. As children, we took the standard IQ tests, which pigeon-holed us into categories predicting our ability to succeed in life.

However, anecdotal evidence and long-term studies began to appear indicating that the smartest kid in the class may not have ended up as the richest kid. People began to question the value of these IQ tests since they did not necessarily predict success, even in the academic environment. It was clear that other qualities were just as vital to success, even other forms of intelligence.

The Different "Types" of Intelligence

Here is a quick review of these other forms of intelligence:

1. Linear Intelligence

This is the form of intelligence measured by IQ tests. It is the logical, linear thought that is adept at using numbers and words in a step-by-step process to solve problems. Linear thought depends upon information that is given or stored to reach these logical conclusions. This intelligence is vital to a trader's ability to handle market data and to design and test a trading system.

2. Street Savvy

We all know someone who has more street sense than anyone else. This kind of savvy or intelligence is vital to survival in risky situations. Yet, highly "intelligent" individuals are often at a loss to quickly solve the problems of survival on the streets of their real world. The sources of information used in street savvy are not obvious, nor are the conclusions logical or arrived at in a step-by-step process. This intelligence is vital to a trader's ability to pick up the minute-by-minute cues in the marketplace based on a synergistic understanding of what is available.

3. Wisdom

This kind of intelligence is a deep knowingness, which appears to be an intellectual gift just as math or language intelligence is a gift. Some small children seem to be wiser at four years than their grandparents at sixty. This type of intelligence is vital to a trader for developing a deep understanding of the markets. It also creates an awareness of the trader's role in the marketplace that allows a trader to make the right decisions and take appropriate actions. This is what I call being in tune with the markets by having the probabilities of market action available to you.

4. Emotional Intelligence

We know that some people are completely lacking in emotional intelligence. These individuals cannot learn how to detect social cues, develop relationships, or appropriately handle their emotional states. Other individuals are geniuses on the social and emotional level of human interplay. This type of intelligence is absolutely vital to success as a trader and is the key to self-discipline. Emotional intelligence provides the ability for an individual to manage his emotional and social life so that he can follow his trading rules. In addition, it enables one to get support from the significant people in his or her life to follow the passion for trading.

5. Mechanical/Spatial Intelligence

Have you ever had a great mechanic work on your car? I mean someone who was literally a genius with machines. If you ask him, he will probably tell you how poorly he did in the classroom. This type of intelligence allows individuals to understand how things work and/or to see things in spatial terms, but not necessarily in numerical or intellectual terms. Great athletes like Michael Jordan fit into this category. It is not just training and physical prowess that allows him to judge the distances in the air for those jumps and shots which take our breath away. This type of intelligence is vital to traders and investors who study charts, work with mechanical systems (no pun intended), and are adept at using computers.

6. Creative/Artistic Intelligence

Artists, musicians, and all other creative people use their senses in variable combinations to enhance and restructure information. Creative people have the ability to go beyond a linear and structured view of the world. This form of intelligence enables them to see and discover opportunity in trading and investing.

Which Form of Intelligence Does a Master Trader Have?

A Master Trader does not have any single type of intelligence, but several of them combined, if not a bit of all of them. Most good traders and investors have a high linear intelligence, but are lacking in creative and emotional intelligence. Developing any new aspect of intelligence will increase your ability to earn greater profits and enjoy the process of trading more. With a new dimension, you will increase your self-confidence and gain more insight for making the best choices.

Chapter 26

PASSION: THE DOUBLE EDGE SWORD TO SUCCESS

To reach a high level of competence or to complete any great achievement in life you must have passion. Passion, that build-up of emotion and intense feeling, is the main ingredient of motivation, and motivation is the thrust which pushes you through the obstacles on the way to great success.

As necessary as it is to success, however, passion comes with a caveat. On the one hand, life without passion is boring and meaningless for people who know its stimulating emotional drive. On the other hand, all intense feelings need an outlet for expression and those outlets can be negative, as well as positive. When passion is misdirected it can lead to obsession and addiction. It is for this reason that passion is a double edge sword to success.

Developing Passion

The strong feelings associated with passion develop when your senses are highly stimulated. The more detail you give to your senses, the more stimulation you will feel in your body. This stimulation can come from both positive and negative detail. The manner in which that stimulation is created will determine whether or not, and in what way, a person will be passionate about life, about a particular direction and about feelings for their own sake.

The following stimulating experiences will create passions for positive outlets in these three arenas. You can see how the lack of these experiences can create passions for negative outlets.

How to develop passion for:

1. Life

- A child is raised in a family where traditions are practiced with enthusiasm and effort.
- There is high value and praise given for the contribution of each family member.
- Positive conversations, positive action and, as a result, positive thinking is a way of life.
- Everyone in the family is made to feel special, smart, talented and attractive.
- Schools, religious teachings, clubs, camps, military and business experiences promote creative thinking as well as logical thinking, the importance of each individual and a win/win attitude.

2. **Positive Direction**
   - Individual achievements are rewarded and the rewards themselves are given great value.
   - Talents, abilities and skills are nurtured, supported, praised and celebrated.
   - Discipline, purpose and planning are a way of life.

3. **Feelings**
   - Emotions are dramatically expressed in rejoicing, laughter, hugging, kissing, and praise.
   - These same emotions, when expressed, are rewarded, encouraged and supported.
   - Stimulating, positive and natural sights, sounds, smells, and touches to the senses are used to induce pleasurable and happy feelings.

If you have experienced the positive aspects of developing passion, you are less likely to fall victim to obsessive behaviors. When a person has a history of successes, his neurology is programmed to take him in the direction of more success. Creativity and opportunity are then part of your daily experience and obstacles are seen as stepping stones on the way to the next level of success. You know how to attach rewards to success even if it is just the stimulation of your own feeling of completion or hearing a voice which sounds like your father saying, "Good job."

Positive Outlets for Passion

Once you feel the thrill and rewards of victory, for the rest of your life you will want to experience those feelings again. That new aliveness of the senses opens you up to a new dimension of yourself in which your goal will be the mastery of your potential as a human being. At this level of awareness, new possibilities and opportunity become available to you because you are developing your spiritual dimension.

Events leading to a passionate life:

- The child who works endlessly on a project for science and wins a prize for his efforts is the adult who finds ways to solve problems, come up with new ideas and complete difficult assignments.
- The child who is held over other children's heads as the hero of a game is the adult who accepts the reward for excellence for a job well done.

- The child who builds a small paper route into a large paper route is the adult who becomes top salesman.
- The child who delivers a motivational speech amongst his peers is the adult who leads a company to success.

The more of these positive, passion-creating events you experience, the stronger will be your anchors for the need to be a high achiever. Two examples of individuals, whose list of positive childhood anchors led to higher and higher achievements, are Ronald Reagan, whose athletic achievements led to broadcasting opportunities, which led to acting roles, which in turn led to greater opportunities and Terry Sandford. His strong family role models led to his war heroism and passionate political views, which led to political opportunities, which led to the presidency of Duke University, a shot at the U.S. Presidency and finally to the U.S. Senate.

Nearly forty years ago, a young boy was given a gift of a small, amateur movie camera along with the encouragement and support to have fun with it. His passion for his pictures led him to creating small films, which increased his passion for the craft he was developing. Now, Steven Spielberg is making some of the greatest movies of this century and thanking his parents for their support, encouragement and gift with nearly every award he receives.

The Dark Side

When you feel continuous, strong emotions as a child, you can become addicted to feeling those feelings again. Anything less than those states of high emotional arousal are boring, even if those feelings are uncomfortable or terrifying. When a child grows up in a family where there is both tremendous joy and sorrow, these feelings will need to be expressed as the child reaches adulthood. In a family which expresses mostly pain, this feeling can also come out in the form of passion. Naturally there can be many other psychological reasons for these negative behaviors. The need to re-create high emotional feelings is one of them. Two other psychological reasons for expressing negative passion are:

- A child who is abused needs to control everything and everyone because he feels out of control.
- A child who achieves and does not get the reward of praise will sabotage his efforts as an adult by being on a win/lose cycle.

Some examples of people with passion which directed them to the dark side are: Adolf Hitler, Saddam Hussein, Ayatolla Khomenei.

Negative signs for needing an outlet for passion:

- If you are addicted to food, alcohol, drugs or sex.
- If you have obsessions such as being a perfectionist.
- If you are abusive to your self or others.

- If you gamble.

Patrick had a pattern of making a great deal of money and then losing or squandering it. Once he had gone through his money, he would then live off of borrowed money until he reached bottom. Then, at the very bottom, he would find the emotional and physical resources within himself to create a great success once again. Patrick was only motivated when he experienced certain emotional states: he had to be deeply and desperately alone and at the point of being thrown out on the street.

From where did this negative pattern come? Patrick's father was a gambler and an alcoholic whose vices would force the family into flight in the middle of the night. Patrick would be awakened from a deep sleep by an hysterical mother as the family fled to a relative's house for temporary shelter. In the heat of all the emotion, his father would find a way to "save the day." As an adult, Patrick was addicted to nearly anything you could be addicted to and stay out of jail. His home was so neat and orderly that his friends used to tease him that he lived in a department store. In the meantime, Patrick's personal eating obsessions placed him on the end of a pendulum that swung between binge eating and grueling fasts. No one doubted that Patrick was a passionate man. The problem was that his passions were so out of control.

Negative Going to Positive

Not all negative, emotionally charged experiences leave negative anchors. Sometimes, a child has internal resources which can translate that experience into a passion for positive action. When this happens, it is usually because the child was exposed to positive models early on or from another source. For example, a child is rewarded at school for achievement and punished by his peers for the same achievements. If the feelings he experiences when he is rewarded are deeper than the ones he feels when he is punished, his passion will lead him on the path to achievement. Some other examples are:

- A child who has faced difficult struggles, but there was joy in the accomplishments.
- A child who became a contrarian to a negative environment.

Abraham Lincoln faced so much loss, rejection and humiliation on the road he traveled, it is difficult to imagine what passion drove Abraham Lincoln to the White House. He was raised in abject poverty, grew into an awkward and unattractive man and lost nearly every election he ever entered. Yet, he turned each negative experience into the motivation to try harder. Other examples of people who turned adversity into triumph are: Helen Keller, who was a blind and deaf mute and then became a world-famous communicator; Thomas Edison, who was sent home from school because he was too stupid to learn and then became the greatest inventor in history; Irving Berlin whose immigrant family was too poor to send him to school to study music and then composed some of the greatest songs of the 20th Century.

Positive Going to Negative

Unfortunately, the reverse process can occur from positive to negative, as well. If someone who knows a high level of success suddenly gets caught in a downward spiral and cannot recover, the passion for success can be transformed into a passion for self-immolation. Going down in flames often becomes the goal for the once highly successful individual who sees no way out of his problems. When that happens, he will consciously, or unconsciously, choose actions which accelerate the process of loss or defeat.

Individuals who are at risk for reverse motivation are:

- The athlete who wins the award but has never trained himself for anything else.
- A person whose health has failed him and cannot accept achievement at a lower level than he experienced in the past.
- The film star who cannot make the transition from the femme fatal to a character actress.
- The person who was extremely successful but for various reasons has to change his environment. In his new circumstances he does not adapt to the requirements of success.
- The person who changes professions and believes that because he was good in his former profession he does not need to do the work involved to be successful in the new profession.

A young man in Chicago developed himself into an exceptional floor trader. He was so successful that, by the time he was in his late twenties, he was living the high-life, wearing expensive clothes, driving the best cars and living in the most expensive condominiums. The continued stress made him decide to change professions. One day, he decided that he was tired of trading and that he would take his considerable talents and apply them to other businesses. Unfortunately, he was never able to translate his trading success into another field. The result was that he fell into a pattern of self-destructive behaviors which were designed to create failure. The drive which compelled him to success was now carrying him to one disaster after another. Eventually, he lost all of the self-disciplines and positive habits which had created his initial success. Now, fifteen years later, he is talking about becoming a trader again. The prognosis is not good.

Channeling Passion into a Positive Direction

If the outlets for your emotional expression are not healthy, or producing a positive outcome, you can choose to do something about it. Here is a strategy which is designed to divert those passions into positive outlets.

Write down a plan for your life which balances your activities in a way so that each part of your life will support each of the other parts of your life. For example, if you are neglecting your home life and your family, eventually the problems at home will negatively affect your business, or if you are not taking care of your health, it will affect every part of your life. And if you don't have a social life, you will find yourself wondering, "What's it all about?"

As you develop this plan for your life, fill your activities with a lot of tasks which are attached to small rewards along the way as well as a large reward when you have completed them. Your activities must be stimulating, exciting and meaningful and the rewards must be very compelling.

This plan works because passionate people love a challenge. They also love to plan because developing a plan provides details for their senses which stimulate feelings, which creates passion. When people feel deeply, they are motivated to act and if there is a reward at the end of it, the combination not only propels them forward, but it makes them more likely to stick with the plan, making it a self-reinforcing loop. In other words, it's the perfect diet.

Conclusion

Although passion is essential to success, passion that cannot easily find an outlet will sabotage your goals. For this reason, passion is a double-edged sword. Positive experiences that are filled with positive emotions help to build the passion that is supportive of success. However, many of us were raised with experiences that created passion based on very negative input. Fortunately, it is not essential to have the right experiences or the benefits of positive emotional anchors to direct your passion in a positive direction. By following a carefully crafted life plan such as the one described above, you can re-channel your passion to lead you to success.

YOU'RE THE BEST

Chapter 27

NEEDING VALIDATION

How do you know that you are worthy of achieving success and you are valuable to yourself and others?

You know you are valued by being told through words or actions by someone who is perceived by you to be an authority in your life. At first, your parents have the strongest influence on how you feel about your life. They are not just the final word when you are young; they are the only word. Eventually, new authorities follow in their influence: other family members, your peers, teachers, coaches and mentors. These new authorities may influence your feelings and beliefs about a host of issues in your life. But the one area they have a limited influence on is the feeling you have about your own worthiness. If you have learned from your parents' words and actions that you are unworthy at critical developmental stages in your early years, the messages will take permanent root. Regardless of the positive messages from them at other times and from those authorities who follow them, your parents' early words and actions can have such a negative influence on how you feel about yourself that you spend the rest of your life looking for validation. The extent of this deficit is so great that even when you get validation from many other people and go on to prove yourself worthy by exceptional accomplishments, it is never enough.

Winning in the Markets

So, where does a bright and capable person who needs validation look for it? Public venues like politics, show business and professional sports are excellent stages for approval and validation on a major scale. Of course, these venues also provide opportunities for disapproval and rejection on a major scale. In addition, few people are cut out for public life. Another excellent venue for finding validation is one in which you have opportunity to win and advertise your winnings if you choose while generally being able to conceal your losses. What better place to find validation than winning in the markets. Money is the language of the markets and when you win in the markets, money speaks volumes that validate you as successful in one of the most difficult professions you can enter.

Unfortunately, the problem with having a need for validation that can never be fully satisfied is that, in order to continue to feel the impact of validation, wins must be larger and larger. Larger and larger wins in the market require wider contrasts of wins versus losses to feel the impact of a bigger validation. Wider contrasts require greater and greater risks, with the high probability of wider and wider emotional swings, as well.

Even when you win, it still is not satisfying. How can a win in the present time satisfy the child within that needs validation from the mom and dad of your youth? As an adult your parents might be giving you all the praise that you missed when you were a child, but that will not reach the wounded child in you. So, you trade in the markets with the best system that your conscious mind can develop to achieve wins that never satisfy you. In the meantime, your unconscious mind is figuring out ways to sabotage your efforts because you do not feel worthy of achieving success.

When More is Never Enough

Jack grew up in the shadow of his brother David. David was handsome, bright and the object of both parents affection. Jack's plain looks and awkwardness were amplified by his belief that his parents did not value him. He would do anything to please his parents in order to get their attention, but his actions were met with criticism at every turn. Jack represented to his parents their own inadequacies. They did not like that reflection of themselves. On the other hand, their son, David, could do no wrong. When they spoke of Jack publicly, they bragged about his accomplishments as their own personal medals of honor. But, when his parents had no audience, Jack could clearly see the difference between their feelings for him and for David.

When Jack grew up, he took on the traits of his parents, even the ones that he hated the most. He would vehemently deny the similarity if you pointed it out to him in conversation, but would point it out himself when he was in an emotionally vulnerable state of mind. When Jack was vulnerable, his sense of his own unworthiness and weakness surfaced. For this reason, Jack hated his vulnerable side. Woe be to the person who witnessed it, especially to those people in his life who were close to him. His defensive strategy would be an attack, such as finding a reason to get angry at them and point out their weaknesses. These aggressive behaviors made it difficult for Jack to maintain good relationships at work and at home. In spite of his social handicaps, he was an exceptional scholar and became a high ranking corporate executive. While he earned his living in the corporate world, Jack longed to get out of what he thought of as a political rat race and be "free and independent." While dabbling in stocks, he found that he had a knack for making a profit in long-term investments and began to work toward the goal of being a full-time investor.

Meeting His Waterloo

As a very competitive person with an insatiable need for validation, Jack decided to raise the bar to the next level of investing. In other words, Jack decided to become a short term commodities trader. What Jack did not know was that he had chosen the very career which would force him to deal with all of the issues he worked so hard to avoid.

For most people the shorter the time frame in which they have to make trading decisions, the more likely psychological issues from the past will rise up to haunt them.

Trading for Jack was a war which pitted him against the markets. The markets represented validation of his worthiness, but looking for validation in the markets is guaranteed to sabotage profits. The human mind and body are designed with systems which provide immunity and protection from injury. One of these systems is a self-repairing system which keeps us constantly looking for opportunities to heal wounds of the past, both physical and emotional. The mind uses any situation where emotions are expressed as an opportunity to heal. Therefore, it is particularly helpful for us to see what the mind is needing to heal by looking at the situations we set up for ourselves and the emotions we express as a result. Most of us bury or repress these long-forgotten feelings, stacking them as ammunition for further outbursts in the future. With longer-term investments, Jack was less likely to let his emotional side affect his decisions because the emotional pressure was lower. As long as he did not bring up emotions in his decision making, he followed his strategy without conflict.

Conversely, commodity trading kept flashing a reflection of his past in his face which brought up his repressed emotions. Jack felt those old feelings of unworthiness and sadness, and in typical style again repressed them into his stomach. He used antacids to quell what was really emotional pain rather than deal with his real problems. Emotionally, Jack continued his life-long pattern of stacking situations and issues that were filled with repressed emotion, waiting for another opportunity for healing to surface. Eventually, he was forced to give up commodities. Then, the only place left for his emotions to surface was in his close relationships.

Looking in the Mirror

As we have seen in Jack's situation, when you do not feel validated, you cannot satisfy this need by validating the adult self. What needs to be validated is the wounded child still inside you. Thus, winning in the market is not going to satisfy this need. In fact, winning in the markets may actually make the emotional climate even more unbearable by creating a sense of dissonance and uneasiness, leading to a need to sabotage your success.

To validate that inner child, you must begin to feel good about yourself, when you are actually feeling unworthy. These feelings of unworthiness are very difficult to express. The sadness, fear, self-loathing and anger associated with feeling unworthy, if expressed, make us feel more vulnerable and more unworthy. To make matters worse, the expectation of being validated also brings up these same emotions, which are also not ones that an invalidated person wants to feel or express. So, it becomes difficult to express nearly any appropriate and deeply felt emotions, with the possible exception of anger, which has the effect of protecting us from feeling vulnerable.

If you have a deep, unfulfilled need for validation, you are probably avoiding unpleasant issues from the past which created the sense of being unworthy. As a result, you will have problems expressing emotions and you will avoid negative feelings. This repressed emotion, in turn, will cause you to create different forms of sabotage, both in your professional and personal lives. Although there are many, many issues which can adversely affect your trading results, the feeling of unworthiness and all of the repressed issues and feelings associated cannot fail to sabotage your trading.

If you are in need of validation, you will be repressing emotions and sabotaging your trading and your personal life. If so, you will likely see yourself in the following survey.

1. Are you earning the rewards of your system? (If you are, then this is not an issue that you need to explore.)

2. Do you have pain in any part of your body or inflammations of any sort while trading or at the end of the trading day. (stomach, headaches, hemorrhoids)

3. Do you take any kind of medication to overcome stress or a repeated pain?

4. Do you have a continuous appetite for simple carbohydrates? (foods and drinks made from refined sugar, pasta, rice, bread)

5. Do you tighten up any part of your body? (teeth, fingers, neck)

6. Do you repeatedly have a need to demonstrate nervous behaviors? (tapping, pacing)

7. Do you have a need to repeatedly give a blow by blow description of your trades to anyone who will listen and those who pretend to listen?

8. Do you blow up at slight inconveniences or minor unfulfilled expectations? (roadside mates that drive inconsiderately, the guy that brought in donuts to the office and did not offer you one)

9. Does your self talk condemn you or the people around you?

10. Do you repeat stories of the past thinking of how it coulda, shoulda, woulda turned out if better choices were made?

11. Do you often feel that life is a burden and you are a victim?

12. Do you find reasons to find fault with everyone in your life and resent them for not being the way you want them to be?

13. Do you notice a trading pattern of the more you are emotionally distressed the more your trading does not reflect what you should make from your system?

14. Do you believe that this is your lot in life and nothing can be done about your behavior?

While many of your answers could be "yes" at one time or another, it is the accumulation and frequency of these symptoms which indicate that there is a problem which needs to be addressed. Most people can identify with some of the symptoms of such frequently diagnosed psychological disorders as “Bipolarity” and “Attention Deficit Disorder,” without actually having these conditions. The collective symptoms, on a continuous basis, which create dysfunction and disruption in your life, are required for a diagnosis. The same standard needs to be applied to a diagnosis of "Needing Validation."

Conclusion

It is all too common to reach adulthood with a deep sense of unworthiness, with all of the attached emotional baggage. A trader carrying this burden is at a great disadvantage in short-term markets that create stress and emotional intensity. For this reason, it is important for traders to seek out help with this problem before they find themselves, like Jack, fighting unsuccessfully to stay in the game. What they don’t realize is that, instead of fighting with the markets, they are really battling their own demon.

SECTION 5
Balance...

EL DORADO
SINCE 1935
JOE'S BAR

Chapter 28

BAR BY BAR

One of the market wizards once told me that he covered his walls with commodity bar charts and went over each chart, bar by bar. Then, he would ride the waves of each market until he knew them so well that one could bring out a chart and he could tell you which commodity it was from. This exercise allowed him to feel the probability of market movement in the future.

It was not an intellectual understanding that allowed this great trader to predict future market movement but a sensorial one that came from his neurology.

Taking the Shortcuts

While computers service us with shortcuts for processing information, the old-fashioned hand written charting methods provide some benefits which should be considered. We train the nervous system and mind by processing material through all of our sensorial modalities, sight, hearing, taste, touch, and smell. Physically developing a chart with each daily change in the markets sends a message to our nervous system which translates to our neurology the sense that we are one with the markets. The comparison of following charts on a computer and physically compiling them is like learning to surf by watching someone else instead of actually having the experience of surfing the waves on the surfboard yourself. The more senses which are directly involved in your learning process, the more you will have the ability to "feel the markets." Charting by hand is more time consuming, but it adds a discretionary/intuitive indicator to your methodology.

My experience with traders has taught me that the traders who trade from a good technical base, adding discretion as a final indicator, are consistently the best traders.

Risking the Farm

Troy came from three generations of traders each possessing different styles and abilities. Grandpa Harry, who farmed wheat, was one of the first farmers in his region to hedge his crops. He made friends with some of the "Big Bucks" from Chicago. Harry used to walk the fields with them, a sprig of wheat in his teeth which to him was the perfect toothpick, spinning tales that stirred the emotions of even the most calculating bankers and traders. What grandpa did naturally was to create in others the buying state of mind. He was also gifted in developing in others the love of the land, the harvest, and the sustenance it provided for people.

Harry's son, Jack, followed him on these walks, soaking up the love of the land while learning the art of the trade. By the time Jack was a young man, he had learned to plot the course of his father's own farming fortunes on bar graphs. Then, he extended his study to the local farmers. Eventually, he branched out into other agricultural commodities in the region. By the time he graduated from high school, he had begun reading about commodities trading and was placing his own trades. Jack had such an intuitive feel for these agricultural markets that he made enough money to pay for his college education. In time, Jack became a highly successful trader, moving his family into Chicago to be closer to the markets.

Jack's son, Troy, was eager to begin his own trading career. Bypassing the "boring and useless" hands-on work of creating bar charts, Troy went straight to using his computer. Not only did Troy lose touch with the hands-on work of the farm, he lost touch with the hands-on work of trading. Troy, an intelligent and hard working mathematician, was desperate for a mechanical or mathematical solution to his trading dilemma. However, his background made him a hard-sell for his father. Now, it may simply have been a coincidence that Troy was struggling to make it as a trader, but his trading took a serious turn for the better after his father convinced him to go back to the basics of working with bar charts. Afterwards, he became one of this process' most ardent proponents.

The Reckoning

In his best selling book, *The Reckoning*, David Halberstan details the rise and fall of the American automobile industry in the mid-1980's. The early American automobile makers were nothing but gifted mechanics with a love for machinery and a hands-on understanding of the workings of their creative offspring. If a car didn't work properly, the man or men who designed it would figure out why it didn't work and repair the problem - after all, the buyer was likely to be someone they knew. This close, hands-on association between the designer, the manufacturer, and the salesman made the American car maker the world's dominant producer of cars.

By the 1960's, the dominance of the design people over business executives had begun to reverse. The bean counters had no interest in the design of the car except in its eye appeal which attracted buyers into the showrooms, or where costs were reduced while increasing profits. Unfortunately, while the accountants and business executives focused exclusively on the bottom-line, the bottom-line began to shrink rapidly. The cause, the Japanese auto makers, who had been trained by the old American manufacturer that was ridiculed by the new American car makers for his emphasis on quality and design. The Japanese plunged ahead by putting design ahead of profit. The result was a reckoning that nearly destroyed an American industry which had once employed, directly or indirectly, one out of every six workers.

Three-Dimensional Thinking

Most intellectuals spend a lifetime developing two dimensions of their thinking. Our educational system trains us to focus our attention on the process of cerebration (absorbing information, analyzing, discussing, studying, readying, and synthesizing it.) This process does not necessarily develop wisdom. When individuals focus on learning instead of knowing, they are usually limiting their brain function to the left-brain thinking that helps us to analyze and formulate sequential, logical thoughts. This process allows us to see the world in essentially two dimensions, the width and height of what is in front of us. However, in order to know that the object is a box, and not merely a rectangle, we must be able to think in three dimensions. To accomplish this, we must be able to use the right side of our brains as effectively as we use the left. This right brain thinking, which is characterized by intuitive and illogical leaps of understanding allows us to "see" the back of the box, to see its depth, its third dimension. This kind of thinking can be incredibly useful to traders, like Troy's father, Jack, who have a "knowingness" about the markets which is not derived from logical processes.

Unfortunately, many traders avoid this right brain thinking. Some avoid it because it feels uncomfortable and threatening to think differently. Others are conditioned to avoid this kind of thinking because they have learned to associate it with things that are feminine or "arty." But, try telling that to the "macho" men who work with their hands and their senses and unwittingly access their third dimensional thinking daily. For example, your average "great" mechanic may study the workings of an engine. When you talk to him though, he has a feel or sense of what is wrong with your car and goes on intuition when the cause is difficult to diagnose. Draftsmen, doctors, musicians, chefs, cabinetmakers, builders, tool and dye makers, farmers, cattlemen, and veterinarians must be able to access their intuitive, sensorial thinking in order to anticipate and solve problems. Most of these men have mastered their field by a combination of study and hands-on learning.

Science is another field that appears to be dominated by left-brain thinking. Science cannot advance without 3-dimensional thinking, either. In their undergraduate and graduate work, young scientists must master the techniques at the bench in order to have their experiments produce appropriate, consistent results. No amount of reading about an experiment can help you duplicate its results if you haven't mastered the hands-on techniques. Once a scientist has advanced to running a laboratory, he must be able to think in 3-dimensions in order to create a thesis and design the experiments to be carried out by others. Albert Einstein was a classic right-brainer who credited the origins of his theories to illogical leaps of intuition.

Achieving a Balance

As important as it is to develop the right side of your brain to create depth in your thinking, it is equally important for right-brainers to use the logical part of their brains. Successful floor traders are often highly sensorial in their moment-to-moment decision-making. They must be reflexive and intuitive to respond instantly to the movement of the market. However, if they fail to keep flexing the left side of their brain and leave the floor for an off-floor day-trading career, the results can be predictably disastrous. Achieving a balance by effectively exercising both types of thinking is important, regardless of the type of trading that you do.

Taking the Long-Run

It's not difficult to see why people want to take the short-cut to mastery. The case for taking the long-run is rarely made except in certain fields where long experience has taken the shine off the short-cuts. Actors can choose two basic methods to develop their skills. Method acting requires years of study and training to allow an actor to connect the feelings and experiences of his own life with the role he is given. A technician can use an onion in a handkerchief to instantly create the same tears, however, the audience doesn't feel the same connection with the young technical actor as it does with the young method actor. Young technical actors like Clark Gable and John Wayne started out playing roles in predictable performances, while the young method actor, Robert DeNiro, wowed audiences from the start with his performances.

Getting It Right

How do you develop 3-dimensional thinking and increase your sensorial skills? The first step is to identify your weakest senses and find ways to develop them. One of the easiest and most pleasurable ways is taking classes in hands-on activities you would normally pay little attention to. For example, sign up for classes in acting, pottery, clay-casting, painting, drawing, cooking, woodworking, gardening, or dancing. Then, return to the act of physically drawing bar charts without the use of a computer. This strategy does not mean that you can't use a computer eventually; but, you must first get the physical sensations that connect you with the market. These physical sensations will give you a sensorial base and a unique understanding of the markets.

Conclusion

Whenever you develop a new skill, you will master it if you take the time to develop a sensorial base for that skill. To be complete, this sensorial base should include each of the five senses (sight, sound, touch, smell, and taste). In trading, this sensorial base could include:

1. watching skilled traders as they go through their day
2. hearing the crowd like a floor trader or listening to stories of traders on tape, in workshops or seminars describing how they developed their careers

3. putting in a system that goes directly to the floor or developing your trading plan by physically writing it out before computerizing it
4. going to the floor of an exchange and taking in the smell of the crowd from the beginning of the day, and
5. licking your wounds after a bruising trade (just kidding, but you get the idea)

A trader who relies only upon cerebration and logic, is listing to the left in his thinking and seeing his trading in only two dimensions. Successful trading requires a balanced mind.

BUY PORK BELLIES!

Chapter 29

SEX AND TRADING

Sex is an important part of a trader's life. Refreshing one's mind with a diversion that is all consuming enhances the ability to perform as a trader. I can think of no better diversion than sex. Yes, it's true that sex can help you make more money in trading.

Do I have your attention?

Of course, making a trader want to get out and make more money is not the only reason that sex is important. The sad truth for some traders is that if a valuable activity in their life does not enable them to earn more money, they are not interested.

As a coach, I am privy to all aspects of a trader's life. One would think that with all of the sexual references in the media today there would be more sexual activity. Perhaps that might be true for some people in the single world, but if the information I receive from young married men is a current reflection of our society, then this article is very necessary.

The Honeymoon Is Over

Remember, as a child, when you could not wait to open up a special present at Christmas? As the initial excitement gave way to familiarity, the gift was often left forgotten with other toys on the shelf. Does this sound like your sex life?

Bob and Laura fell in love at first sight. Both of them knew immediately that they wanted each other for a life time. They both wanted to develop their relationship by the book, so there would be no chance of sabotaging the relationship in any way. The book they used was written by family, friends and all of those women's magazines with articles about "how to get a man and make it last." While Bob was playing the part of the gentleman who would not take advantage of a sweet, almost innocent lady, Laura was playing the part of the lady who was holding out as long as she could without pushing her man away. The truth was that neither could wait to make love, and when they did, they were unable to get enough of each other.

One year after Laura and Bob married, they had a daughter, Tammy. Bob was determined to give his little family all of the advantages he could provide as a floor trader. A new home and son, Gregory, followed in the next year. Once Gregory was old enough to allow Laura to work, she began a successful career in real estate. All of the elements of success were there, but the honeymoon was over.

Sex Snatchers

There are many sex snatchers which can creep into a young family's life before anyone recognizes the symptoms or realizes the damage that can be caused by them. Before long, a young couple has to schedule sex on a calendar of events if it is going to happen at all. And, very often, when couples do have sex (please notice that we are not talking about making love here) the man is in a "wham, bam, thank you ma'am," mode. The woman, meanwhile, puts on the two minute performance of her life while thinking to herself, "I had better satisfy his needs or he might find someone else who will." One or both of these unfulfilled people will wake up one day to the fact that something is missing - the thing that once brought them joy, passion for each other, and a sense of closeness that nothing else ever did. At this point, the serious marital problems begin. Like many young couples, Bob and Laura fell a victim to these sex snatchers.

What are these sex snatchers?

Expenses and Clutter

The American Dream keeps getting more expensive. Only 100 years ago, indoor plumbing was a luxury. In the 1920's, you were considered "The Cats Meow" if you owned a radio. Then, in the1950's, owning a television was a luxury. Just think of how we have come to expect certain things to be a standard part of our living! Now, the average family has indoor plumbing and electricity, plus, three television sets (one wide screened, of course), two computers, and every new gadget shown on television infomercials. Additionally, each member of the family wants and expects his own room, bathroom, telephone and car.

To support and maintain this lifestyle, it has become necessary for both spouses to work. And, with so much entertainment readily available to stimulate the senses, making love is reduced to just one more activity.

Time

Dad has to be Mr. Mom and Mom has to earn a large piece of that loaf of bread. Juggling nursery schools and class activities for children, as well as your own activities consumes all of your time. As each member of the family fights to control their time, he or she starts to feel resentful of the other family members. Cooperation tends to disintegrate, and counseling needs to be added to the already crowded schedule, if the family is going to survive.

As a responsible and devoted parent, you want to be involved with each and every family activity while meeting everyone's needs and wants, but it all becomes too much. And, guess which personal activity is the first to be eliminated?

Energy

In order to be good at anything, a certain amount of energy must be expended. Caring for the house and children requires the expenditure of tremendous amounts of energy. When a woman adds a career to this mix, it is a wonder that she is able to make it out of bed in the morning. And is it any wonder that all she wants to do in bed, after she finally collapses on it at night, is sleep. Furthermore, a career mom will soon be demanding support around the house from her husband, who as a trader also expends a great deal of energy. When both career parents involve themselves in household upkeep in addition to the other activities, there is little energy left for romantic activity.

If you recognize this scenario as all too familiar, you are probably feeling a loss of interest in romance. You have been robbed of the energy required to feel the passion needed to sustain it. Although you remember romance as being a satisfying activity, in this state of mutual exhaustion, you start to build bad psychological anchors because the romantic response you remember is not what you are receiving.

Fear

When a child is born, there is a lot of pain, inconvenience, and sacrifice. Parental tasks, such as changing diapers, nighttime feedings, and listening to a baby with colic scream are not fun and certainly are not a prelude to romance. Not only do you add a host of activities to your life when a new child comes to your home, you find that you are missing many of the spontaneous activities with friends which once brought pleasure to your life. To compound matters, you must now be content with an erratic income, which probably had not been an issue before the baby came. The lack of a steady dependable income can also create feelings of vulnerability. For some, the fear of having another child is frightening, and this fear can be related to making love because the sexual act is closely associated with the production of babies.

Men have to deal with their own fears. The responsibility of earning an income for a family can be especially frightening for a trader whose income can be unpredictable and erratic. With each new monetary responsibility, a trader can start to feel life's burdens closing in on him. He works harder, exerts more energy and time, and when everything becomes overwhelming, he has only room for fear in his mind.

Children

When children come into this world they need to feel that they are the center of the universe. Loving parents willingly become the slaves to tend to their baby's demands. After a child advances through the crawling stage, the walking stage and the "why" stage, parents take on the roles of chauffeur, tutor, and Little League coach. A new national focus on education has teachers giving demanding homework to young students, forcing parents to become even more involved in the nightly homework ritual. And when your child gets sick, you stay home from work as a nursemaid. While there is great joy in raising a family, the fact remains that children will deplete your sexual urges.

Beyond Normal Everyday Challenges

While Bob and Laura are typical of an average, loving family with no obvious major problems, consider other families who add a variety of scenarios to the mix of sex snatchers.

Psychological Problems and Behavioral Problems

Couples are often blinded by physical and emotional attachment and believe everything else will work because they have been taught "love conquers all." Current divorce rates illustrate the point that it takes more than just love to make a marriage work. Couples can find themselves in a relationship where psychological issues from past events can consume their attention. Some common issues are control, manipulation, depression, and sexual issues. Behavioral conflicts can be equally disruptive: for example, if one person is a slob and the other person is overly neat, or if one person wants to save every penny and the other wants to spend more then the budget will allow.

Psychological and behavioral problems lead to a lack of sexual desire.

Commuting & Business Travel

When couples are physically separated because of business travel and too much responsibility falls to one party, there will be additional problems in the marriage, to say nothing of the fact that opportunity for sexual activity within the marriage is cut to a minimum.

Illness

Children or a spouse who needs additional care because of illness creates a tremendous strain on a marriage. Multiply expenses, energy, time and other demands by three and then some for the additional stress on the family.

Addictions & Other Major Behavior Problems

Drugs, alcohol, and legal problems are some of the major addictive and behavioral problems that place serious strains on family life. In addition, addictions alter the body and brain chemistry and inhibit libido and performance.

How to Make Love and Sex Work

In order to make sex work, you must start by making love work. Both men and women must turn off their brain from other daily activities and connect with each other. Think in terms of what will please the other person and take joy in creating an atmosphere of love. Before this can be accomplished in your lives you must clear the clutter:

What is Important

In order to bring passion back to your marriage, you will need the cooperation of your entire family. Without this cooperation, you will find yourself putting out fires instead of starting them. Leadership will determine how much cooperation is gotten.

The first step is to refocus family attention on the things that matter to happiness. It is important that your family understand that family happiness is a function of the well-being of your marriage. Since this process of redefining values has to start somewhere, you will have to convince each family member that you are concerned about the true happiness and durability of the family.

Have each family member define what is the most important thing about life, what is important to him as an individual, and what is most important about family. Put each item in order of importance. Then discuss how each person's life can become more streamlined so that more energy and support is given to the most important parts of everyone's life. This might mean a smaller house, fewer toys or less scattered time together but more quality time. It means more consideration for the needs and desires of each individual and more cooperation and support rather than competition for time and energy.

Manage Time and Energy

Since a lack of uninterrupted time together is a major sex-snatcher, you can reverse this problem by scheduling to include two hours before sleeping on a few days of the week without work, telephone, television or any other interruptions. Allocate this time for sharing loving positive conversation with your partner.

There will always be unscheduled time grabbers such as a friend who calls unexpectedly, an unavoidable business appointment, or a forgotten classroom assignment that must be completed by tomorrow morning. Plan for these contingencies by changing something in your schedule like not going to work the next day or staying home from basketball practice. You will be amazed at how time grabbers disappear when you take drastic action. For example, your friend gets five minutes of your time to talk because you have told her in advance your time allocation. Your son stays up on his own doing his project and listens more carefully about his assignments the next time. And after that out of town meeting, linger on the phone with loving conversation.

If you have small children, you will have to manage their schedules for them. A way to have more time together is putting the children to bed earlier. Decrease stimulation in the evening and slow them down by not giving them sugar products after dinner, turn off the television, play slow soothing music and read stories to them. When starting to read, be dramatic and loud, slowly get softer, slower and speak in a monotone pattern.

Conclusion

The secret of keeping sex alive in a marriage is making love. Making love binds a marriage together and helps to overcome the challenges of life. Sex relieves tension and helps to make problems seem more manageable. You get better sleep when your mind is cleared of the day's activities. And the only way to make love and have healthy sex is by clearing your mind. You must plan your activities to have a transition time of relaxation in order for both parties to have desire. In order to turn someone else on, you must turn yourself on first. The best way to do this is to think in terms of how you will please the other person. This focus will stimulate thoughts, which in turn will stimulate action. Good performance in sex is dependent on the creation of an atmosphere with the least amount of stress. Good performance in trading is also dependent on decreasing life's stress. Why not choose to enjoy the process, become stress free, enliven your marriage and earn more money from trading in the process?

Chapter 30

THE BIG PICTURE

When times are bad, most traders worry themselves through difficult periods of trading. Focusing on their powerlessness and pain, they are unable to see the Big Picture. They are immersed in the minute-to-minute act of survival and neglect to look past the moment. What would happen if they could put each trade into its rightful context and see that it is part of the big picture of a working system?

Of course, loss and failure are not the only things that lead us to focus on the small picture. Bill Gates once said that success was a poor teacher because it seduced people into believing they could not lose. People who are in the midst of great success are often unknowingly working their way through success to the other side, while focusing only on their invulnerability. Their newly found arrogance often blinds them to the larger picture, setting them up for a fall from grace as they fail to see what is coming.

The Wake-Up Call

Ted was lucky enough to receive the wake-up call that accompanies a lack of attention to the "Big Picture." As a very successful money manager whose company grew too fast for him to manage, Ted lost control of everything in his life. He drank too much, and abused his personal life in many ways.

Inevitably, Ted started losing money. Up to this point, money had always been there and was the one measurement Ted had used to justify the way he was living. Like many other successful people, Ted had to go through a very bad period in his life to wake up. Now, he is taking care of himself, has regained his health, and his business is making money once again.

Labeling Life

Another way to limit your ability to see the Big Picture is to get trapped by your values. For Vinny, who needed to have the right labels on everything, success had always come easily. His definition of success meant that he had the right clothes, the right friends, the right car, and membership in the right country club. When Vinny lost his money and, consequently, everything he had, he lost all of his friends, who also defined their friendships through the "label-system." Vinny's trip out of bad times was an arduous one until he redefined success and was able to see the "Big Picture." Now, Vinny is as financially successful as before, but he lives his life differently based upon a larger set of values.

Restricting Opportunity

A third way to restrict your ability to see the Big Picture is to restrict your opportunities. Just as Vinny was trapped by his values, Gwen was trapped by her concepts. Gwen was a commodities trader who had only one idea of how her trading was going to be done. She had to trade on her own and there was no other way for her to do it. The problem was that she was not suited to trading successfully on her own. She had limits on her capital, on her training and expertise, and on her ability to run her own business. Because of her limiting notions, she could not see opportunity around her and found herself cornered in a position where she could do nothing.

Once she was cornered, Gwen was forced to look around and rethink her assumptions. Within a short time, she found a job trading for a company and was making far more money than she could have ever made on her own. She is no longer working from early in the morning until late at night, and she has a family life once again.

Stuck in the Problem

When we are stuck in the problem, it is difficult for most of us to see the way out. We are so close to the situation that we cannot step back and see that the final outcome is better than we could have imagined.

One of the reasons that we get stuck in the problem is that we extrapolate results from what is happening right this minute. If things are going well, we cannot foresee failure. When things are going terribly, we cannot imagine times improving dramatically. Whatever we see now is what we see in the future. A part of this lack of foresight is due to a lack of imagination. Few people have the imagination required to create in their minds the completed picture of a house from a set of plans or the final cut of a great movie from the original screenplay. This skill is called vision and can be identified in a handful of individuals commonly referred to as "visionaries."

Planning for the Best and the Worst Outcomes

Since few of us are visionaries, one of the best ways for us to gain a grasp of the Big Picture and its outcome is the act of planning. Learning to plan for the best possible outcome can bring you out of a downturn faster and take you to the best possible outcome faster than staying stuck in the problem. The process of planning requires you to ask questions that can generate new ways of perceiving a problem, which will remove limiting notions about the way things have to be done. For example, you might ask yourself:

- How can this problem be turned into an opportunity?
- What can I do to solve this problem on my own?
- What can I do to solve this problem by getting outside help?
- Is there another way to look at this problem - how would a very successful person look at this problem?
- In the past, have I observed anyone else resolve this problem successfully?
- Have others who are now successful had to resolve this problem?
- Have I ever experienced a similar problem and if so, how did I resolve the situation?

On the other hand, getting a grasp of the Big Picture also requires you to plan for the worst possible outcome as well. By anticipating the worst thing that could happen, you are in a position to:

- Soften the blow
- Avert the problem altogether
- Put into place a set of defensive strategies
- Create an alternative to what you are currently doing - an escape route
- Prepare yourself mentally and physically
- Create a totally different reality and/or outcome

In the event planning for the worst possible outcome worries you, it does not insure the worst will occur nor does it create pessimism or depression. In fact, it is a very liberating experience to develop the worst case scenario and your response to it. This process tends to give you a sense of security while it frees your focus to solving the problems confronting you. Planning stimulates the imagination so that you are more likely to see opportunity in the guise of a problem.

Taking the Long View

Bruce went to work every day fearing that he would lose his job. The sad thing about the situation was not that Bruce's job was in jeopardy, but that after ten years at the same job, Bruce could barely support his family and could not see past the limitations of his present situation.

When Bruce asked me to help him find a way to hold onto his job or find another job, he was shocked and hurt when I refused. I told him that I would not honor his request because he was stuck in an old way of thinking. Instead, I offered to help him set up his own business so that he could use the vital industry information and contacts that he had developed to become a successful supplier. At first, Bruce was resistant to the idea and came up with reasons that he would fail (the worst case scenario). We worked through the reasons and found ways to overcome them. Within three months, Bruce was not only in business, he was solvent. By the end of the first year, he was making three times what he had been making as an employee of the same company he was now supplying. The Big Picture was that Bruce was in an industry where he could play any role he chose to play - and he could play a minor role or a starring role with the same amount of effort.

Preparing for Success

Part of planning your way out of the small picture is to keep yourself conditioned for success once opportunity comes your way. People who are stuck in the problem often let themselves go physically and emotionally because they see no way out. Keeping your eye on the Big Picture will help in maintaining good physical health and in avoiding the self-destructive behaviors that will tempt you when you are feeling helpless and hopeless. Then, when opportunity presents itself, you will find yourself in the right condition to meet the challenges that both the bad times and the opportunities will present to you.

The Past and the Future

If you consider your past, your future will fall into one of the following categories:

Same - Generally, people will place themselves into the same monetary and social category they have been accustomed to when they do not add resources to their situation. Whatever you have been accustomed to in the past will equal the future if you continue to do the same thing you have always done.

Better - If you want the future to be better than the past, you must expand your resources and add new ones to your situation.

Worse - Tragedy, trauma, a loss of physical health, or marital problems are generally the only factors which will pull you into a lower station than you have formerly experienced.

Resources

Adding resources to your life or utilizing the resources you already have is the single most effective method for improving your circumstances. It is also the fastest way to pull yourself out of a bad spell. People often ask me what I mean by resources. All too often, people who are stuck in a problem fail to recognize that they even have resources to draw upon. The life resources to which I am referring are your:

- Skills

- Talents
- Experiences
- Training
- Contacts, friends, family, and social support network
- Capital in liquid and non-liquid forms, i.e. bank accounts, investments, property, loans to others, etc.
- Education
- Knowledge of specific ideas, strategies, etc.
- Character strengths - for example, if you have been working on your courage to handle difficult situations, your willingness to stick to a long-term plan, your commitment to goals

The Friendship/Mentor/Coach Resource

These resources are what you can draw upon when you are stuck in a problem and unable to see the larger picture. If you add resources to the mix, the equation changes. One of the very best resources you can add is a special person who brings problem-solving skills and important contacts. With this resource, your view will widen and dramatically improve your chances of solving your problems. Even if this special person has no contacts or important resources to bring you, he or she may bring you the important resource of a new perception of the situation. Sometimes, it takes another person to tell us that we are suffering from self-inflicted wounds when we are convinced that we are victims of a particular situation. He or she may offer simple encouragement or faith in our abilities to handle the problems at hand. The added emotional support can give us the strength to periscope up and look at the Big Picture for a brief moment and change the entire situation. For most people, the skill of a professional counselor who becomes this special person usually provides the best resource in solving this problem.

Conclusion

When we are experiencing a bad time in our lives, we tend to constrict our vision and limit our ability to solve problems. Under stress, we lose the imagination to see that what is happening now is not the only thing that can and will happen. Often this myopia prevents us from seeing that our troubles are often a needed wake-up call that can bring far greater opportunities and happiness than what we have lost. Stepping back and seeing the Big Picture will result in being able to plan for the best and worst scenarios. A view of the Big Picture with a solution to our problems can come from using the resources we currently have or adding new ones to our situation.

ANYONE HAVE SOME GREY POUPON?
THE ROCK OF GIBRALTAR

Chapter 31

THE STABLE TRADER

Stable traders thrive because stability builds strength and overtakes weakness. There are many different types of strength and the right combination of strengths is important to winning in each situation. When looking at countries, military power was once the answer to stability and strength. Now, a nation needs more than weaponry to maintain its strength. A country needs to be economically and technologically strong to be stable. For an individual to have the stability of a consistent professional trader, the strengths to survive in the trading arena must be developed. Some of the characteristics that are necessary are knowledge of the markets, a good business plan, and a balanced life.

Stability Breeds Success

This principle works everywhere you look. Banks lend to people who are wealthy and avoid lending to people who need money the most. Being needy, which is a classic weakness, is the surest and fastest way to get people to avoid you. People who are self-sufficient and healthy are perceived to be more attractive, and for that reason, they are likely to get jobs, promotions, and opportunities.

Trading Brothers

Michael and Martin grew up in a household where each person was expected to carry his own weight. Their father, Max, who worked as a butcher, took the boys to work at his shop once they started school. Their mother, Martha, did not think the kids should take on such responsibility at a young age. In fact, Martha resented the stern work ethic imposed on the family by her husband. She loved to spend the money she made on the side on indulgences that her husband refused to buy. Martha worked in the shop during the peak hours and also had a small business preparing and selling dinners from the leftover meat at the shop to her working neighbors. With this extra money, she indulged her appetite for expensive, personal luxuries that brought her pleasure.

When Michael and Martin grew up, they both developed an interest in the markets. Michael traded commodities from his home office while Martin traded on the floor of an exchange. While Michael followed in his father's footsteps, Martin modeled his life on his mother. Michael was frugal with the money he made from trading. He lived in a comfortable, but modest house, and put his profits into very safe investments. He practiced the personal disciplines of eating healthy food, exercising, and taking care of his mental health. Martin, on the other hand, lived beyond his means in a lavish style. He wore designer clothes, drove expensive cars, and lived in a mansion. After seeing the pleasure his mother derived from indulging herself when compared to the dour life his father lived, Martin was determined to enjoy his life. If it felt good, Martin was a devotee.

Over time, however, Martin's life began to unravel. Because he spent every penny he made on luxury, Martin had nothing to fall back on when his health began to interrupt his trading performance. He began to worry constantly about money. Nevertheless, Martin was unwilling to cut back on the luxuries that he was accustomed to. Eventually, he was forced to go to his brother, Michael, whose pockets were very deep, for a significant financial bail out.

Several years earlier, Michael had come to me for help in improving his trading performance. He considered the cost of getting coaching a business investment since his goal was to improve his bottom line. We worked to make him more aware of the fact that he would increase his profit margin if he traded his better trades. To reach his goal, Michael had to learn to trust his system, follow his trading rules, and stay disciplined. Michael also needed to learn to balance his life and learn to enjoy and reward himself. This emotional balance served to create a positive feedback system in his neurology that supported his success. The result was that Michael's profits improved well beyond our original goals. When Martin asked his brother Michael for help, Michael called me for advice. Michael did not want to loan money to his brother only to watch it spent on luxuries. If Martin's situation continued, he would soon return to the same situation and would be unable to repay Michael the money he owed him.

After our conversation, Michael agreed to help his brother, but he exacted a steep price, Martin would have to create stability in his life. He would have to set aside a significant portion of his money for the future and would have to reduce the cost of his lifestyle to accommodate his real income less the money he had to pay back on the loan and put into savings. In addition, he would have to create stability in the rest of his life, as well. Martin agreed to join a gym and go every day. He and his wife stopped eating out every evening at expensive restaurants and learned how to prepare healthy foods at home.

Slowly, Martin pulled himself out of financial trouble and his trading results improved dramatically. Now, he is trading electronically, off the floor, with his brother. He had enough money set aside to make the transition, with plenty to allow for time to learn and make mistakes.

Building Stability

Weakness is an invitation for something to go wrong. Stability, on the other hand, is the absence of weakness in the system and is a form of insurance. Removing and fixing any weaknesses in the system is the first step in creating stability. In the real world, these steps translate into mending holes in the fence, beefing up security, identifying and remedying weaknesses, reinforcing foundations, laying in supplies, creating resources, building sustaining relationships, buying insurance, and developing escape routes.

The Recipe for Maintaining Stability as a Trader

Any good recipe involves blending ingredients. Stability is the result of a combination of the following ingredients in ample quantities.

Energy
High energy builds physical, emotional, mental and spiritual strength. The result of having positive, high energy keeps you healthy. An unhealthy person diminishes his stability as a trader.

Knowledge
Knowledge gives a trader the confidence and competence to make his own decisions knowing from his own authority that he is right. Those who follow other people's advice are dependent and, therefore, vulnerable.

Wisdom
In order to use the wisdom that is a part of you, you must develop and balance right and left brain thinking. Statistical, mathematical people cannot work beyond a mechanical system. Creative, people often want to trade using only discretion. If you do not develop the wisdom that whole brain thinking provides, you will not optimize your trading ability.

High Self-Values
High self-values such as self-esteem and self-confidence increase your stability by giving you the psychological advantage. You perform better when you have these high self-values, which are a result of developing and using your resources. All skills, abilities, abundance, and positive relationships will add to your resources account. People who are not constantly growing will lose their ability to maintain self-values.

Discipline
Discipline is about following the rules and guidelines set up for yourself in all areas of your life. Keeping to a predetermined winning course is the essence of stability. When you are on course and the outcome is not what you want, you will know what not to do and be willing to try other tactics.

Prosperity Consciousness

Prosperity consciousness creates stability for traders by increasing the probability of success. Prosperity consciousness increases financial strength by keeping the mind focused on maintaining a positive mental outlook and positive expectation, while taking action on creative ideas within a plan.

Flexibility

Flexibility promotes stability by allowing you to adapt to change. Strength cannot exist without flexibility. Without flexibility, you cannot fight the long battles. It keeps you young, fresh, and open to opportunities and growth.

Environmental Support

Stability is created externally as well as internally. The environment where a trader lives and works must support him physically and emotionally. If it is hostile, unsafe, or unhealthy, he is operating from a position of weakness that will eventually undermine his efforts. Another factor in his environment that can weaken his defenses is inadequate resources.

Financial Security

For a trader, no single ingredient builds stability as much as financial security. You must build your financial strength on diversification. This strategy must include long-term investments for retirement, education for the children, and insurance to secure present lifestyle in the event of sickness or disaster. It must also include mid-range savings and investments for the realization of dreams and short-term fund allocation for enjoyment of life in the moment.

According to a recent television news show, a segment of American workers most at risk of losing their jobs are middle managers in their forties earning over $100,000 per year. Companies are letting these valuable employees go to replace them with younger workers that can be started at $40,000 to $50,000 per year. Far too many of these middle managers are living right up to their incomes and putting nothing back in reserve. When they are released, they are at immediate risk of losing their homes and everything they have. To make matters worse, they find that they cannot replace their jobs at the salaries they had once commanded. One former executive sent out nearly 300 resumes without receiving a positive response. Nevertheless, if you had asked him before he was fired how stable his employment situation was, he would have given himself high marks.

Liquid assets are the very definition of financial stability. Money that is tied up in hard assets, even when they are appreciating rapidly, can disappear in a matter of days if a market goes bad.

What is your capital accumulation plan? Capital cannot be accumulated if it is not being saved. Unfortunately, most people who have money to spend do so with a vengeance. Few of us have developed the self-discipline to save because the nature of our culture is to consume. Our economy thrives only as long as everyone keeps buying and we are constantly bombarded by the unconscious manipulation of advertisement to buy things that we do not need.

Attractiveness

If stability is measured by strength in any situation, then beauty and attractiveness are important ingredients for increasing stability. Attractiveness increases the chances of survival, health, and money. Studies have shown that more attractive people get jobs, service, and opportunities at all levels while their less attractive and possibly more capable peers are turned away. Opening many doors of opportunity might require a plastic surgeon and good packaging, but keeping the door open requires the attractiveness of high energy, capability, and character.

Aggressiveness

Aggressiveness is a factor, which increases a trader's stability by increasing his strength in any situation. I have made the distinction between aggressiveness and aggression. Aggressiveness is assertive personal power that does not step on the rights of others or take unlawful action to reach a goal. Nevertheless, the aggressive are perceived as stronger than the passive and non-assertive. They are more likely to win battles and are, therefore, less vulnerable. They are also less likely to be afraid, which makes them stronger in most situations.

Health

How healthy is your health account? Many people tolerate feeling uncomfortable as a part of their lot in life. While there are people who cope as best they can with conditions that are chronic, most people choose to ignore the fact that they are not operating from their optimal health potential.

We often admire the thirty-year-olds burning the candle at both ends while managing to turn out good performance. These bon vivants are borrowing on their future energy supply and will pay the price with their health when they are in their fifties. There are those who have been gifted with unusually strong immune systems that seem to thrive no matter what their choices and live to be centenarians, but these supermen are the exception. Others with the strictest health regimes are sickly all of their lives. Most of us, however, reflect our choices in our health and appearance.

The stable person, who is not a superman, makes healthy choices in food, drink, exercise, rest, and relaxation. To achieve stability in your health, pay attention to the signs that your body gives you. Aches, pains, and negative behavior are signals that your body sends to let you know that you need to take notice and act on better choices.

Relationships

Harmony with others surrounding you is necessary for the welfare of your stability account. Most people habitually interact in set patterns of conversation and behavior. When you recognize and notice negative patterns and make a conscious choice to change them to positive interaction, you add to your stability account. You will notice how everyone around you will follow suit and what follows is a volleying effect of even more positive relating. Each major relationship is a like a living system. If there is bad feeling in an important relationship, either expressed or unexpressed, the system is weakened and can become unstable. Pushed far enough or neglected too long, the relationship can spin out of control causing havoc in the lives of those it touches. Building a healthy marriage or partnership will add a significant number of stability points to your account.

Conclusion

The stable trader operates from a position of strength, which allows him to fight the long battles and emerge victorious. The trader whose life is stable can weather losses, bad markets, and change because he has the resources to grow and adapt. Any trader who wants to stay in trading for the long haul must make a commitment to increasing stability in all areas of his life. Michael and his brother, Martin, learned that the cost of stability is years of self-discipline, but the cost of instability can be the loss of all we hold dear.

HOME
RUN

Chapter 32

THE ABLED TRADER

If they search hard enough, most traders will find that they have one form of disability or another. This is because people start out with their own unique genetic makeup and develop some problems along the way. These anomalies, which interfere with the perfect functioning of our minds and bodies, can be physical, emotional, social, and/or neurological. They can range from something so minor that they rarely surface to the trader's conscious awareness to disabilities so major that everyone cannot help but notice them.

The physical and immediately obvious disabilities that need to be addressed often come with terrible baggage creating enormous hurdles for the individual to overcome, but they do get the attention of the people around them. On the other hand, the disabilities that are emotional, social, and neurological can be just as difficult to live with because they are often overlooked and never addressed.

What do these disabilities have to do with making money in the markets? Sometimes, they represent the keys to success or failure. While some traders are disabled by their limitations, others are actually "abled" by them. Their disability provides them with winning strategies, experiences, and character traits that help them overcome obstacles and reach their goals. What makes the difference? It is the programming about success that a trader accepts or rejects from his parents, teachers, and other early influences in his life and how he feels about himself that determines if his disability helps or hinders his efforts. The remaining question is: Can this programming and its accompanying attitudes be changed?

The Gifted Problem-Child

The first-generation American parents who raised their young son, Tomas, and his siblings adhered to the strict and conservative values of their own European-born parents. Displays of praise, encouragement and affection were rare. Each family member had a role to play and any deviation from that role was unacceptable. Tomas' father's job was to go out into the world each day, work, and bring home the money to support his family. His mother's function was to feed the family, keep the house clean, and make certain that the children's behavior conformed to the narrowly-defined, acceptable ways that would bring no shame to the family.

This fear of shame meant that no one in the community could have anything negative to say about the children. Although Tomas' father loved his children, he would never demonstrate his love with affectionate actions or words. Instead, he proved his love by supporting them and his wife proved her love by giving them the proper foundation of values and behaviors in order to function in their world.

There is a great deal to be said for the stability that results from this type of highly conformist upbringing. Children have no confusion about who they are, what they are supposed to do, and what is right and wrong. If everyone follows the rules, everything runs smoothly. Hilda and Rainer, Tomas' siblings, were the perfect children to thrive in this "don't rock the boat" environment. Unfortunately, Tomas was not.

Tomas was a hyperactive child who was unable to stay out of trouble in school, at home, and in the community. He had difficulty learning in school, although he appeared to be very bright. He was constantly getting in fights because his classmates would make fun of his accent, his dress, and the twitches in his face. His dominating mother was very angry with Tomas for bringing trouble to her household. His father and siblings resented him because of the uproar his antics created in their home life. Tomas found no relief from this rejection in school because his teachers would disparage him for his behavior and his classmates would soon follow suit.

Because Tomas had difficulty learning, he cheated his way through school. Eventually, when he was a teenager, he found an activity at which he could excel. He became interested in bodybuilding and devoted every ounce of his energy to this activity. As a result, he won a title and created a good anchor for the feelings of success and self-discipline. While working out in the gym, he met a man who was in the vitamin business. While still in his teens, Tomas took over this business, and in a short time, was earning several hundred thousand dollars a year.

Suddenly, Tomas was a success. He knew what it felt like to make money and to be an entrepreneur. But, instead of his parents and siblings being proud of him, they resented him even further for not being the failure that his non-conforming behavior should have predicted. His success threatened to make them wrong.

From all of this childhood rejection and unhappiness, Tomas took one lesson that supported his future success. Tomas' father had been in the construction business. After working in the homes of the wealthy, he would tell his children that money was the most important thing in this world. Tomas' father had so much respect for a person with money that Tomas decided that making money was the most important thing in life.

Tomas discovered the trading world through a friend who became his mentor. He taught Tomas in a style of learning that was easy for Tomas to comprehend. To his great surprise and gratification, Tomas found that when concepts and information were presented to him in this way, they made sense to him.

One day, Tomas and his mentor were going through the list of symptoms of Attention Deficit Disorder (ADD). ADD is a common neurological impairment where the central nervous system is not able to sensor out all of the sensory inputs that come your way, moment to moment. The results of this disorder are that the individual has difficulty concentrating, has limited short-term memory, and difficulty learning. However, just because a person has ADD does not mean that he is unintelligent. In fact, many people with ADD are highly intelligent. Suddenly, Tomas realized that what he had experienced all of his life was an Attention Deficit Disorder (ADD).

Once he was able to find a learning style that worked for him, Tomas was able to turn his disability into ability by using the strategies that he had developed in order to overcome the obstacles of his disability. In fact, Tomas went on to be one of the most successful traders with whom I have ever worked. When he hired me as a coach, he was not hiring me to deal with his trading issues; he was hiring me to deal with the imbalances in the rest of his life. Unfortunately, although his father had given him the motivation to be successful materially, Tomas' parents had robbed him of the ability to relate successfully to the people closest to him.

The Hidden Cost of Designer Labels

Tomas' story is not at all unique. In the past few years, I have worked with a significant number of traders who have ADD or other neurological disabilities. Only one was fortunate enough to have had parents who recognized his problem without labeling him a "bad" child. Instead, they took the trouble to find out about his condition and helped him develop strategies that would allow him to succeed. They also took the time to teach him the social skills that often do not develop in ADD children. By missing the social cues necessary to develop childhood friendships, the child with ADD or other conditions like it becomes even more isolated and rejected. This cycle of failure and rejection often causes these children to act out in anti-social ways, especially if they do not find the area in life at which they are "abled." This explains why there are so many adults with ADD in prisons.

Like Tomas, many young children grow up with undiagnosed neurological, emotional, and social disabilities. While they are suffering from these conditions, the people around them do not understand their special needs. Then, one day, the families, doctors and teachers of these children discover that the condition exists and give it a label. Now, the child learns all about his condition and begins to live the condition and understand all of his experiences through this new paradigm. With this label, he gives himself a reason for being the way he is. Unfortunately, instead of giving the child a tool for living, this new label gives him an excuse for being one way and an invisible barrier that prevents him from being any other way.

When a child is growing up with a disability, there can be a lot of pain. The process can create breakdowns in the important relationships in his life. This trouble is especially prevalent in families where the other children behave normally, while one is constantly getting into trouble, failing to pick up social cues, or unable to learn through standard teaching models. This "problem" child will most likely not get appreciated, loved, or noticed for the exceptional talent he is.

Occasionally, a child with what appears to be a learning disability is actually a genius. He is labeled a "problem child" or a "slow learner" because he is trapped in a school system that is limited to the learning models that work for average children. As a result, the exceptional child becomes bored, the teachers become frustrated, and the child is treated like an outcast in his family. If he manages to survive through high school under these conditions, sometimes he is lucky enough to find either a mentor or an activity that sparks his interest.

When that outside influence allows him to express his latent talents and interests, he is capable of reaching greatness in his life. What makes the difference between success and failure is the early programming from this parents about success and its value and if he has interpreted that information in a way that would bring him high self-value.

Lessons from School

What I have found in working with top traders is that school was often a painful experience for them. This is despite the fact that it takes a high level of native intelligence to become a successful trader. The reason for this apparent inconsistency is the fact that the gifted child with anomalies is often drawn to trading as an occupation. The personal freedom that is enjoyed by traders permits an individual that is not like everyone else to excel to his full potential without the inhibiting influence of social pressure.

If you were to look at "normal behavior," you would be able to pick these individuals out as "disabled." However, if you were able to find the learning model that was right for these individuals, they would reveal themselves as gifted. Unfortunately, the average public or private school is not designed to identify and nurture these individuals. Instead, they are left to their own devices to sink or swim. Fortunately, like water, they often find their own level through trial and error. This process of finding some way to learn and to achieve seems to be instinctive for many, as though they are internally driven to find a way out of their disability. The result of their effort is to create strategies for coping that create, in turn, distinctive strengths and resources. And instead of being disabled, they become "abled" in their own unique way in the world of trading, where being unique is a great blessing.

The Great Disabled

Once a child or adult has labeled himself as "disabled," it can be a difficult challenge to undo the associations he attaches to his "disability." Most of these associations come in the form of self-imposed limitations. If an individual buys into these limitations, they become self-fulfilling prophecies. At this point, I like to tell traders who have fallen into this self-sabotaging trap about the world of great achievers who stretched the envelope for all of us despite the fact that they carried the heavy burden of disabilities that should have slowed them to a crawl.

For example:

1. Thomas Edison - the world's greatest inventor was thought to be unteachable
2. Franklin Delano Roosevelt - led this country through the Great Depression and World War II; he was crippled by polio and confined to a wheel chair
3. I have a very long and distinguished list of disabled individuals who were so "abled" by their limitations that they changed the course of history. I especially like to tell traders about the world-famous trader, teacher, and mentor, Joe Ross. Joe is so dyslexic that he has difficulty reading 25 words per minute and must read in special, large type. In addition to all of his trading and speaking functions, Joe has written eight important books on trading. Instead of being disabled by his dyslexia, Joe has been "abled" by his condition.

Conclusion

For the present time, there are literally millions of individuals who think of themselves as less than intelligent and not cut out for success because they have some form of disability that makes it difficult to learn and decipher social cues in the usual way. Some day, we will learn to identify these anomalies early. Instead of limiting potential, we will know how to use these "disabilities" to enhance human capacity for achievement.

In the meantime, it is important for all of us to realize that finding the right learning modality can unlock the enormous learning potential hidden in each of us. The strategies for overcoming a handicap often create strengths that can enable us to be better traders. The key to making this transformation lies in our attitudes about success and our attitudes about our selves. The decision to rebuild our sense of self-worth is the first step in making this change.

SAME LOW
BUILD STRENGTH
BUILD VITALITY
BUILD
HEALTHY HAPPY FOOD
ERGO CHAIR
LIGHT YOUR FIRE

Chapter 33

THE BORED TRADER

Making money in the markets, even making a great deal of money from trading, must fit into a life that is filled with other fascinations. Otherwise, a trader who seemingly has everything can end up with nothing. After more than a decade of working with traders as a trader's coach, I have seen men and women who have placed trading, not at the center of their lives, but over the entire picture. The net result has been that, even if they become very successful, their lives can be undone by boredom.

The Trader with No Time on His Hands

Twenty-five years ago, Mike entered trading from a successful career as an engineer. With his savings and profit-sharing proceeds, Mike was well positioned financially to trade. Additionally, he had spent three years in preparation for full-time trading before he made the career move. He had developed a unique mechanical system that he tested and re-tested. Although Mike entered trading when the field of trading psychology was in its infancy, he was fortunate to have been a highly disciplined individual from childhood. He was not greedy, and he did not undermine his efforts with baggage from traumatic events or from an un-supportive home environment. Thus, he did not need coaching or counseling to undo destructive patterns of behavior and thought.

Mike was free to trade and that is what he did, morning, noon, and night. He loved doing research to improve and modify his system and trading. He especially loved the challenges that the market presented. The result was that he made a great deal of money. He loved that, too.

Why did Mike become so absorbed in his trading? Soon after he began trading full time, Mike took a loss that frightened him. He had never felt a significant loss before this trading loss. Up to this point, his life had followed a very predictable path of positive experiences. Although he knew intellectually that trading inevitably involved taking losses, the idea that he could lose everything suddenly occurred to him on a deeply emotional level. He could feel it and see it, and he was frightened by the experience. Mike was determined to make certain that he would never allow himself to suffer a major loss again. Driven by this unconscious fear, Mike focused on his research and system. His problem was that he forgot that there was anything else in life besides trading.

When Mike began trading, he had a wife and three children. As the years passed, his total absorption with trading began to take a toll on his family. Left to raise their children without assistance from her husband, Mike's wife, Emily, began to feel resentment towards him. By the time the children were in high school, Mike barely saw them. They, in turn, had little interest in their father except for the money he made. Once the children were in college, Emily went to graduate school to earn an advanced degree. Afterwards, she left Mike and moved back to her hometown in Indiana.

By this time, Mike had been trading for fifteen years. Now, he was more able to concentrate on his trading. For the next few years, Mike traded without the interruptions from wife and children. Trading was the only focus of his life. He rarely spent time with friends, he did not attend church or social clubs, and he had no pets because Mike knew that pets died after a few years and he was not willing to deal with that loss. As time passed, Mike had fewer and fewer exchanges with the outside world. The only thing that mattered to him was his trading. Then, something happened that changed everything.

One day, Mike awoke and walked straight into the trading office that he had built onto his home. He flipped on the lights and felt something that he had never felt before. He felt a lack of desire to spend the entire day in his office. In fact, he almost felt a tinge of revulsion. Instead of getting started, he returned to the kitchen and made himself a breakfast for the first time in many years. The thrill was gone and Mike was bored. Unfortunately, he had no concept of how to handle this situation. Suddenly, he wanted more from his life, but he had no idea what that could be.

As the days passed, Mike found it more difficult to concentrate on his trading. After fifteen years of nearly obsessive trading and research, it was hard to find a new challenge in his trading. Because his trading system was highly refined and predictable in its results, Mike could have hired someone to place his trades for him. But, he had always been afraid to let anyone handle his affairs.

What many traders fail to understand is that the time you spend when you are not trading is actually necessary to support your trading. The joy, health, peace, fulfillment, and growth you gain from these activities are deposited into your life account. The capital maintained in this life account is the other type of capital needed for trading. When you continue to trade without making deposits in your life account, you will eventually come up dry.

Mike decided to take some time off from trading, which was another first for him. In the past fifteen years, he had not taken a single long vacation and had only taken a handful of long weekends at the insistence of his wife. Mike was afraid to leave his office for fear that the markets would move and he would lose money or a great opportunity. He called his aging parents and booked a flight to visit them. In the past, the only way they had seen him was when they made the trip from Indiana to visit. Now, they were too old and infirm to travel. The visit with his family was a revelation for Mike. He had no notion of how to relate to his family. With time on his hands, he was even more bored than he was with trading. Sensing his need for something to absorb him, his brother suggested they get on a plane and go to Las Vegas.

In Las Vegas, Mike discovered gambling and many other ways to occupy himself. The fact that he won quite a bit of money was also attractive to him. Mike was not a fool and he knew that gambling was self-destructive. So, he and his brother flew home. When he returned to trading a week later, he approached it differently. Now, he was interested in putting more action in his trading as a prescription for boredom. A year later, Mike had lost nearly all of his trading capital, but at least he was no longer fighting his boredom. He didn't have time. He was now desperate to survive.

How Boredom Creeps In

Many traders are like Mike. They fail to develop any of the other parts of their lives beyond their trading. As a result, their lives do not possess the richness of relationships, social activities, travel, vacationing, or hobbies. Concerned for their security, all of their actions come from a state of fear:

- They don't take vacations for fear of missing something
- They don't have relationships for fear of being hurt or of being abandoned or giving up some of their money
- They don't have a pet for fear of it dying
- They won't eat at expensive restaurants because it's cheaper to eat at home and why should they pay "for a candelabra and linen napkins"?
- They don't join any social groups for fear of being disappointed or criticized
- They don't have children for fear that they will take drugs or in other ways make their lives miserable

When traders find themselves trading on "emotional empty," they suddenly lose the passion they once felt for trading. This loss of interest can come very suddenly, as it did for Mike, or it can creep up on a trader like a slowly growing tumor. Regardless of its speed, a trader will reach a point where he has nothing upon which to draw for inspiration, support, or escape. Without a life outside of trading, a trader cannot feel interest in trading indefinitely. But, like a Catch-22, without that outside life, there is nowhere to go once he loses interest in trading.

Now, he is bored with his professional as well as his personal life. He keeps asking himself, what is the point? Why have I given everything up to do something so meaningless? Often, there is no one nearby who cares about him to answer, since he has isolated himself in his quest for success.

Not only do traders become bored when they isolate themselves from others; they also become boring. They often find that they have little to talk about with people who are not in their field and they lose the necessary social skills that allow them to interact well through lack of practice. In a downward spiral, this withdrawal from social interaction feeds upon itself, so that these traders rarely find themselves invited to join others.

Getting into Trouble

One of the major traps that bored traders fall into is that they are likely to lose sight of their goals and their values and the instant fix for boredom is excitement. Once a trader begins to look for excitement, he will do things that are very risky and self-sabotaging. Like Mike, bored traders will find themselves gambling instead of trading, taking risks in order to feel the adrenal pumping. Unfortunately, the pumping sound is usually that of their assets being pumped out of their bank account.

If the risky behavior is not confined to their trading, bored traders may look for excitement in risky sports and risky social behavior, including heavy drinking and drugs. A bored trader may look around for the reason that he is bored and conclude that there is nothing that he has done to cause the problem. He will then look for a culprit and find his wife and children to blame. Without any warning, they will suddenly find themselves replaced by a bright, new, exciting, young creature named Tammy or Tiffany.

The problem is that boredom is not an external problem and cannot be fixed by radical, external changes or by blaming others. It can only be corrected from inside the person who is experiencing it.

Pulling Out of Boredom

The first steps out of boredom are the very hardest ones. Long entrenched habits make isolated traders fearful, embarrassed, and uncomfortable in taking the first steps to create a life outside of trading. Initially, they may be met with rebuffs, especially from the very people they have ignored or pushed away. They may have to reach out to complete strangers, which can be uncomfortable. One of the easiest ways to take that first step is to join a group that is traditionally welcoming such as a church or a charity that is looking for a helping hand. Getting on the phone is another first step. Making calls to old friends can open up a lost world. Getting on the Internet is another relatively easy step.

It is important for a trader who has reduced the size of his world to figure out what is important to him. Since time is a limited commodity, he should carefully select activities, hobbies, and social experiences that will give him pleasure as well as a sense of fulfillment. He should also attempt to fill out his time roster with physical activities as well as social and spiritual ones to prevent burning out from too limited a focus. An internal journey of discovery is one of the best antidotes to boredom. So is the quest for personal growth.

Once a trader has started to fill his world up outside of trading, he is likely to find that he can return to trading and find pleasure, meaning, and reward in the process.

Conclusion

At some point, traders who limit their activities to trading hit a wall. If they are the lucky ones, they are knocked into consciousness: a person can make money being a trader, but if they don't have a successful life, what is the point? What are you doing with the time when you are not trading? If you do not cultivate that time with the same commitment that you utilize the time when you are trading, you will have nothing to fall back on when you stop trading. Furthermore, what you do with your non-trading time actually supports your trading. When you don't cultivate the other parts of your life, you will eventually sabotage your trading because you will fail to see the point of it.

SECTION 6
Life Phases...

THIS END
UP

Chapter 34

THE PHASES OF A TRADING CAREER

For each phase of a successful trading career, there is a beginning, middle, and end. While some traders are good at starting a project, others are good at sustaining a project, and still others are good at completing a project. The problem for traders is that, if they are to make successful transitions to a new phase, they will have to have the skills needed to complete beginnings, middles and ends.

No End in Sight

This fact was underscored recently when a trader named Harry called for help. Harry was very upset at the prospect of going into the next phase of his life. This long-term, successful trader and money-manager felt old. Life was no longer exciting for him. Harry knew that changes would have to be made in his life, and he was keenly aware of the promises he had made to his wife and family about his departure from trading. In fact, he was at the point of selling his business to his partner and phasing out of the business completely. So, why was Harry in a panic?

Harry was frightened thinking about his friends who had retired from trading. According to Harry, they were either bored with life or dead. Of the retired traders who still had a pulse, all wanted to get back into the game to feel alive again. Harry was also aware of the fact that he had never learned to enjoy life beyond his trading. He had difficulty relating to his wife, Edie, who hoped that when Harry gave up trading, their fighting would stop. Her reasoning was based on the fact that Harry excused his lack of loving involvement by saying that he was under too much pressure from trading. Harry would placate Edie with the promise, "One day, when I give up trading, everything will be all right." But Harry did not know how to stop and smell the roses along the way. He had been highly skilled throughout his career as a trader, and then, as a money manager, but Harry had no concept of how to end things.

Successful endings are critical to a trading career because they set the stage for the successful beginning of the next phase of life, whatever that might be. If a trader is afraid to end something and holds on too long, serious losses can result, not just from a single trade but from a transition that must be made. Fear is usually the issue as it was in Harry's case. The solution is a new set of associations framing ending and closure as a source of opportunity and forward movement rather than a source of pain and loss.

Beginning Phase

Of all of the traders I have worked with, Charles is one of the most skilled at completing the beginnings, middles, and ends of things. While he was still in college, he had started up a small business with a family friend, which he leveraged into a flourishing operation. Several years later, when Charles decided that he wanted to be a floor trader, he realized that he would need a mentor. Charles found a mentor by spending time observing floor traders while considering, "Who do I want to be like?" When Charles identified the trader he wanted to model, he found someone to introduce them. This introduction launched a life-long friendship as well as the start of Charles' career on the floor. The young trader read all of the books his mentor read and, as quickly as he could, he molded his every action on his mentor's pattern. For the next fifteen years, Charles was very successful, in his trading, in his marriage, his relationships with his children, and with the other people in his life. Charles was definitely a good starter.

On the other hand, there was Todd, a trader who wanted everything now. From his need for instant gratification, Todd wanted to experience the feelings of success before he had actually achieved success. While he was skilled at creating these good feelings in his own mind, Todd forgot to put into his imaginings the details and steps needed to reach his goals. When Todd came to the floor of the exchange, he had no plan for learning his new profession, which required study and preparation. Instead, he felt he could learn by trial and error. The result was that Todd experienced so much error that it wiped him out of the business.

Unlike Todd, successful beginners have a different set of associations, which make them willing and eager to do the things necessary to make this phase successful. They see beginnings as exciting and challenging. In addition, they see beginnings as the foundation for their project - not as an inconvenience or as the end in itself.

Mid-phase

After fifteen years, Charles, our successful starter, realized that he had to get off of the floor. At forty years of age, Charles' back and feet were aching and he felt that he was wearing out. So, Charles did what many floor traders do, he became an upstairs trader. Instead of resisting the change and clinging to the past, Charles saw the ending of his career as a floor trader as a step toward a new challenge which he eagerly anticipated.

Charles was also aware that the transition from floor trader to upstairs trader is often called "the kiss of death." To avoid sabotaging himself during this transition, Charles decided to approach this change as though he was starting a new career. Using his pattern of seeking the right teachers, he attended conferences, seminars and read books on trading. Once again, Charles succeeded in completing the transition. Within a year, he had developed himself into a good discretionary trader off the floor.

Along the way, Charles had also learned about successful middles. He understood that there would be a second phase in his trading, after the exciting beginning period. During this phase, he would have to give up the excitement of trading on the floor, and develop his craft off of the exchange floor. During this mid-phase, Charles would accept the fact that his system and trading methods worked and that he would need to be content to reap their rewards. Now, he was in a new period where he just had to follow his plan. Many traders find this phase boring, so they sabotage their efforts, wanting to go back and rediscover the early excitement. When he looked at his life, Charles saw the rewards that becoming a successful trader brought to him and his family. He was exceptionally good at aligning his excitement with following his rules and the rewards he would get from being a good trader. Charles was a good, mid-phase man.

The mid-phase of a trading business requires these qualities of character, which are needed for a successful trader. When trading gets boring, a trader must persevere. When inevitable losses occur, a trader must stick to his commitment. When the temptation is great to break your rules, a trader must have the integrity to hold fast to his trading rules and to his word to himself and others. He must respect the foundation in market study and research that helped him to get where he is. At the same time, he must be flexible in order to deal with the inevitable changes that will be encountered. He must be willing to continue to refine his system to make it the best it can be. And finally, he must be disciplined enough to keep his business afloat every day, which means that he has to attend to his physical and emotional well-being and do the things that are hard, but necessary for continued success.

Like Todd, the "instant gratification" guy, Elliot wanted success immediately. Fortunately, he was also willing to pay the price and do the things that it took to launch his trading career and become very successful - until the period of routine set in. Then, Elliot found ways to create excitement by sabotaging his results. He would do this by changing his system, adding new rules and generally experimenting with what was tried and true. Inevitably, Elliot's trading career was lost.

Interestingly enough, Elliot not only acted out this pattern in his trading, but also in his personal life. He loved romance and seduction. Elliot wanted each romantic encounter to be another "Titanic" affair. However, when he finally did extend his honeymoon into a real honeymoon and married the love of his life, the routines of everyday life and dealing with the emotional issues that couples face daily, led him to separation and, finally, divorce. Isn't it interesting how new romances no longer produce the same impact for Elliot because he sees them through the eyes of a wounded lover?

End Phase - to a New Beginning

Charles, our successful starter and mid-phase trader, had a good life with his family because he knew how to balance his life. Charles had come to a point where he wanted more special moments with his children and grandchildren. To accomplish this, he would have to phase out some of his career as a trader. In typical Charles fashion, he decided to become a long-term investor. While he was still a day-trader, he looked into long-term investing and began investing in tandem with his day trading. As a result, making the transition to full-time investor did not involve learning new skills, but giving up one of his careers. Now, you can find Charles with his son and his grandson on the golf course, or with his wife in exotic places where they are experiencing the beauty of this planet and enjoying themselves.

Conclusion

The beginning, middle and end of each phase of a trader's career are important to the long-term success of his overall career. A trader must be able to carry his ambition to trade past the first few hurdles of learning his business, doing his research and building his system if he wants to have a trading career at all. A trader can not rest once his business is established simply because he likes the challenge and excitement of starting up his business. He must sustain that trading business through its development and day-to-day activity even though it may become routine and boring. And finally, it is important to a trader's life to know when to end his trading career. For a trader to make these transitions requires a tremendous commitment to his goals, a willingness to model those traders who are successful in each phase of the business, and the flexibility to make the adaptations required for that next step forward.

YEAH... YEAH... UH-HUH.

Chapter 35

MID-LIFE TRADING

"No, nothing's wrong. I'm doing fine. Really," Jon responded to my questions. His answers were encouraging except that, if everything was fine, why was he phoning for help with such urgency?

Actually, on paper, everything was fine with Jon. He had come far from his early days as a young, poor and thoroughly wild-eyed trader. He and his family lived in a beautiful home in the Chicago suburbs, his children were preparing to go off to college, Jon had a solid marriage, and he had plenty of money in the bank. Who could have a problem with that scenario? Jon did.

At forty-nine years of age, Jon had fought the trading wars and won. He had once risked his entire capital base, including his first house, his car, and money he had borrowed from his aunt on a single trade which had, luckily, gone his way. "I wouldn't dream of doing anything that stupid anymore," he told me, somewhat wistfully.

"Then, why are you here?" I asked. "Do you want to reach the next level of your trading? Have you reached your ceiling and want to break through it? Are you beginning to break your rules? Have you suddenly lost energy? Are you suffering from stress or burn-out?" I went through the standard list of trader problems, but Jon kept shaking his head.

"I guess I'm just hitting a mid-life crisis," he told me. "Nothing's wrong, and that's the trouble. I have nothing to worry about, or to look forward to overcoming. I need to know that there is something else." Jon's face expressed pain as though he had come to the end of his trading career.

The Passion's Gone

Remember when you were the risk taker, the one who was out there without a net, just for the challenge? Maybe you were considered the black sheep in the family. You went against all of the odds and decided you were going to be a successful trader. You disciplined yourself to do the right things, experienced the ups and downs, made the mistakes, and learned the lessons. Now, you are respected. You can count on a good income and you're proud to call yourself a futures trader.

But, something is missing. The passion is gone and you have reached the light at the end of the tunnel. It's not as bright as it used to be, though, and you wonder, "So, that's all there is?" This is the same feeling many people experience after a number of years in a happy marriage. Ennui is a primary reason for infidelity and the reason the betrayed spouse suffers so much pain. The question remains, "If I did everything right and we were so happy, why did he/she leave me for someone else?"

The Conquest of the Hunt

Human nature evolved over millions of years for one primary purpose, and that was the survival of the species. The characteristics that promoted survival were the ones that were retained. In order to survive, people had to have food, shelter, and protection from the elements.

For early man, the first order of business was finding something to eat. Without food, he wasn't going to have to worry too much about shelter, and just about anything would do. Research has shown us how important human blood sugar levels are to our brain and heart function. Hours past mealtime, a highly intelligent, energetic and rational person can turn into a desperate, weak and inarticulate wreck, operating at a fraction of previous levels of performance. The internal drive to feed themselves stimulated early man to catch that wild game, or spear that fish, or find that source of fruit or plant food. In that time, eating may have meant stealing or fighting someone to get that meal. Thus, there was a daily problem to solve, obstacles to overcome, and victories to achieve just to survive another day.

The Hunter

Once man became a hunter, the natural inclination was to go for conquest. Once the prey was down and victory was at hand, there was an immediate need for another conquest and another victory to provide for continued sustenance. This pattern of chase and conquest continues in us to this day, since we are, in evolutionary terms, not that far from the hunt.

For many traders, the great conquest is mastery of their trading. The market is the prey to be vanquished. This quest proved to be sufficient to keep them going through the endless hours, then months and, finally, years of hard work and research. The adrenaline continued to pump during this period, especially when the prey looked to be within reach and the danger of loss was imminent. But, what happens when there is no longer a need to go on the hunt, and there is nothing left to conquer and bring home as the victor? When the market appears to have been tamed and there is no conquest left in your work?

The Builder

Not all traders are dominated by the hunter instinct. Some are more evolved as builder-types. At some point in history, humanity reached a critical population and hunting was no longer able to supply the needs of all of the people. Then, small villages and, eventually, cities began to appear. This urge to build and create is much different than the urge to conquer.

For many traders, the early part of their career represents the building phase of their life, which satisfies their innate need to be building something. Perhaps you have known someone like Jack who with his wife has built several houses. Once they had completed and moved into their most recent home, Janet announced that she would refuse to move again. Since that time, Jack has been remodeling their house. He built a garage, added a third floor, a screened in porch, and a fully heated gazebo. Currently, he is remodeling the bathrooms. Jack cannot stop building because, like a shark, which needs to move to exist, Jack needs to express his need to build.

But, what happens to a trader who has built his system and, subsequently, built his career?

The Explorer

Once man had conquered his backyard and built a city in it, a handful of men had the insatiable urge to explore new worlds. This urge to explore is also very deep in our psyches. When local hunting grounds, pastures, and orchards were depleted, man needed to be willing to move on. With few uncharted lands left to discover, we still have explorers among us who are at the cutting edge of scientific, intellectual, and technological exploration. To interview young scientists is to get a clear picture of this human urge to discover and explore the unknown.

For some traders, the lure of the markets has been about the urge to explore and discover. Researching the markets offer to many, the possibility of finding the secret of its workings and the discovery of knowledge that no one else possesses.

What happens, however, when a trader who has come with the need to explore and discover decides that there is nothing left for him to understand or discover about the markets?

The Mercenaries

Mercenaries were a primary component of the expeditions to the New World in the 1500's. They came strictly for the gold. Their hearts were filled with greed and they plundered whatever they could find. These men were not hunters, because the hunters do not hunt out of greed. The hunters seek the challenge of the hunt. The trophy head represents the challenge and its conquest - it represents a genuine achievement. But, like the hunter, mercenaries are not content with their first pot of gold and need more and more material treasures to produce the thrill. Their coffers are full, but they need more to feel the desired chemical rush to the brain produced by the satisfaction of greed.

Let's face it: many successful traders come into the business because they are mercenaries. After all, the markets are where the money is. Unfortunately, the syndrome of non-fulfillment applies here, as well. Once you have it all, where do you go from there?

Why do traders stay in the game when they have reached the points set as their goals? There is so much time, passion, energy, and emotion invested in that deeply worn path that most traders lack the reserves of energy required to leap out of the path or change its course.

So, here we have a significant group of mid-life traders who have achieved their goals, conquered their foes, discovered their uncharted lands, and built their empires. What is left for them? Like Jon, they feel empty, without a goal and without the passion to make them want to wake up in the morning and get to work. A great danger is that they will suffer depression, let go of their disciplines in despair, and seek out challenges that are essentially self-destructive in order to recreate a sense of excitement. The alternatives are common ones, but they are not positive and constructive ones. In addition, they are not the only ones available.

Spiritual Quest

In recent years, a new spiritual awakening has appeared as a cultural force. This spiritual quest has grown in influence because people are receiving limited satisfaction from the toys, luxuries and free time, which have come with their increased wealth and technology. For the first time in human history, great numbers of people are able to satisfy, and even vastly exceed, the deep urges for conquest that were once necessary for survival. With their material needs being met, people began to realize their connection with who and what they were as spiritual beings. In a recent survey reported in *Newsweek* magazine, 58% of all adult Americans which represents over 100 million people, feel the need to experience spiritual growth - not religious growth, but spiritual growth. And what is most amazing is that these people on the spiritual quest are seeking answers from metaphysical or mystical sources. Once on this quest, they begin to realize they are connected to everyone and everything and that this connection is what is needed to feel fulfilled in life.

Rediscovering Your Passion

In order to rediscover your passion, you must be willing to step out of your comfortable routine, which means making changes. Of course, change, both positive and negative, comes with risk, but, when you are in the mid-life doldrums, this element of risk is one of the many benefits of change. Clearly, some changes are either too destructive or superficial to be worth the temporary excitement that they create. Change is always uncomfortable even if it moves you towards a positive end. Nevertheless, the rewards of change are passion toward life and a feeling of aliveness. Incidentally, in recent studies of successful aging, one of the qualities shared by people who were alive and active into their tenth decade of life was the willingness to change and to accept change.

Some suggestions:

If you have reached the mid-life doldrums, consider the following strategies:

1. Become a mentor or teacher to passionate motivated people. When you teach others, their enthusiasm will be infectious. Mentor unmotivated people. In order for you to be effective with unmotivated people, you must become motivated and passionate yourself.

2. Choose an avocation that will stimulate the hunter, builder or explorer in you. For example, write a book. Reliving your life will drum up old feelings. Teaching what you know will make you feel good about yourself and what you have accomplished. Establish a service for other traders based upon your own fount of experience and research.

3. Change careers. It could be time to find another career, which will bring out the passion in you. A caveat to consider is that you may not be able to recreate the financial success you currently have, so be prepared for a change in your life-style.

4. Change your environment. Just by changing your environment, everything and everyone will change around you. We virtually stop seeing our environment when it becomes completely predictable to us.

5. Master what you are doing. Mastery in trading at each new level of success is like rediscovering yourself.

What Happened to Jon?

Out of desperation, Jon had been considering a host of destructive alternatives to his state of living. Once he was presented with this list of alternatives, however, he began to consider a new set of strategies. One thing he did was to begin exploring his spiritual life and was soon on an exciting quest. Then, he decided to become a mentor to a young trader he had recently met at a seminar. He and his wife discussed their living situation and decided to move to that home on the beach that they had always dreamed of owning. Jon has taken up fishing, which, he tells me, has become both his new passion and part of his daily spiritual journey.

Conclusion

It is common, and possibly inevitable, that mid-life success in trading will result in the loss of passion for your trading and market studies if you do not have ongoing goals. When there is no new goal to achieve, you need to redefine your life in terms of what is truly meaningful, decide how you can contribute to the world around you, and determine how you can create constructive change in your life.

BOVINAVACA

Chapter 36

THE PROFESSIONAL INVESTORS OF THE FUTURE

What is an interesting, financially rewarding and flexible career for women who want to run a business from home? An answer is professional investing. Until recently, women have not been a major force in the trading and investing community. This fact is changing because of a rapid shift in career dynamics for women caused by a recent combination of historical forces and changing role models.

For the past decade, I have worked with hundreds of professional traders and investors from around the world. A very small percentage of these professionals have been women. Over the last several years, I have noticed a significant change occurring in the numbers of women who are seeking a new model for their career goals. More women are suddenly seeing the potential of professional investing. This awareness is significant not only to this new segment of the investing population, but to the entire investment community.

What Happened

The role of women in our society has undergone tremendous change in the past one hundred years. When women left their homes in the 1940's out of the patriotic duty to work in war supporting jobs, they had already started to alter their model of who they were and what they could accomplish. Their mothers and grandmothers had recently won the right to vote granting women political equality. Now, their daughters began to want economic and social equality, as well.

In the 1970's, the role model for women had undergone even more dramatic changes. Women were entering the workplace in unprecedented numbers, while their children were still young. Women were working, not because they had to work, but because they wanted to work. Young women were inspired by the role model of the "Supermom," who was a perfect creature who had it all and could do it all. Without breaking a sweat or losing her sex appeal, "Supermom" managed a successful career and was also able to care for her home and family with precision and doting attention: a perfect blend of Hillary Clinton and Donna Reed.

Struggling through the 1980's with this implausible model, many women began to work while their children were infants. By that time, however, they were working not just because they wanted to work, but because many of them had to work. The economic forces of inflation and government policy had made it difficult for the average family to live on one income. The "Supermom" model was rapidly being replaced with the "Supercareer" model, which was the aggressive and independent single or married woman without children who jet-setted around the world, closing deals and eating power-lunches without anyone to hold her back. This new model was a response to the enormous pressures involved in building a truly successful career while raising small children and keeping the perfect home. As a result, many young career women delayed marriage and beginning their families as they established the foundation for successful careers. Unfortunately, many discovered too late the window of opportunity for these delayed goals had closed to them.

The Battlefield

By the late 1980's, many women had decided that it was impossible to do it all and that a choice to focus on career or family would have to be made. When large groups of women had made their choice, they found themselves warring collectively over the choices they had made individually. The women who returned to their careers often expressed public concern for their counterparts who remained home choosing to raise their children rather than return to their careers.

Meanwhile, the small but growing number of women who gave up their careers to work full-time for their families lost touch with their former independent and confident corporate selves. While they raised their families, they were forced to take on the social and community burdens that were left to them by the women who were "too busy" with their careers to volunteer in the schools, churches and hospitals. They found that they had as little time for themselves as their detractors. As a result, these stay-at-home mothers developed negative feelings for the women who returned to their careers while leaving their children in daycare.

The Problem

By the time the 1990's were in full swing, most women realized the truth: regardless of the choices they were making, they still wanted these two seemingly incompatible things:

1. A husband, children and home – and the freedom to be at home to take care of the children while they were small without feeling overwhelming loneliness and loss of self-esteem.

2. The desire to be financially independent, productive and a recognized part of the working world without feeling guilty for neglecting the home responsibilities.

Openly or secretly, the women with whom I have worked want it all. They want to be both the city mouse and the country mouse, or at least they want to be able to alternate at will. They are tired of feeling guilty, on the one hand, for neglecting their families and pretending that "quality time" is equal to being there; and they are tired of feeling apologetic, on the other hand, for not being an achieving, financially independent player in the game.

If a woman wants the entire package, she has to get up at 5:00 A.M., put the laundry in the washer, get the kids dressed for daycare, transport them on her way to the airport, and pick them up at 7:00 P.M. with a take-out meal on the front seat. By the time she gets the kitchen cleaned and sits down to read the paper, she is too tired to focus. Her kids barely know her, her married life consists of e-mailed messages during the day, her blood pressure is dangerously high and she has long stopped enjoying her enormous, but, unused house. Or as one frustrated, overwhelmed woman told me, "I need a wife, but the problem is I'm supposed to be one."

The Solution

The situation appeared to languish for nearly a decade: How to work and be at home with the children at the same time? Behind the scenes, an amazingly simple solution was beginning to take shape: Working from home.

The stage was set for this exciting option through the television shows from a decade ago, which periodically featured success stories of women who had developed businesses in their kitchens and basements. Mrs. Fields' Cookies started in a kitchen and within five years had become the fastest growing cookie baking company in America. Also, in the early nineties, a set of kitchen-based industries were taking off as women advertised and made fortunes with their handmade dolls, designer craft kits, and home-decorating companies.

Women whose families needed the second income and/or who were desperate for an outlet for their self-expression found an answer to their prayers in the new communications technologies. It was not long before women were moving the base of their operations from their kitchens into their guest bedrooms cum home offices along with a second telephone line and a computer. Affordable home computers, printers, FAX machines and e-mail systems suddenly presented women with two options that allowed them to work at home:

1. They could link up to their offices from their bedrooms or home-offices via their computers and FAX machines.

2. Or, they could start up their own businesses from home.

The Computer Revolution

What surprised many women was the ease with which they could learn to use their computers. Fortunately, most schools had required students to learn typing so that they could go on to college or into the business world. For many of the women with whom I have worked, the transition to their first word processor was easy and welcome.

The computer was a natural next step. One woman took her two small children out of daycare after they had developed chronic infections. She had worked on a word processor for her employer typing manuscripts. For Christmas, the family bought their first computer and soon she was freelancing her typing of manuscripts from her bedroom. The money she saved on daycare and work-related costs balanced the loss in her income. I have stories of other women in their seventies and even eighties who bought their first computer, taught themselves how to use it, and are now managing the business affairs for their favorite charities, in addition to their own finances.

Enter "Super Investor"

As women become more and more sophisticated in running computer-based businesses from home or simply in learning how to use computers, they are discovering that professional investing offers many attractive benefits.

1. **Your working conditions are flexible**
   The hours and investment style are completely flexible, to be determined by you. For example, if you decide that you do not want to be tied to the office all day long, you can focus on long-term trading and investing in low-volatility investment vehicles, etc. If you want to day trade and never take your investments to bed with you, you can close out positions each day and decide when it's quitting time. You determine the number of hours spent on this business.

2. **Your overhead and start-up costs are low**
   The hardware and capital investments in setting up an investing operation can be very low. A computer and a phone line, plus some software and a library of investment books and newspapers are probably the most expensive initial office investments. (Of course, people were professional investors long before the introduction of the computer, so even this piece of equipment is not absolutely necessary, but recommended.)

3. **You need no previous experience**
   There are no advanced degrees, educational requirements or previous experiences that are necessary in order to begin. In fact, essentially all professional investors are self-taught. In the meantime, hundreds and hundreds of books and journals are available for the motivated student to read and study.

4. **You determine your level of isolation**
   You can be as isolated or involved with other investors as you want to be. You can invest on your own or be part of one or many investment clubs or organizations. You can network with other investors on the Internet or at seminars and workshops.

5. **You can invest in your pajamas**
   For at home mothers, this is one of the most important advantages of investing from home. You are not going to be bothered by occasional salesmen and clients who might stop in unexpectedly. If you have been up all night with a sick child and are 24 hours from the nearest shower and shampoo, no one will ever know.

6. **The baby can be crying in the background**
   Most home-based businesswomen live in mortal fear that their small child will decide to cry in the middle of an important call. As an investor, the person on the other end of the telephone line works for you and you do not need to answer to anyone if your child is screaming in the background. You will still get your order executions.

7. **Your start-up capital is lower than for most businesses**
   You can start by investing with a small amount of money or a large pool of capital. The more you have to invest, the less risk you must accept with good money management rules.

8. **Your investment vehicles are your decision**
   You can invest in stocks, bonds, commodities, etc. You can invest in collectibles or art or gold coins. You can also invest in real estate. However, whatever area you decide to invest in, become an expert in that area. If you decide to invest in stocks, you must study the stock market so that you know as much as anyone in the business.

9. **No one can limit your earning potential**
   You can make as much money as you are able to make. Since you are self-employed, your earning potential will not be limited.

10. **You'll be the life of the party**
    When you go to parties and people ask what you do, you can proudly say that you are a professional investor. Instead of yawns, people will respond to you with intense interest. The problem will not be in trying to get people interested in you, but in dampening their interest and limiting their questions.

The Drawbacks

Not all investors make a killing, regardless of their sex. Some just limp along and a few lose their investments entirely. This description is not materially different from the prospects of starting any new business. Most new businesses fail because the entrepreneur did not complete the homework and/or because he or she was undercapitalized. These two factors are just as vital in becoming a professional investor. Without committing time and effort to learn about investing and the markets, an investor is merely a gambler. Fortunately, the need for education is so immediately obvious that most women are willing to put in the time to learn.

You need a methodology to invest that is well tested and the necessary trading capital to give you the confidence to start investing money.

The Right Psychology

Performing well when there is risk needs a healthy psychology. What is the right psychology for investing? Simply defined, it is the ability to manage your emotions and maintain a dispassionate focus on the moment so that you stick to your investing rules regardless of what is happening or what has happened in the past. Then, once the investing is done for the day, the right psychology allows you to have a balanced life so that your home life, your community life, and your work life all support each other. The disciplines required to raise a family, maintain a home, and build a career are an excellent starting place for the disciplines needed to be a successful investor. While women are typically more disciplined than men, they are not as confident about taking risk. It is especially important for a woman to have the belief that she will make money from her methodology before she starts investing with real money, and be very stringent about her money management.

Conclusion

The time is right for women to enter the world of professional investing as a career, which allows them to stay at home and make a comfortable, if not highly profitable income. The flexibility that appeals to many men who enter this profession is the very quality, which makes investing such a perfect career choice for women, as well. With the advent of computer technology, women are ready to learn about investing at a level that was never available to them before.

Chapter 37

THE NEXT GENERATION: MODELS FROM OUR FAMILY

Do we limit our success because of the psychological wounds inflicted on us by our parents?

Each generation bestows on its children a legacy of its resources and its limitations. It is the wise parent who develops the natural, good qualities of the family and transforms family limitations into lessons through counseling. It is the wise child who has the desire to develop genealogical gems and who understands the lessons passed on by his parents. Unfortunately, it is likely that a child will take on these psychological limitations, despite recognizing them as limitations, because they feel comfortable or natural. When a child develops into an adult, these limitations will limit success potential.

The process of passing on a good model to the next generation has the added benefit of transforming those limitations in yourself.

Here, then, are eighteen ways to both prevent the contamination of the next generation and to transform the present one:

Discipline

Children who know the boundaries of reasonable discipline feel secure in good leadership from their parents and the knowledge that their parents care about their welfare. Since discipline is a key element of success, once established at a young age, it will form a comfortable habit when a child reaches adulthood.

Effective disciplining of children requires a model of discipline.

Consistency

Through consistency, children learn that they can rely on themselves to complete tasks and reap the benefits. The quality of consistency builds trust within the individual resulting in support from his neurological system. Consistency also builds trust between family members because expectations are realized. When a child feels trusted, he develops self-confidence, which is a key element in building success.

Children will take on the quality of consistency if they learn it from their parents. When parents follow through on good decisions, it builds psychological strength in both the parents and the children. It is important to say what you mean and mean what you say.

Love

Love begins for children with the selfless love that is demonstrated to them in a nurturing environment. In his first year of life, a baby has to feel that he is the center of the universe and that all of his needs are met. In the second year of life, a baby has to learn that he is not the center of the universe and yet his needs are still met. This process makes children love themselves and learn to love others.

To experience true love, one must give selflessly to others. Children and people who have special needs offer us an opportunity to discover this gift of selfless love. Children must learn to love themselves before they can learn to love others.

Environment

The environment in which children are raised must feel safe and comfortable. Certain rooms may be placed off limits to children, but space must be available for them to play and explore without retribution if something is broken.

When you create a comfortable environment for your children, you are also creating one for yourself. Surroundings nurture emotional states thereby preparing you for upcoming challenges.

Negative Talk

When children are raised with positive, optimistic conversations they develop thinking which supports positive action. Criticism and gossip should be reframed to give self-talk a positive model to follow. Children who are raised in a home which limits critical self-talk will have less conflict within themselves. A low level of internal conflict is another ingredient to success.

Service

Children learn the value of giving when they learn to be of service to themselves and their community. Serving themselves teaches children independence. Serving others teaches them prosperity-consciousness. Serving others develops abundance-thinking, which leads to abundant living.

Developing service-oriented children requires the development of this skill within you; the benefit of being of service is that it attracts opportunity by expanding limited thinking.

Time

Children must learn the importance and use of time in order to appreciate it. An appreciation of time develops an appreciation of life and cultivates the desire to limit wasted time. Children who appreciate time will develop resources, which will make their lives more valuable and create joy in the process of life.

Teaching others to manage time will make time management more important to you.

Energy

Some children are blessed with abundant amounts of energy while others have less than abundant energy. Parents can add or subtract available energy for their children by the choices which they make for the child. Eventually, children make their own choices, which add or detract from their energy reserves. The amount of energy a child accumulates will determine the level of his health, developmental skills and success in life. As a parent, you must teach your children to make the best choices in food, thinking, interactions, physical exercise, and spiritual growth. All inputs will influence the amount of energy that is available to enhance their lives.

While teaching your children to make better choices, you will become aware of better choices for yourself.

Control

Children develop a sense of control over life when they experience parents who have a plan for their life and live their plan. It is important that children learn planning skills for goals, tasks, and rewards. With these planning skills, they will not feel out of control in life.

Developing a life plan for yourself will help you learn to control yourself and your environment without the need to control others.

Special Times

Children must learn that they are special. One method to develop this resource in children is by spending "Special Time" with them. Give a child the opportunity to express himself fully and praise him for good ideas and actions. A child will look forward to receiving your praise and will choose behavior that is praiseworthy.

When you create special times for others, you also create it for yourself and receive the benefit of feeling special.

Develop Talents

Developing the natural talents in children makes them feel capable. From these skills, they can develop resources to expand their horizons, allowing for success in ever expanding talents. Children who learn to expand beyond their comfort zones are able to expand their abilities to meet challenges when they are adults.

When you surround yourself with others who develop their skills and experience the rewards of achievement, you exist in an environment that will nurture your own development.

Distinguish Roles

It is psychologically healthy for children to understand the appropriate role for each area of their life. As children, they learn the leadership role of the parent as well as the playful, spontaneous role of the child. Many adults find it difficult to be a model of carefree playfulness for their children or to take the responsible role of the adult to support their family. Learning all roles enables children to be well-rounded adults who act appropriately in all situations.

In distinguishing these roles for your children, you learn, or relearn, them for yourself. Each role will enable you to be a well-rounded individual who has more of an appreciation of life.

Rewards

Children need to be rewarded with demonstrations of love such as hugs, kisses, or an emotional demonstration of pride. They need to be told specifically what they did well and be allowed to observe your good feelings about their achievement. Rewards of gifts, time and special privileges are important to their motivational learning. Children who are motivated will learn to be self-motivated as adults.

Rewarding others will most likely cause a chain reaction leading them to want to reward and encourage you. Rewards will motivate you to complete the tasks required to attain your goals.

Budget

When children learn how to handle money, they are less likely to waste it and more likely to appreciate its value as an adult. Children should have money to manage and be responsible for how it is spent. You need to show them how to use and how to save money. Good money management skills are essential for anyone who wants to accumulate wealth.

It is likely that you will want to be more accountable for your money management when you develop the skills in your child.

Chores

Family chores should be written as part of a family time management plan. Each member should choose the chores for which he or she would be happy to take responsibility. The remaining chores should be negotiated and divided, making everyone a part of the family unit. Rotation of responsibility will give each member an appreciation of the duties involved in less desirable tasks. School and work responsibilities should be taken into consideration when creating the plan. Chores are a good way for a child to earn money; however, some chores should be part of their contribution to the family. Another benefit derived from chore planning is that children learn to negotiate.

Dividing chores among family members frees time for more productive uses and instills family unity.

Teaching Influences

All teachers influence children and their development. While a teacher can be skilled to teach many children, that particular teacher might not be suitable for your particular child's ability to learn. Know your child's teachers and monitor the results with each teacher. If there is a problem, change teachers or classes for the benefit of your child's future, if change is possible.

Being proactive in your child's education can make a major difference in how much energy and money have to be utilized for their higher education.

Peer Groups

One of the biggest influences on your children is their peer group. When you direct young children to other children who are a positive influence on their development, they are more likely to make better choices in companions when they are older. Children who are nurtured in a positive, supportive environment seek out positive influences as they develop into adults.

Helping your children to make better choices in companions will make you think about your choices for companionship. A nurturing, supportive environment will give you a sense of well being and will enhance your performance.

People and Etiquette Skills

The way a child behaves in public will influence his acceptance by others and, therefore, his self-esteem. It is important to take cognizance of your own etiquette skills. If you find it necessary to take lessons yourself in order to develop etiquette and personal skills in your children, it is important to do so.

Teaching new skills is the best way to learn new skills.

Conclusion

We are not condemned to pass along to our children the limiting patterns we inherited from our parents. The process of passing on negative, success-sabotaging models from one generation to the next can be transformed in a single generation. If we are willing to take personal responsibility for our own actions and consciously model new, positive behaviors and attitudes for our children, we not only build the foundation for their future success but rebuild the foundation for our own.

Trader's Conclusion

Note the resources passed on from your family, whcrc improvements need to be made in your own life and your children's lives. Your personal resources will enhance your trading resources, and therefore the bottom line.

Epilogue

The goal of this book is to inspire you to create a balance in your life between the demands of your professional and your personal life. Not even a Holy Grail system can achieve results for a trader who has not handled his psychological issues over the long haul. Fear, greed, impatience, lack of planning and the biggest saboteur of all, stress, are lurking behind every trade to undo potentially winning trades and traders.

After your initial reading, reread the chapters you identified with as being areas you need to work on. Complete the exercises, even if you think you don't need to. Update your business plan and review your trading plan. Take care to balance all of the areas of your life. Make the decision that it is okay to be very successful while enjoying the process as you share your abundance with others.

Best wishes for a happy and prosperous life.

Adrienne would like to thank the following magazines and newsletters that have published articles and interviews:

Applied Derivatives Trading

Financial Trader

Futures Magazine

Money World

Technical Analysis of Stocks and Commodities

The Bridge Trader

The Sentinel

The Individual Investor

The Technical Trader

Trading on Target Newsletter

Traders'Catalog and Resource Guide

OTHER SERVICES & PRODUCTS AVAILABLE

FROM ADRIENNE LARIS TOGHRAIE

TradingOnTarget.com

SERVICES

• **Private Consulting**	Remove the Barriers to Each Level of Success in Trading and All Areas of Your Life
• **Institutional & Corporate**	Increase Production, Trading Ability and Teamwork

SEMINARS

• **Top Performance**	For Discipline & Overcoming Sabotage
• **The Winner's Edge**	Gain the Technical & Psychological Tools for Becoming a Successful Investor
• **Intuition/Discretionary**	Develop & Use Reliable Intuitive Indicators
• **Building a Capital & Client Base**	Build Sales, Increase Production
• **Creating Affluence**	Increase Resources & Balance Your Life
• **Enriching Life Seminar**	Build Success by Making Better Choices and Gain Control Over Your Life

PRODUCTS

• **The Winning Edge 1, 2, 3, 4** How to Use Your Personal Psychological Power to Succeed in Trading & Investing	A Series of Four Books on the Psychology of Trading

• **Traders' Secrets**	A Book About Real People Becoming Successful Traders
• **Business Plan for Traders** Book & DVD	A Plan for Your Trading Business
• **Dear Coach-Book** Potty Training for Traders, Brokers & Investors	Psychological Questions & Answers with a Humorous Twist
• **Getting More Out of Life-Book**	Building Self-Confidence
• **Trader's Evaluation**	Pinpoint Psychological Issues
• **6 Steps to Great Success** 1 DVD	A Model for Reaching Success
• **Trading on Target III** 4 CDs	4 Interviews
• **Trading on Target IV** 4 CDs	7 Interviews + Fear Workshop
• **Discipline Workshop I** 1 DVD	A Model for Discipline
• **Discipline Workshop II** 2 CDs	How to Follow Your Rules
• **Discipline Workshop III** 2 CDs	Motivation to Light Your Fire
• **Stress Relief for Traders** 2 CDs	Overcoming Stress; Building Success; Daily Trading Rules
• **TOT Newsletter** **4 Quarterly Issues**	Discipline Perspective

For additional information about our services, please contact us. Be sure to ask about the savings available when you purchase one of our packages or the Home Study Course.

Trading on Target
100 Lavewood Lane
Cary, NC 27518
Call (919) 851-8288
Fax (919) 851-9979
Email - Adrienne@TradingOnTarget.com
Website - TradingOnTarget.com